Doing Sociological Research

Doing Sociological Research

Edited by
Colin Bell

Professor of Sociology at the University of New South Wales

and

Howard Newby

Senior Lecturer in Sociology at the University of Essex

London
GEORGE ALLEN & UNWIN
Boston   Sydney

First published in 1977

Introduction, Epilogue, editorial matter and arrangement
© C. Bell and H. Newby 1977.

Chapter 1 © J. M. Atkinson 1977; Chapter 2 © C. Bell 1977;
Chapter 3 © S. Cohen and L. Taylor 1977; Chapter 4
© R. Moore 1977; Chapter 5 © H. Newby 1977; Chapter 6
© R. Pahl 1977; Chapter 7 © R. Wallis 1977.

Editorial note to Chapter 2 © H. Newby 1977.

Other material © George Allen & Unwin (Publishers) Ltd.,
1977.

ISBN 0 04 300070 3 hardback
      0 04 300071 1 paperback

Printed in Great Britain in 10 on 11pt Times

by Biddles Ltd, Guildford, Surrey

Contents

Acknowledgements

As the Epilogue to this book indicates, editing the following collection has not been without its difficulties. Moreover, as joint editors we have had to overcome the logistical difficulties of functioning 12,000 miles apart. Eschewing the temptation to acknowledge the lack of help received from errant postal services and nervous lawyers, therefore, we shall confine ourselves to thanking those who have helped us to overcome the many obstacles which this book faced on the way to publication.

Michael Shaw originally encouraged us to pursue our half-formed idea and we are deeply grateful for his understanding, good humour and constant encouragement. Frances Kelly has been indefatigable in her efforts to ensure that the book has been published in a form which bears some resemblance to our original conception.

Our thanks are also due to Michael Holdsworth of Allen and Unwin for his patience in the face of so many problems.

We also gratefully acknowledge the permission of Paul Barker, editor of *New Society*, to reprint material in Stanley Cohen and Laurie Taylor's contribution, 'Talking about prison blues', which was taken from their article, 'Prison research: a cautionary tale' (1975).

Finally, we would like to thank Nadia Massoud at the University of New South Wales and Linda Peachey at the University of Essex for all their help in the typing of the manuscript and the associated correspondence which made this book possible.

COLIN BELL
HOWARD NEWBY
Kensington, Sydney, New South Wales
1976

Introduction: The Rise of Methodological Pluralism

COLIN BELL and HOWARD NEWBY

THE THEMES AND PURPOSE OF THIS BOOK

'Idiosyncracies of person and circumstance are at the heart not the periphery of the scientific enterprise' (Johnson 1975, p. 2).

This remark, which was recently found in a thesis written by one of our students, is also at the heart of many of the contributions to this book. It is now that there are no previous accounts of these 'idiosyncracies of person and circumstance' (most notably Hammond 1964; Vidich, Bensman and Stein 1964), but that the lessons to be learned from them have been but imperfectly assimilated into the sociological enterprise. It is our contention that accounts of doing sociological research are *at least* as valuable, both to students of sociology and to its practitioners, as the exhortations to be found in the much more common textbooks on methodology. The real key pur-. pose of these texts was, we would argue, to provide *some* standard, *some* set of procedures, *some* method by which research practice could be evaluated. Yet it is common knowledge that there has always been, perhaps necessarily, considerable divergence between how sociological research has actually been done and what is found in the textbooks. So the first purpose of this book is the very *practical* one of providing evidence that sociological research is very different from what anybody would believe after a close reading of books as different as C. Moser and G. Kalton's *Survey Methods of Social Investigation* (1958) and A. V. Cicourel's *Method and Measurement in Sociology* (1964).

Vivien Johnson's remark quoted above refers to the 'scientific enterprise'. There are many accounts written about the normative underpinnings of this enterprise, yet one of the problems that has to be faced as we currently look around the sociological enterprise is that it is not *one* but *many*. Moser and Kalton's and Cicourel's books can hardly *both* be taken as exclusive guides to action. This book is, then, necessarily dedicated towards what, at the very least, is a decent methodological pluralism. This pluralism has emerged out of the ruins of the former positivistic hegemony in sociology. No longer can there be only one style of social research with *one* method that is to be *the* method. Rather there are many. This, of course, is a view which would be disputed by those – as far apart as ethnomethodologists and Althusserian Marxists – who believe that they have discovered *the* method. Our position of methodological pluralism rejects this methodological exclusivism and is cautious about the new methodological anarchy advocated by Paul Feyerabend (1975) – who claims that, for the success of the scientific enterprise, there should be no method, and who is therefore *against method*. (We return to this below.) Our second purpose is then *philosophical*, or more strictly speaking epistemological, in that we believe that these accounts of doing sociological research show that at the very least there are a variety of methods. We also suspect that there are no clear ways of choosing between them.

To read what we call *normative* methodology, be it ever so positivistic or ever so phenomenological, it frequently would seem as if much, if not all, sociological research was 'context-free' – i.e. carried out by non-people in non-places. As the accounts printed here amply display, however, sociologists too are people, and so, in order to be of practical use, such prescriptions as the textbooks provide must be personally operable (cf. Fletcher 1974, p. 68). Almost invariably, for example, sociological research takes place with some sort of political context; yet how many of the normative textbooks take account of this? We do not just mean that we need to appreciate that we, too, are all part of the state's repressive apparatus along with the police and the media, or that we should decide whose side we are on – not that these are not extremely important issues that are deserving of a far more central place in the teaching and the doing of sociological research (Becker 1967; Gouldner 1975). By political context we mean everything from the micropolitics of interpersonal relationships, through the politics of research units, institutions and universities, to those of government departments and finally to the state. All these contexts *vitally* determine the design, implementation and outcome of sociological research. So our third purpose is the overtly *political* one of displaying openly and centrally that politics, defined thus widely, pervades *all* sociological research. The 'idiosyncrasies of person and circumstance' referred to by Vivien Johnson were frequently political by our definition. Indeed that may be one good reason for the failure successfully to apply and enforce one and only one 'scientific' method on to the social sciences.

Our chosen medium *here* for achieving our practical, philosophical and political purposes is through the reproduction of eight personal accounts of doing sociological research. This does not mean that there are not and could not be other ways of achieving these purposes. For instance, it might be possible eventually to produce a far more *analytical* account along the lines so brilliantly pioneered by W. Baldamus (1972) in his reanalysis of the accounts published in Philip Hammond's *Sociologists at Work* (1964). This could be a task that eventually faces the editors of this volume. Another way perhaps of achieving our three central purposes would be to do research on sociological research; Jennifer Platt (1976), for example, has done just that. However, doing research on research does have certain problems as we see it, in that the research (to be done) can most likely only be done within one epistemological framework, so that though our *practical* purposes could be served by such research (to show how research is actually conducted) our *philosophical* purposes could not, for the imposition of one epistemological framework would necessarily mask the very issues which we wish to bring out into the open. However, we recognise that our *political* purposes could be amply served by such research — which is one reason why we regard the publication of Platt's monograph as a welcome addition to our knowledge of research methodology. She was much more in control of her data than we are — that is just why her research cannot serve all of our purposes. Her survey methodology has, for example, hindered her examination of research as a deeply social *process*, something to which all the accounts which follow strongly bear witness. On the other hand, her treatment allows many problems to be discussed far more systematically than we could ever hope for here. Indeed we have exerted very little editorial control over the essays which follow (though no doubt our contributors at times felt otherwise). Certainly we have tried to encourage our contributors to write about what they *personally* saw as important in how they did particular pieces of research.

Since we have committed ourselves to reflexivity, perhaps we should say something about how this book was conceived. In the letter which we originally wrote (in August 1974) to our potential contributors we stated:

'Our ambition is to edit a British *Sociologists at Work*, which we have provisionally entitled *Doing Sociological Research* . . .

'We are now seeking your formal agreement, having made informal approaches, to produce a contribution between 20 and 30 pages (some degree of flexibility is probably desirable) along with seven other similar essays. We intend to contribute individual pieces ourselves, as well as write a long introduction about what can be learned from this kind of methodological essay. Would you be prepared to write a piece on the background to [here we referred to a piece of research] — about how the research was done, and its consequences and so on?

'One reason why *Sociologists at Work* is such a successful book is that in the main, important sociologists own up about important pieces of sociology — and without appearing to be unduly flattering we have high hopes that you could produce a significant piece for our book. We hope, of course, that the book will have some lasting significance and will be widely read by all practising sociologists in Britain. We are aiming for both the post-graduate market but we also want a work that is going to be read by under graduates on their methodology courses. We want a work that can be put alongside the "normative" cook-books that tell us how research *should* be done – a book that will describe how research is actually done. In other words, we are asking you to contribute to what we hope will become the standard work of "descriptive" – as opposed to normative methodology. It is the intellectual justification and the implications of this kind of approach that we will write in our introduction.

'No doubt you will expect some editorial guidance – and obviously anything we can do to help we will do. At this stage all that we would like to say is that we feel that you should if possible write yourself into your account – the best essays we know on this topic are quasi-autobiographical, e.g. Whyte's account of doing *Street Corner Society*. Some account of the "institutional" setting of your research – be it university, research unit, or the whole complex of problems associated with being a research student or assistant (power and authority in research) – would be helpful. Why did you do this or that piece of research, when you did it in the way you did? How did you actually go about your research – what were the false starts, brilliant ideas and so on? What were the reactions, if any, to publication? What have been the personal consequences for you for the research? These are the kinds of things, by no means an inclusive nor an imperative list, we would like to encourage you to write about.

'Our project of *post hoc* essays is very different to the kind of project that Jennifer Platt is currently engaged in (you may well have been one of the sample) – where she is interviewing people about their research in order to write a book about doing research. This is in some ways much more ambitious (and hazardous) than what we are up to, yet obviously very interesting and important. We would hope that these essays would also lead to a wider understanding of the nature of sociological research which relate at a number of levels: to the sociological enterprise; the epistemological (see Baldamus' speculations in "The Role of Discoveries in Social Science" based on *Sociologists at Work* in Shanin's *The Rules of the Game* (Tavistock, 1972); theoretical – on the role of what passes for sociological theory in research; and practical – on how research gets done. Indeed we hope that all these essays will lead to a wider understanding of research that is already published in most cases and will lead to a more realistic appraisal of *Doing Sociological Work*.'

Two people whom we originally approached eventually turned us down, both claiming pressure of other commitments. We chose those whom we knew had interesting and instructive tales to tell. Of course we realise that the lessons to be learned for sociology are *crucially* affected by those whom we chose. There were also obvious (to our publisher at least) limits to the number of accounts of doing research that could be published in any one book and that allowed the contributors a reasonable length over which to write. Our difficulties as editors have stemmed principally from two problems. The first has been to persuade, as gently as possible, our contributors to cut their pieces. The second has been to trip as delicately as possible through the minefield of the British libel laws. To our chagrin, these contributions do not tell all that they might – and we are not referring only to constraints on length. However, there is no reason at all why further collections such as this should not appear – indeed it would show a very healthy reflexiveness in British sociology if every few years such a volume appeared. Over the decade or so that we have been actively buying and reviewing British (and other) sociology books we have obtained eighteen social-research methods textbooks published in Britain (and of course there may well be many more, for it is hardly a genre that excites us eagerly to rush to the bookshop anymore). Such, however, is the power of normative research methodology that over that time there have been *no* books such as ours published in Britain on how research actually gets done – with the partial exception of Platt's (1976) book mentioned above.

In this Introduction we shall look in more detail at these themes; in particular we shall show the value of accounts of doing research through careful attention to Elenore Smith Bowen's (Laura Bohannan's) remarkable anthropological novel, *Return to Laughter* (Bohannan 1964). Then we will consider again the problems raised by accounts such as *Return to Laughter* for method; in particular for the various methodolatories – as Alvin Gouldner called them in his rather overlooked *Enter Plato* (1967) – that are being hawked around the sociological enterprise. For that is really our central argument and why we are entering the *methods* marketplace. Our *practical, philosophical* and *political* purposes are vitally inter-related. This is what the accounts published here demonstrate again and again. Yet they also show that it is through the personal and the private that these purposes are achieved.

All of us who have written for this book were personally changed by the experiences described; they are parts of our biographies.

THE PERSONAL AND THE PROFESSIONAL IN SOCIOLOGICAL RESEARCH

In the early 1960s J. W. N. Watkins broadcast a talk with a title close to the themes of this book: 'Confession is good for ideas' (1963). He advocated what might be called investigators' confessional colleagueship. Of course like so many philosophers of method he was concerned with the natural sciences, but we believe that his arguments apply even more strongly to the social scientist where, as David Reisman has written in his introduction to Laura Bohannan's *Return to Laughter*, 'the observer's participation inevitably evokes certain orders of data and closes off other orders' (1964, p. xi). This is an epistemological point of great importance. *Return to Laughter* is so so different from the accounts in, say, *African Political Systems*, which reveal virtually nothing of how the data published therein were gathered

(Fortes 1940). Instead Bohannan reveals at least some of the human costs, passions, mistakes, frailties and even gaieties which lie behind the erstwhile antiseptic reports of most social scientists. We do need to reveal more so that we can learn more and teach more. If mistakes are creative why not reveal them? Yet even when they are not – even when they have been destructive and crisis-producing – they still should be revealed. Perhaps others too will learn; that surely is one of the points of *Return to Laughter* as well as of this volume. We share Reisman's view that:

'Any assumption that an autobiography of affective experience is an ethnographic irrelevancy would ... be setting a wrong model for what is truly scientific – a term I would define as a canon of ethical scrupulousness and choice of the most appropriate methods, not allowing these methods to be monopolized by any particular sect of methodologists.' (p. xvi)

Bohannan (in 'an author's note' in the paperback edition, under her real name rather than the pseudonym under which *Return to Laughter* was originally published) tells us that: 'There I have written simply as a human being, and the truth I have tried to tell concerns the sea change in oneself that comes from immersion in another and savage culture' (p. xix). We take it as one of the main causes of impoverishment of sociological monographs that their authors have not written 'simply as a human being'. The divorce of the personal from the so-called scientific means that the scientific has not been scientific at all.

What in particular can be learned from Bohannan's marvellously instructive account? Look at how she tells us about fieldwork *roles*, especially those that followed from her sex:

'I should have been content, and I was – as long as I thought only in terms of enjoying myself and of feeling at home. My dissatisfaction lay wholly in the part I was being assigned. I was rapidly being absorbed in the life of the women and children. All the magic, all the law, all the politics – over half the things professionally important to me – were in the hands of the men, and so far not one man had been willing to discuss such matters with me, not one man had taken me with him to the meetings of the elders which, I knew, often took place. Was there a moot? I was at a wedding party. An inquest? I had gone to visit my namesake. A ceremony? I heard women gossip of it, afterwards. I had been identified with the women: unless I could break that association, I would leave the field with copious information on domestic details and without any knowledge of anything else.' (p. 79)

It is not only that the normative textbooks on fieldwork do not tell their readers something to the effect that 'to observe you need to be adopted in some on-going pattern of social relationships' (though many, especially the more anthropologically inclined, do not), but also that data in the final monograph are published about which we have no idea how or why they were collected. They certainly give no indication of how to solve the problem outlined in the above quotation. Nor do they indicate how you can, say, exploit the local political structure for scientific ends (let alone struggle with the ethical problems involved in so doing). Here again Bohannan's experiences are instructive. She tells us that she:

'. . . learned that I could play Yabo and Kako off against each other, though not, as yet, very skilfully. Yabo would take me any place to show that I preferred his company to the chief's: Kako could not bear to let Yabo take the lead. Neither Kako nor Yabo was, by himself, willing to tell any European anything: neither Kako nor Yabo could stand the thought that the other was more valued, by anyone or for any reason. Yabo had set the first, necessary precedent. From then on Kako and in his wake all other notables, told me of funerals and expected me to attend them. Again after Yabo set the example, I was notified of moots and inquests. Some of the elders always – and all of them sometimes – were amused or annoyed by my new role, but none disputed it. Not for any merit of mine, but because of the relationship between Kako and Yabo, my work flourished like the green bay tree.' (p. 83)

Later we are told, very wisely, that 'One cannot make friends with a community. One has to make friends with individual people' (p. 99). This is a good example of the practical purpose served by such accounts. She also stresses the depressing consequences of getting too involved when she 'dived too deep. To breathe again I must stay on top for a while. I had allowed myself to become too absorbed in the personal affairs of the few homesteads I knew best' (p. 156). But as she herself knows it is not that simple. The following passage shows that Bohannan faced difficulties and situations considerably more harrowing than most of us face, but their very extremity graphically raises questions about the morality of social science research:

'I stood over Amera. She tried to smile at me. She was very ill. I was convinced these women could not help her. She would die. She was my friend but my epitaph for her would be impersonal observations scribbled in my notebook, her memory preserved in an anthropologist's file: "Death (in child birth)/Cause: witchcraft/Case of Amera". A lecture from the past reproached me: "The anthropologist cannot, like the chemist or biologist, arrange controlled experiments. Like the astronomer he can only observe. But unlike the astronomer, his mere presence produces changes in the data he is trying to observe. He himself is a disturbing influence which he must endeavour to keep to the minimum. His claim to science must therefore rest on a meticulous accuracy of observation and on a cool objective approach to his data".

'A cool, objective approach to Amera's death? One can, perhaps, be cool when dealing with questionnaires or when interviewing strangers. But what is one to do when one can collect one's data only by forming personal friendships? It is hard enough to think of a friend as a case history. Was I to stand aloof, observing the course of events? There could be no professional hesitation. I might otherwise never see the ceremonies connected with death in childbirth.' (pp. 184–5)

Actually there was no personal hesitation and Bohannan strove (unsuccessfully) to persuade Yaba and Amera's family to take Amera to hospital. We know of few better accounts of the tension between scientific normative prescriptions and what social scientists actually (and ought?) to do. That is why we have quoted it here in its entirety.

Return to Laughter is full of delight and useful information. It would of course be very difficult to systematise. We are told of the value of 'Mrs Grundys' who are often fieldworkers' best informants and of the 'velvet curtain' of polite silences that are the means of defence of those being studied. There is also very good advice on how to cut through such silences. The book's deep strength comes from its author's clear articulation of the stresses and tensions that all fieldworkers face. How important it was for her to remember what she was 'an anthropologist, and an American and heir to civilization' (p. 238). And just how difficult it was for her to achieve survival in the field. This is the title of Michael Clarke's (1975) perceptive article on the more general nature of the problem discussed with such feeling by Bohannan. As he points out, social research is considerably more difficult than was suggested by E. E. Evans-Pritchard when he said: 'Anyone who is not a complete idiot can do fieldwork' (1973, p. 3). Rather ironically in the light of the themes being articulated in this Introduction, Evans-Pritchard then proceeded to give the *norms* of fieldwork, which are summed up by Clarke as 'behave like a gentleman, keep off the women, take quinine daily, and play it by ear' (p. 105). Anyone who reads *Return to Laughter* will know that this will not do, even as a joke.

Our accounts, frequently more prosaic than Bohannan's, show that as research workers we also became different people through the process. This point is totally and necessarily ignored in the conventional methodology texts. Our practical purposes are to make our readers more aware of just these points and to increase the attention paid to them in doing sociological research.

METHODOLOGY AND METHODOLATRY

Basil Bernstein has recently pointed to some of the consequences of the state of methodological pluralism that characterises current sociology:

'In a subject where theories and methods are weak, intellectual shifts are likely to arise out of the conflicts between *approaches* rather than conflicts between explanations will be weak and often non-comparable, because they are approach specific. The weakness of the explanation is likely to be attributed to the approach, which is analysed in terms of its ideological stance. Once the ideological stance is exposed, then all the work may be written off. Every new approach becomes a social movement or sect which immediately defines the nature of the subject by redefining what is to be admitted and what is beyond the pale, so that with every new approach the subject starts almost from scratch.' (1974, p. 154)

This is a key aspect of what might be called, after C. Wright Mills (1959), 'sociology's troubles'. Moreover, this raises the whole question of the applicability to sociology of T. S. Kuhn's book, *The Structure of Scientific Revolutions* (1962). This is not the place to rehearse (again) the whole debate about whether or not Kuhn's work also provides more than a metaphoric model for the social sciences. This has already been admirably discussed by, among others, Herminio Martins (1971) and John Urry (1973). Our point here is a slightly different one. If Bernstein is right – and we believe he is – then, at the very least, sociology is *pre-paradigmatic* in Kuhn's terms. Yet for the reasons argued by Urry, that centre on the inadequacy of a largely 'internalist' account of the growth of knowledge *and* the qualitative difference of social science data from data of the natural sciences, it would seem sensible to argue directly for the inapplicability of Kuhn's approach to the concerns of this book. Certainly we would wish to make it quite clear that a Kuhnian position – e.g. that adopted by Robert K. Friedrichs in his *A Sociology of Sociology* (1970) – is *not* compatible with that adopted here. We are, we repeat, arguing for methodological pluralism, yet paradigms (which all agree are necessarily part of Kuhn's approach) imply exclusiveness, imperialism and certainty. To be sure, there are many sociologists around who do espouse epistemological exclusivism (and who may well see, therefore, the discipline of sociology in Kuhnian terms); for example, this is true of traditional positivists as well as of those who now assault that position from both ethnomethodological and structuralist standpoints. We do not share these certainties. Our position is that there may well *not* be a discipline- or even speciality-wide paradigms in sociology. And so we are *against* methodolatory (rather than method) and certainty, and *for* a constructive scepticism and ethical and logical scrupulousness. This is not compatible with the self-confident espousal of paradigms.

Alvin Gouldner has a brilliant discussion of 'Method versus methodolatory' in his *Enter Plato* (1967). He articulates the basic dilemma between 'intuitive insight with enriching novelty' and 'a reliance upon a disciplined method with controllable and reliable results'. He stresses that 'without method there is no reliable way of resolving competing claims to truth' (p. 337). That is indeed our position and we would say that that is just how sociology currently is. Gouldner notes that with method alone we all too easily sink into ritualism, and in what is a precise indictment of much positivistic sociology he notes that 'it sacrifices the venturesome but chancy insight for the security of controllable routine, the penetrating novelty for the shallow familiarity, the broader for the narrow circumstances'. He warns that it is very easy for reason to become 'methodolatorous' – 'compulsively preoccupied with a method of knowing, which it exalts ritualistically and quite apart from a serious appraisal of its success in producing knowledge' (p. 338). He characterises methodology as the anxiety of reason and as the scholarly style of those who fear, and thus cannot come to terms with, themselves.

Nevertheless, reason, naturally enough, *does* have functions for 'it sets limits on men's actions, it does not permit them to do whatever they wish. . . . Reason is impersonal, also, in the sense that it inhibits or forbids wilful capriciousness or arbitrariness. It erects a barrier against the flux of mood.' Our personal accounts would lead us in some instances to doubt the impersonality of reason, but surely Gouldner has a very penetrating series of points when he writes:

'Reason as method disestablishes inner conviction, or strength of feeling, as the basis of a claim to knowledge. The truth of reason is no longer held to be vouched for by a sense of intuitive certainty. This further implies that "common sense" – common in being widely held and settled opinions – is no longer perforce correct. To secure consensus concerning a view, therefore, is not to prove it correct. Reason as method says that people are not right because born to high station, and further, neither does majority agreement among the many make something right. In this way, reason is both anti-aristocratic, and it has begun to become *depoliticized in principle*.

'Above all, reason as method is a constraining force, leading men to conclusions that they did not know or believe in the beginning and, sometimes, to views opposed to those they held initially.' (p. 338; our italics)

We would urge a careful consideration of these arguments but conclude that our essays show that, notwithstanding reason's ability to be depoliticised in principle, it has actually been *politicised in practice*. We should like to note further that Gouldner felicitously points out that 'if methodolatory compulsively constricts intelligence, method may, however serendipitously, generate novelty by requiring conformity to disciplined routine' (p. 339). Our question now would be: to precisely *what* routines should the sociologist currently conform? And as Gouldner argues elsewhere in *Enter Plato* (e.g. in his discussion of 'knowing and awareness', pp. 267–73), the purpose towards which we should work – i.e. why in this case we do sociological research – is also the subject of some considerable tension.

This tension Gouldner sums up, following Plato, as the tension between some very high knowledge: *epistēmē*, 'which embodies awareness of the known, of the knower and of knowing'; and *technē*, 'which consists of the lessons of experience of trial and error, of clever skills refined through diligent practice' (p. 268). Much of the assault on positivism is an assault on *technē* from *epistēmē*. As Gouldner ably shows, the tension between these two counterpoised ways of knowing is far from an archaic distinction and still lies at the root of many of the major controversies in sociology today: between those who emphasise the *scientific* nature of sociology and those who do not. And we can agree with Gouldner when he writes that 'in their polemical opposition to the naturalists, what the humanists oppose – for example, "methodology" – is often clearer than what it is they favour'. It is clear that the various critiques of positivism which have recently been articulated have increasingly sensitised us to the weaknesses of sheer information (see, for example, Derek Phillips's *Knowledge from What?*, 1971, as well as the phenomenological critique of P. Filmer *et al.*, 1972). This has led to an increasing stress on *awareness* as a form of knowledge.

Yet both forms of knowing have certain pathological tendencies. The pathology of rampant fact gathering is described by Gouldner as follows:

'... knowing as naturalistic information gathering (*technē*) tends towards narrowness. Its characteristic product is the brief and direct technical article capable of being understood only by a few other specialists. Its tendency is to commit itself to a metaphysics which believes that the complexity of the world is undesirable and unnecessary and that things are really simpler than they seem. It consequently has a more hopeful and optimistic view of human ambitions. It is intolerant of intellectual ambiguities and builds intellectual structures into which all things can be fitted neatly, seeking for the simplest and most elemental units of which things are composed. It can, in brief, be naive and simple-minded.' (p. 272)

On the other hand, the pathologies of knowing as awareness (*epistēmē*) are different:

'... it enjoys the shiver induced by a sense of mystery. Loving the smell of incense, it has a tendency towards mystification and a preference for mood-resonating obscurities. Awareness is committed to a metaphysics in which things are felt to be much more complex than they seem, in which simplicitly is only appearance deep, and awareness seeks to capture and portray the complexity of things. Enjoying the mystery of life, it seeks to protect it, and it can therefore become the enemy, not only of science, but of reason as well. Believing the mystery impenetrably complex, it easily sinks into pessimism about the human prospect.' (p. 274)

These pathologies come, we would argue, from not maintaining these two forms of knowing in some form of tension or even in some sort of dialectical relationship. We believe that the essays published in this book show through their autobiographical accounts that it is possible *both* to illustrate the relationships between *epistēmē* and *technē and* to show how these tensions can be creative in the doing of sociological research. Our accounts indicate that in actual sociological practice *epistēmē* and *technē* can be kept within some controllable and creative dialectic. The virtues of these essays are that autobiographical accounts do allow us to learn about doing sociological research, despite Gouldner's claims that *epistēmē* cannot be taught nor handed on in any straightforward manner and that *technē* when usually taught suffers from all of the sterility that comes from its divorce from actual sociological practice. All these reflections on doing sociological research *without exception* demonstrate clearly for the benefits of others that it is possible to avoid the pathologies of the various ways of knowing.

THE PUBLIC AND PRIVATE MILIEUX IN SOCIOLOGY

At the beginning of the previous section of this Introduction, we referred, after quoting Basil Bernstein (1974), to 'sociology's troubles'. This is deliberately echoing the influential distinction drawn by C. Wright Mills in his book, *The Sociological Imagination* (1959). Mills wrote that 'perhaps the most fruitful distinction with which the sociological imagination works is between the personal troubles of the milieu and the public issues of social structure' (p. 8). We want to apply this distinction in order to talk about sociology's troubles as opposed to its issues. As Mills reminds us, 'a trouble is a private matter: values cherished by an individual are felt by him to be threatened' (p. 9). So in this section we are emphasising private matters as opposed to public ones. The frequently heralded 'coming crisis' in sociology has overly focused our attention on sociology's public issues – its political crisis. Mills tells us that these issues 'have to do with matters that transcend these local environments of the individual and the range of his inner life' (p. 9). So when Alvin Gouldner (1967) tells us somewhat melodramatically that we are theorising within the sound of guns (perhaps it would have been more accurate to say within the sound of cash registers) he is commenting on the public issues of sociology. If the sociological imagination of an individual sociologist feeds on, and must finally transcend, this further tension between personal troubles and public issues then we want to argue that sociology as a whole does too – that it is possible to distinguish, analytically at least, between the local milieu of sociology and its social structural location in society. This, of course, parallels the old disputes in the history of ideas between internalist and externalist accounts that are central to the debates, referred to above, about the applicability of the work of T. S. Kuhn (1962) to sociology.

Much of the speculative or reflexive comment on the state of sociology is not on the troubles of the milieu of sociology but on its political crisis. In no way do we wish to deny the relevance and significance of these recent discussions – indeed a full discussion of our concerns here would necessitate an inclusion of these too – but we think that this concentration on public issues has obscured the scientific crisis that sociology is facing within its private milieu. This was a key motivation in producing a book such as this. Sociology's troubles are more private but nonetheless significant and interesting, for we would argue that sociology is facing a *scientific* crisis of considerable intellectual importance. Certainly values cherished by individual sociologists are felt by them to be threatened by some recent developments within sociology's milieu.

It is our contention that the common themes running through sociology's private troubles can be subsumed under the general heading of 'the assault on positivism'. This assault has come both from within and from outside the camp. By positivism we mean simply (or oversimply) working as natural scientists are believed to. It may well be that sociologists no longer believe and practise all of the following: the absolute distinction between fact and value, value-neutrality, predictability with its consequent emphasis on measurement, and so on. However, much of this remains in sociology's research practice, at least implicitly. Positivistic sociology's examplar is Durkheim's *Suicide* (1952), and it is no accident that for years this book was regarded as the seminal work in American graduate schools. So naturally enough many of the disparate assaults on positivism spend a considerable amount of their energies on this work. For example, P. Filmer *et al.*, in their *New Directions in Sociological Theory* (1972), devote themselves *ad nauseam* to disconnecting the social (should we say the human?) from the natural sciences through a demolition job on Durkheim's *Suicide*. Jack Douglas's (1967) criticisms are also well known and take a similar, but more historically informed, line.

However, if positivism – the tried and trusted model of the natural sciences for producing (or was it only certifying?) knowledge – is successfully undermined in the social sciences, what are we left with? To start with, as we suggested in our comments on Gouldner's (1967) discussion of the role of reason, there would be no longer any obvious criteria for adequately certifying knowledge nor for judging the appropriateness of methodological procedures, nor even for what are suitable topics of investigation, let alone for how they should be studied and how we should know anything about them. In the past positivistic methodology did all these things; it no longer does so, hence sociology's troubles. Positivism, articulated to various degrees, provided the normative standards by which sociological research was both judged and practised. Perhaps we should note that the usual term for normlessness is anomie and that this may well be how the epistemological state of current sociology should be characterised. We are, therefore, commenting in this Introduction on a situation that can be called epistemological anomie. This we see as a symptom of sociology's scientific crisis.

For the sake of ease of presentation we shall concentrate on three main assaults on positivism: first, those from *within* the tradition; then those from the phenomenologically influenced ethnomethodologists; and last, those from the Althusserian Marxists. Cumulatively these three very disparate attacks are to a large degree responsible for what we are terming the epistemological anomie of sociology.

The most familiar assaults on positivism are the conventional criticisms that come from within the tradition itself, and they are frequently concerned more with reliability than with what is usually called validity. Ironically, this assault has been stimulated by the very success of positivism in conducting a rigorous pursuit of its own weaknesses. It might be objected that this is not, strictly speaking, part of the assault on positivism so much as reformism from within. Yet we all know that reformism can lead to the subversion of the original aims of any movement, and that is what has happened here (see, for example, the position that Derek Phillips works himself into in his *Abandoning Method*, 1973). Thus, the conventional criticisms of, say, survey research may be seen (indeed are seen) as so massive an indictment of positivism as to fundamentally undermine it. Here, what is emphasised is not that the social world is unavailable to current techniques but rather that our techniques are not yet refined enough. Hence the popularity of books like E. J. Webb *et al.*'s *Unobtrusive Measures* (1966) and the persuasiveness of Phillips's *Knowledge from What*? (1971). Furthermore, the searching out of alternatives to surveys has led some sociologists to conclude eventually that social knowledge itself is of a nature so fundamentally different from that of the physical world that true alternative methodologies should be discovered (see Phillips 1971; Fletcher 1974). Let us hastily add, lest we be misunderstood, that many alternatives to conventional survey research are no less positivistic; facts are still facts and they are still there to be described, but perhaps with less reliance on, say, numerical measurement. Of course, there are some who would argue that the second and more radical assault on positivism is, despite its pretensions to be otherwise, just as positivistic as old-style positivism. This brings us to a consideration of an important attack from outside on traditional positivism.

Sociology's scientific crisis was recently exemplified by a remark which we overheard at a conference. The future of sociology, it was stated, rested upon whether we – i.e. those still prepared to call themselves sociologists – could 'hold the line', attacked as we were by phenomenologists from one side and Althusserians from the other. For this eminent British sociologist the crisis was not coming; it had arrived. Let us start with the phenomenologists, e.g. A. V. Cicourel's well-known *Method and Measurement in Sociology* (1964). This is a somewhat emasculated ethnomethodological attack on conventional positivistic research techniques. However, its main consequence seems to have been to make research methods themselves a subject of sociological inquiry. Cicourel seems to be advocating that instead of doing a survey, for example, the ethnography of doing survey work should be collected – not with the objective of increasing the reliability of social research data, but in order to show that positivistic research methods would *for ever* produce invalid data (so we should note that his purposes are very different from ours in this book). He himself has subsequently done just this on a study of Argentinian fertility (Cicourel 1973). This is a particularly good example of what we may term phenomenological slippage, where the practice prescribed moves the sociologist's interest away from the phenomenon that he or she was originally interested in (be it suicide, crime, fertility or whatever) to the social production of what passes among members for knowledge about that phenomenon. Perhaps it is with Cicourel's assault that we meet one of the central causes of sociology's troubles. For if the assault of positivism is successful and one way of reaching knowledge is undermined, cannot they all be undermined? How then do we know anything? For the ethnomethodologists' assault has not been without success, and they have contributed to a shattering of what remained of an epistemological consensus over the promise of positivistic sociology.

It is particularly instructive, though, to consider the treatment of Cicourel by another ethnomethodologist, Jeff Coulter. Take, for instance, some remarks in his *Approaches to Insanity* (1973). Coulter tells us that, for Cicourel, the emphasis is upon the researcher's having to make explicit remarks as to the communication exchanges he encounters between the people he studies. Yet Coulter goes on to claim that:

'For most other ethnomethodologists, the emphasis is upon analysing the formal procedures and background cultural knowledge informing a given reading, whether or not *that* reading was the one employed by the members whose communicative exchanges constitutes the data for analysis. Such analysis aims at *the highest level of abstraction and generality*. Whilst Cicourel remains at the level of warranting a specific reading or account of the 'meaning' of his data.' (p. 159–60).

Cicourel's position, on the other hand, as stated in his book, *The Social Organization of Juvenile Justice* (1968), is on the contrary that:

'. . . in analysing conversations and reports the researcher must approximate a 'rewriting' of the dialogue or prose so that he can communicate the unstated and seen but unnoticed background expectancies for the reader. Such a procedure would enable the reader to understand how the participants and observer made sense of the environments as portrayed by the research. (p. 18)

Now Coulter's reaction to this is to refer to it somewhat contemptuously as *guesswork*. Cicourel is not analysing his data for their most general properties, 'but for purposes of (re)constructing situation and indexical (context specific) relevancies which might be *assumed* to have gone into their original production' (Coulter 1973, p. 160; our italics). So in fact Coulter maintains that 'the rewriting remains in Cicourel's own terms, measurement by fiat or constructivist analysis' (p. 160). He is, as he says, turning one of Cicourel's most famous attacks on positivistic research methodology back on himself.

The radical nature of Coulter's critique can be seen in the following passage:

'It is the easiest possible trap for the sociologist attracted by the ethnomethodological programme to suppose that such work can be used to underpin particular accounts of social situations, communicative exchanges and other surface phenomenon. The participant observer inquiring into the social organization of some institution, residential area, or factory is doing the sort of sociology for which remedies are not forthcoming. Ethnomethodology announces no less than a paradigm shift; a complete reformulation of what is to count as data, researchable problems and findings; it is incommensurate with a substantive topic orientation to social research.' (p. 160)

We have elaborated this issue in some detail in order to demonstrate that some of the critiques of mainstream positivistic sociology are on closer examination fairly diverse themselves. There can, however, be no mistaking Coulter's claims for ethnomethodology. What we might ask is: how might he convince the unconvinced? Are there ways available to us of choosing between positivistic explanations and methodologies and those favoured by the ethnomethodologists. Our answer is to repeat what we have written above: no – or not yet.

However, what we practise, as exemplified by the essays in this book, is from elsewhere dismissed at best as *mere* sociology (Juliet Mitchell's phrase, 1971) but more usually as bourgeois ideology, and our findings frequently are seen as empiricist dross. For the new scientific Marxism the primacy of theory (perhaps we should say *the* theory) is all. Althusserian Marxism is predicated on a belief in science; indeed Althusserian practice *is* scientific practice. It is just as self-confident as the high positivism of the Columbia/Chicago graduate school models. There is one, albeit a difficult, path to truth, a path which avoids the twin dangers of ideology on the one hand and empiricism on the other. Never for one moment is a belief in objective knowledge and the primacy of theory relinquished. In its assaults on the more empiricist aspects of positivism there is even a weird alliance with reformist positivists (see, for example, the reception given by Sami Zubaida, 1974, to D. and J. Willer's book, *Systematic Empiricism*, 1973).

Willer and Willer's case is that sociology as practised is at best a pseudoscience. It is, as their title suggests, no more than systematic empiricism. There are, according to the Willers, three specific types of thought: the *empirical*, which connects observable to observable (which is what sociology does most of the time, claim the Willers); the *rational*, which makes connections only at the theoretical level; and the *abstractive* (or truly scientific), which connects theoretical and observational levels. As Judith Willer wrote in an earlier publication: 'Empirical thought uses only observables, rational thought uses only mental concepts and abstraction uses only mental concepts and observables together' (1971, p. 24). For the Willers no system of knowledge is scientific unless it connects the observational and theoretical levels – and they find most modern sociology wanting by their criteria. Althusserian Marxists are, of course, delighted to discover such criticism coming from within conventional sociology. This is actually even more surprising because the paragon of scientific virtue that the Willers hold up for approval is not Karl Marx, but Max Weber. As their key example of abstractive thought the Willers use (p. 13) Weber on idealtype construction, where Weber wrote that an ideal type:

'. . . is formed by a one-sided *accentuation* of one or more points of view and by the synthesis of a great many diffuse, discrete, more or less present and occasionally absent *concrete individual* phenomenon, which are arranged according to those one-sidedly emphasised view points into a unified *analytic* construct. In its conceptual purity, this mental construct cannot be found anywhere in reality.' (1949, p. 90)

This is surely very different from the current Althusserian critique of social science practice. The latter is founded, firstly, on a close reading of Marx's later writings and a rejection of his earlier writings, summed up in the well-known phrase 'from alienation to surplus value'; and secondly, on the necessity of an epistemological break with bourgeois social science. The radical nature of this break (compare Coulter, 1973, on Cicourel, 1968) is such that it separates Althusser and his followers from even other Marxists; witness, for example, the debate between Miliband (1969) and Poulantzas (1973) on the nature of the state in capitalist society. The protagonists in this debate frequently miss the positions of their opponents precisely because they are arguing from within totally incommensurable frameworks. This means that what is data for the different sides is not agreed and, what is more, that the relevance of any data is sometimes disputed; no appeals to evidence produced will suffice. At its extreme we offer as an illustration Poulantzas's reply to a question put to him by one of the editors of this book. He was asked whether there was anything at all that could be discovered about advanced industrial societies that would lead him to modify his theory about the nature of that society under capitalism. (Note that this was a typically Anglo-Saxon empiricist question.) His answer was that there was not, and could not be, anything at all. At this point it should be realised that there is a considerable distance between this style of social science and sociology as normally practised.

Steven Lukes (1975), in a review of two recent books by Poulantzas, notes that what he calls the underlying and pervasive dogmatism of this school is characterised by defining terms in such a way as to make them true. For instance, he feels that Poulantzas *defines* the state apparatus as either repressive or ideological, rather than shows how they are. Lukes notes that works of this school 'contain numerous interesting speculations, some of them plausible, about trends within the relations between various occupational groups. But these are offered as theoretically derived *assertions* on the basis of little systematic evidence.' With considerable elegance Lukes centres on the question of methods (in the widest sense) and accuses Poulantzas of being:

'. . . one-sided and undialectical *in* his exclusive preoccupation with objective determinants. There is very little sense here of the existence of alternative options *within* the structures and of the role of action, individual and collective in bringing about (or preventing) social change. Marx himself never ceased to feel the conflicting tugs of structure and of agency, of determinism and of voluntarianism.'

These strictures, it should be emphasised, are aimed not at the Althusserian adaptations of Marxist *theory* but at the underlying realism which defines the relationship between this theory and the procedures and practice of actual research. It is not surprising that the most cogent critique of this realism has come from an historian, Pierre Vilar, since the implications of Althusser's notion of science is that history itself is scientifically impenetrable, condemned to a mere sterile empiricism ('events') on the one hand or a vulgar ideology on the other. According to this view, history is a 'mere assemblage of facts, something to be left out of account once its suggestive potential for theory has been utilized' (Vilar 1973, p. 71). Vilar, while recognising that 'the very concept of history has yet to be formulated' (p. 65), chides Althusser for renouncing the concept of history. Marxist historians must, according to Vilar, exclude 'the repetition of theoretical principles combined with criticism of whoever does not know of them all in the service of skeletal and weightless constructions', whilst simultaneously avoiding a vacuous empiricism:

' "Real" Marxist history, by contrast, must be ambitious in order to advance. It must – and no science can do otherwise – move ceaselessly from patient and ample research to a theory capable of the utmost rigour, but also *from theory to "cases"*, in order to avoid the risk of remaining useless knowledge.' (p. 101; Vilar's italics)

The problem, as Vilar acknowledges, is that Marx himself gave very little practical advice on how this was to be achieved. The dialectical structure of Marxist thought, which has enabled succeeding adherents to view Marxism as a philosophical, theoretical and *methodological* totality, tells us *where* to look but not how to look. But Marx, while constantly 'doing' history (and sociology):

'. . . was no epistemologist. He discovered his method by practising it. We can only recover it in his practice. However, his practice as a historian was exercised in response to quite diverse occasions, so that it contains not one but several different types of analysis, not one but several different levels of information and reflection.' (p. 67)

In their actual *practice*, therefore, we find among Marxists an astonishing range of methodologies, many of them reflecting an unremitting positivism which, in other contexts, they are so concerned to decide. Not only did Marx himself produce a survey questionnaire (see Bottomore and Rubel 1956, pp. 210–20) which even Lazarsfeld would regard with horror, but also more recent practitioners, especially in the 'new' economic and social history, have used official statistics with an abandon matched only by orthodox positivism. (However, for a critique from well within the Althusserian camp, see Hindess 1973.) Unlike the ethnomethodologists, therefore, whose theoretical conceptions have guided them in developing prescriptions for both operationalisation and fieldwork procedures (Garfinkel 1967), Marxists generally, and Althusserian Marxists in particular, have hardly addressed themselves to this problem, let alone solved it to their, or anyone else's, satisfaction.

Have we, then, reached a situation where either you believe or you don't? Are there ways to adjudicate between the various epistemological stances that we have outlined? Recently it has seemed as if an increasing number of sociologists have prepared to answer, 'yes' to the first question and 'no' to the second, and to shrug their shoulders at the ensuing impasse. In the light of this it is interesting to see how philosophers of various persuasions have faced a somewhat similar problem; in order to arbitrate between various epistemological disputations in the natural sciences they have investigated actual natural scientific practice. If one thing unites Popper, Bachelard, Kuhn and, more recently, Paul Feyerabend (1975), it is in their appeal to the history of natural science to establish their positions and to falsify those of their antagonists. They, at least, have agreed on the importance of our knowledge of what scientists actually *do* as a basis for formulating an epistemological position on how science *should* be done. Now, while we might mischievously suggest that their historical practice does not always match their philosophical stance – indeed much of their history seems akin to the kind of positivist inductivism which R. G. Collingwood (1943) dismissed over thirty years ago as 'scissors-and-paste history' – we nevertheless take this to be an important point. It is possible, at least, that an analysis of descriptive methodologies *could* help us to overcome our epistemological anomie. Nevertheless, until recently what sociologists actually do – i.e. how they do their research and how this relates to their theory – has been little explored and little understood. But if we are to understand how what passes for sociological knowledge comes to be produced, it is in these areas that we need to concentrate our attention – hence this book.

It is possible, of course, that an analysis of these descriptive methodologies would reveal that there is *no* method, in which case our epistemological anomie would be perpetuated. It may be that sociologists set out to follow certain procedures – whether positivist or antipositivist – whereas in practice they do not. However, even this need not lead to counsels of despair, for a potential lesson that could be learned from such descriptions is that any method is potentially crippling or blinding – that methods produce trained incapacity. Such, for example, is the conclusion drawn by Paul Feyerabend from descriptive accounts of natural scientific practice in his *Against Method* (1975). The audacity of Feyerabend's work is in his argument that there can be no single research technique, no method; indeed his book argues *against* method. From his examination of how scientists actually proceed, he demonstrates that they had no method; they frequently changed what they were doing and how they did it. Feyerabend concludes that the hitherto accepted accounts, like those by Popper (1963), T. S. Kuhn (1962) and I. Lakatos (1970), are more honoured in the breach than as accurate descriptions of how natural scientists worked. Thus Feyerabend believes that the history and philosophy of science can best be conceived of as residing in a state of epistemological anarchy; indeed he himself rejoices in the label of epistemological anarchist. Naturally the other protagonists have hardly concurred with Feyerabend's findings or interpretations, and they have all expended much energy against each other. (There is a witty and irreverent pastiche of this debate in Ford 1975, ch. 4; a more measured earlier version is Lakatos and Musgrave 1970.)

Following Feyerabend, should sociology's epistemological anomie be more accurately described as epistemological anarchy? Anarchy, however, can only thrive in a tolerant political climate, and we do not currently discern this within sociology's milieu; witness the violence with which both the ethnomethodologists and the Althusserians are attacked and satirised with the consequent accusations of bias, intolerance, discrimination and so on among all parties. Certainly our thesis is that a close examination of actual sociological practice along the lines pioneered by Baldamus (1972) will probably show a wide variety of incommensurate procedures. There is at least a possibility that we will find a degree of epistemological anarchy similar to that which Feyerabend seems to have discerned in the natural sciences. Perhaps, however, we should merely retreat to a more cautious epistemological pluralism and face the consequences of that both for our own practice and in how we teach our students. Normative methodologists are currently fighting a battle to retain their all-inclusive empires displaying what we earlier called epistemological exclusivism. The essays presented here, however, display not such exclusivism but rather a remarkable degree of pluralism.

Finally, it remains to be stated that we still need to analyse the relationship, if any, between these private troubles and the public issues of sociology. Given our desire to separate this collection from its prescriptive predecessors we do not intend to impose a set of ethical and political standards for doing sociological research. We would point out, however, that such considerations were at the forefront, rather than the back, of the minds of most of our contributors throughout their research. More generally there is a clear need to know how far the sociologist's relationships to wide political and ethical issues are responsible for the current situation of epistemological anomie and/or anarchy. Perhaps we should simply note that anarchy is difficult to sell and that a lot of sociology is being bought and sold in the marketplace. A loss of confidence in positivism will almost certainly make consultancies harder to obtain, make sociology less demonstrably 'useful', and make the information thus obtained less amenable to forming a basis for social control by elite groups. May it be that alternative epistemologies developed precisely because of a distrust of working for capital and for the state in mixed economies? We do not want to extend this argument here and now, except to recognise that a full account must relate sociology's troubles to the public issues of sociology.

1

Coroners and the Categorisation of Deaths as Suicides: Changes in Perspective as Features of the Research Process

MAXWELL ATKINSON

REFLECTING ON RESEARCH

Essays like the ones in this book can be seen as constituting a form of extended complaint against the normal ways in which research gets written up and published. Thus, there seems to be an assumption that what *really* went on in getting some piece of research done is not fully reported in the articles and books already published, and hence that other intending researchers and/or naive readers may develop false impressions about the processes of doing research. Sometimes the complaint is directed against 'unreasonable' publishers who, in their ignorance of sociology's problems, insist on regarding as an unnecessary waste of paper the more comprehensive methodological appendices that most authors claim they would like to have included.

As a remedy to this, however, the present opportunity to 'reveal all' is not without its own dangers, and readers need to be alerted against viewing papers purporting to do so as literal descriptions of what actually happened. For all that can be offered is one of several possible versions of how the research was done, events of significance and so on, with each version being equally open to the charge of being no more than yet another piece of neatly reconstructed logic. The present story, for example, tells how perspectival or paradigmatic changes took place during the course of doing research into suicide rates, and how these changes affected the way the research problem was formulated and the kinds of solution to it that were sought. Of the various ways in which the events could have been depicted, there are at least two which seem particularly plausible. The first could be called the 'Vicar of Bray' version, and would have as its scenario the intense theoretical and methodological debates of the late 1960s and early 1970s, with the researcher changing perspective to fall in line with each new trend. The second version has the same backdrop, with the 'Vicar of Bray' replaced by the 'earnest empiricist' diligently trying to follow the advice of the methodologists and constantly striving to find a way of doing rigorous empirical research. Not surprisingly, my own preference is for the latter, and it is this version that is expanded in what follows.

Given these cautionary remarks, the question arises as to whether this chapter has any point at all, so it may be as well to comment at the outset on the possible usefulness the account might have for other sociologists. In this context, the first thing to be said is that the problems encountered in doing the research were, and are, fairly typical of those faced by any other researcher attempting to do empirical studies at the present stage in the development of sociology. This is not intended as an exaggerated claim about the importance of the experiences in question, but it does involve a claim about the importance (or peculiarities) of the kind of background to them which was referred to above. For one of the consequences of the intensified theoretical debates which have characterised the last decade or so is that the problems facing researchers have become much more complicated than was the case in earlier periods. Sociologists are now likely to feel inhibited about doing surveys, or indeed anything that might lead to their work's being derided as 'positivist'. As a possible solution, more and more younger researchers have turned to participant observation, but even this is not without its difficulties, as was illustrated in an encounter between a graduate student and Howard Becker during the latter's stay as Visiting Professor at Manchester. The student, who had already obtained excellent access to an organisation and was about to start fieldwork, told Becker that he was still very worried about which paradigm to adopt in the research. Becker was clearly appalled by such hesitation and advised the student to stop worrying and to 'get in there and see what's going on'. But the point about this is that, today, even this methodology which paid such rich dividends in the work of Becker and his contemporaries has come under attack from enough different camps for new recruits to research to feel more than a little inhibited about taking the plunge.

In summary, then, the range of different research strategies currently available in sociology not only ensures that researchers are faced with a difficult problem of choice between alternatives, but also guarantees that whatever they choose they will lay themselves open to attack from all the other alternative positions set aside. One implication of this is that a certain amount of toughness is required if one is to make a choice and follow through some empirical research, and toughness is a quality difficult to sustain without subcultural support and seldom referred to in the methods texts. Given these kinds of constraints, it is perhaps not surprising that various ways of 'copping out' of empirical work seem to have proved more popular. At least three of these can be detected in the recent literature of sociology, and they can be summarised as 'anything goes', 'nothing goes' and 'everything goes'. The 'anything goes' option involves a recognition of the terrible methodological dilemmas associated with doing social research, coupled with the conclusion that, as no method is anywhere near perfect, it does not matter a great deal what scrap of evidence gets used in what way in support of what argument. The 'nothing goes' option has two variants, both of which can be seen as responses to the same methodological dilemmas. In the first of these, hesitation is so great that the researcher never actually gets into the field, while in the second the empirical research gets done but the hesitation sets in afterwards, thereby preventing the study from ever being written up. Finally, the 'everything goes' solution trades off the methodological troubles in the production of synthesising texts, which claim to review every side of every argument in an attempt to construct some compromise which purports to take them all into account. The main effect of such studies tends to be the provision of further 'data' for the next synthesising text.

Part of the advice contained in this chapter, then, is that each of these reactions is worth avoiding. The 'anything goes' principle inevitably leads to sloppy work, and is almost always inferior to good journalism. The non-productivity entailed by the 'nothing goes' option is self-evidently pointless. And the synthesising texts can often appear absurdly overambitious when written by persons who are not old enough to have accumulated the depth of knowledge and experience that might make such ventures worthwhile – unless, of course, there is already good evidence for believing that the person in question is possessed of the kind of genius required to qualify him or her as a paradigm innovator (this and related terms are derived loosely from Kuhn 1962). Unfortunately, however, the temptations to aspire to this latter status sometimes seem to be more attractive to contemporary sociologists than the more modest task of working within one of the variously flawed paradigms of normal science. In the sociology of deviance, for example, symbolic interactionism had no sooner arrived in Britain than it was being summarised as one of several perspectives on deviance, modified, criticised and even discarded – all on the basis of minimal empirical research along the lines of that done in the United States by those who developed it (this theme is developed further in Atkinson 1974a). More recently, it looks as though ethnomethodology may suffer a similar fate and be dismissed before empirical studies have had a chance to get established, given that so much of the debate has been conducted at the level of programmatics (e.g. Goldthorpe 1973; Taylor *et al.* 1973; Benson 1974; Worsley 1974; Coulter 1974; Wilkinson and Grace 1975). A message of this chapter, then, is not simply that certain responses to methodological diversity are to be avoided, but rather that it may be more worthwhile to select one perspective and to work within it. Certainly it may be found wanting, but to be able to discover the limitations in the process of doing the research may prove more rewarding personally and more convincing to others than purely abstract discourse. And there is always the possibility, however remote, that one may stumble across some interesting discovery which, regardless of its general importance, might never have been imagined had the researcher remained behind locked doors to contemplate the problems of studying social reality.

As a final and perhaps more encouraging word of introduction, it may be noted that, in spite of the difficulties posed by the multiplicity of competing perspectives, the newcomer to research can enjoy an important luxury which is less readily available to his more established colleagues: namely, the freedom to change his mind. For, however attractive or convincing some new perspective may seem to someone who is already known as a functionalist or positivist or whatever, it is no easy thing for such a person to espouse it and embark on a new style of work. In the discipline at large he would be seen as being erratic or inconsistent, while on a more personal level a conversion might entail a reassessment of the earlier work as hopelessly mistaken, as well as depression at the thought of so many wasted years. By contrast, the beginner is by definition one who is still learning and who, unlike the old hands, is not expected to have learned already. Changes of heart, therefore, are less likely to provoke surprised or hostile public reactions, while the absence of a collection of earlier work in need of repudiation minimises the problem of personal adaptation.

THE POSITIVIST PHASE AND THE PROBLEM OF ACCURACY

It is possible in retrospect to divide the seven years or so during which my research was done into three main phases, according to the particular perspective which was predominant at the various points in time. But it was, of course, never quite as simple as that, and there were times when I was not always aware of what phase I was at. The issue was complicated further by the fact that the research was a part-time venture throughout and had to be sandwiched between many other commitments, some of which involved awkward inconsistencies. During the second two years, for example, after the suicide research had already entered the interactionist phase, I held a research fellowship under the terms of which I conducted a national random survey of old people and learned how to construct precoded questionnaires, how to feed data into a computer, and so on, activities which contrasted sharply with my other methodological concerns (Atkinson 1970, 1971a, 1971b, 1973a). These experiences, coupled with the earlier training I had had in quantitative research procedures, were also to prove difficult to set aside even after the point of commitment to interactionism, and, as will be seen below, the possibility of using survey techniques was still being considered at a fairly late stage in the project. Thus, while I now tend to present the research as having been divided into three distinct phases, it should be noted that there were also transitional periods during which features and assumptions of the previous dominant perspective lingered on in work which was purporting to be conducted within a new and alternative framework.

At the very beginning of the research I was not only unaware that the problem was formulated in essentially positivist terms, but also more or less unaware that there were any really serious debates about how sociological research should be done. Programmatic disputes between competing perspectives had not been a central focus in sociology courses during the early 1960s, nor were they much in evidence at my first place of employment after graduation, the Home Office Research Unit. Certainly there was a concern there with the problems of measuring the effectiveness of different kinds of penal treatment and the extent to which rates of reconviction were adequate or accurate enough, but that such things were 'in principle' measurable was never seriously at issue. But one thing which was seen as a serious methodological problem at that time was the gap that was supposed to exist between 'theory' and 'research', and the related implication that some kinds of research could be written off as 'crass empiricism'. The few of us at the Home Office Research Unit who considered ourselves to be sociologists came to share a collective guilty conscience about the work we were engaged in, secretly fearing that it fell into this disreputable category of research. One mode of adapting to this was to teach sociology or criminology at evening classes, which provided a way of escaping into the literature as well as an opportunity to learn and talk about theoretical matters. Another was to sign on at London University as a part-time graduate student, and it was as a result of this option that the present research problem came to be formulated.

Among the MSc courses for which I registered at the London School of Economics was one on the Sociology of Deviance. It was just before labelling theory had made its mark in Britain, and there were no references to people like Becker, Goffman, Cicourel, and so on, on the reading lists. It therefore seemed perfectly reasonable that, at the first class, a volunteer should be sought to write an essay which would 'set the scene' for the course by addressing the question: 'How much deviance is there?' Whoever was to do it was instructed to consult the *Criminal Statistics* and other official publications in order to produce an up-to-date statement of the current rates of crime, delinquency, drug taking, mental illness, suicide, etc. Given the excellent access I had to such materials in the Home Office, it immediately occurred to me that I was especially well placed to take on the assignment, and my offer to do so was accepted forthwith.

In the event I never got as far as the official documents, as my first recourse was to the textbooks, which typically included summaries of how much deviance there was as a prelude to the inevitable discussions of competing explanations of such 'facts'. The most noticeable feature of these books was the way in which each chapter would begin with a few brief remarks about the difficulties involved in getting accurate estimates of the rates, and then proceed to the apparently more interesting business of comparing explanations of the same rates which were supposed to be so inaccurate. It seemed intuitively obvious that there was something odd about this practice, a view which could be shown to have respectable sociological support by referring to the Introduction of the then essential collection

Sociology Today, where Robert Merton had written that 'before social facts can be "explained" it is advisable to ensure that they actually are facts' (Merton *et al*. 1959, p. xiii). The apparent disregard for such problems exhibited in the deviance texts also seemed unreasonable when assessed in relation to discussions of sampling in the methods texts, and very quickly the question of how and why such eminent sociologists were ready to bend such obvious rules so flagrantly established itself in my mind as being of greater interest than the question of how much deviance there was. As a result my essay consisted of a series of headings referring to the types of deviance to which I had been directed (crime, drug taking, suicide, etc.), with a page or two on each saying why it was that no accurate estimates could be provided. It was not well received, and I was accused, among other things, of the cardinal essay-writing sin of having failed to answer the question. This was clearly true, but it nevertheless seemed rather unreasonable given that I had attempted to provide a carefully argued account of why the question could not yet be properly answered.

Shortly after this experience an opportunity arose to turn the theme into a research proposal as part of an application for a research job at Essex University. In composing this proposal it was clear that the whole range of statistics on deviance was not studiable, and for various reasons I decided to focus the outline on suicide. One reason for this was that I had been personally involved with a suicide case at about that time, which had led me to do more reading in that area than in others discussed in the original essay. It also seemed that some of the other possibilities (e.g. crime) were far too complicated; there were so many different types of crime, each seemed to have a different 'clear-up' rate, and therefore each would presumably need to be studied separately. In comparison with this, suicide seemed much more straightforward – at least at that early stage. Finally, the fact that Durkheim's *Suicide* (1952) was based on a reliance on official rates gave the subject an added attraction, given that my research proposal was going to be inspected by sociologists. For a while there were relatively few sociologists at that time with an interest in crime and criminology (Cohen 1974a); most claimed some interest in suicide, even if it did not extend much beyond Durkheim. By focusing on the way in which suicide statistics were compiled, then, the hope was that better rates could be computed so that a more thorough test of Durkheim's theory could be carried out, a goal which was later discovered to be similar to that referred to by Jack Douglas (1967, p. vii) as the original aim of his work on suicide.

Initially, the application was as unsuccessful as the essay had been and I was not appointed to the post for which I had applied. But there then followed a stroke of luck without which the research would never have got off the ground. Alasdair MacIntyre had just moved to a chair in sociology at Essex University and, quite unknown to me, was planning to do some work on suicide. He had also been allocated one of the established one-year research assistantships in the department, and having seen my application for the other post he got in touch with me to find out more about my own interests. An interview was arranged in a public house near Trafalgar Square, the eventual outcome of which was that I was offered a post which would involve me in assisting MacIntyre in his work and in doing my own for a PhD. It did mean giving up the security of a pensionable position in the Home Office in exchange for a one-year appointment, but it seems that if a person wants to take the risk of venturing into the unknown on more than a part-time basis, he also has to be prepared to be continually reminded of the risky nature of the enterprise by the temporary contracts typically associated with such opportunities.

At this point, then, it may be noted that the way the research problem was initially formulated was very much within the framework of what, for convenience, can be called the positivist paradigm. Previous investigators were seen as having been overhasty, rather than theoretically mistaken, in their attempts to explain suicide with reference to the social structure. They had been content to rely on statistical data derived from official sources on the assumption that they were good enough samples of the total population of suicides to use in the process of theory testing. The methodological and statistical literature, however, suggested that, in order to be able to arrive at valid generalisations, researchers should first be able to make certain specifications about the relationship between their sample and the population being sampled. Yet as far as the cases of suicide in the official records were concerned, there was still no way of knowing how representative they were of the population of all suicides. At this stage in the research, then, a clear distinction was being made between the official rate on the one hand and some notional 'real' or 'true' rate on the other, the main task of the research being to discover something about the relationship between the two. The suggestion that it might be misguided to regard suicide rates as 'social facts' or to attempt to uncover the social laws determining them was not even entertained. For the concern was with a technical problem, which questioned none of the paradigmatic assumptions, but which sought to improve the way in which this kind of normal science was typically conducted.

It is, of course, much easier to identify a problem for research than to find satisfactory ways of investigating it, and in this context there were many reasons why I was fortunate in having had Alasdair MacIntyre as supervisor. One of these had to do with his general orientation to scholarship, which apparently had started early in life. Thus, he used to tell a story of how he had had a childhood ambition to read every book that had ever been written, and how his first major intellectual discovery came with the realisation that such a project was impossible. An element of this idea had survived, in that I was instructed to compile as complete a bibliography of works on suicide as possible, with a view to reading them all. In addition to being an essential preliminary to my own work, I was also to draw his attention to particular kinds of study that he would specify from time to time. This approach contrasted markedly with another which was in evidence at

Essex University at that time: namely, that of going into the field at the earliest possible opportunity and then doing some reading afterwards. For reasons which will become clearer below, it was to prove just as well that I did not find myself working within this latter camp.

The first discovery was a repeat of MacIntyre's childhood experience, for it quickly became clear that the chances of reading everything that had ever been written on suicide were minimal. The best estimates reckoned that at least 6,000 works on suicide had been published by 1961 (Rost 1927; Farberow and Shneidman 1961), and I subsequently located another 300 or so that had appeared between then and 1967. For some time, however, I proceeded undaunted by these statistics and spent a great deal of time reading obscure articles on suicide, collecting more and more examples of the way in which researchers were prepared to ignore the inadequacies of their data, as well as clues to possible sources of 'inaccuracy' that I might be able to investigate. Particularly interesting in this context was the discovery of an extensive literature on attempted suicide, threats and related phenomena which, with one or two exceptions (e.g. Wilkins 1967), had been largely ignored by sociologists in their almost exclusive concern with completed suicides. These studies also provided some useful hints on the way in which factors like responses to suicidal warnings and the intervention of others in suicide attempts might have important implications for the way in which suicides became officially recorded as such (Atkinson 1968).

The reading was not limited to the suicide literature, however, but focused also on related areas in sociology. The problems associated with official statistics were, as I knew already, not confined to suicide research, and it seemed likely that some useful clues as to how empirical work might be done might be found in criminology and the sociology of deviance. Very quickly, therefore, I was to discover that there were some people, called interactionists and labelling theorists, who not only had interesting things to say about sociological research which relied on the analysis and explanation of rates of deviance, but were also rather dismissive about the enterprise as a whole (e.g. Kitsuse and Cicourel 1963). This led to an immediate realisation that I was not working on as obscure a technical problem as I had thought. There were others who were not just worried about the way sociologists had used official statistics, but who also had an approach to sociology which involved a radical revision of its methodological procedures, the most shocking of which was the suggestion that good empirical research should be done without recourse to statistics and surveys.

As if all this were not disturbing enough, what seemed at first like a disaster occurred with the discovery of an article in the *European Journal of Sociology* by someone called Jack Douglas (1966). His discussion of suicide and social meanings seemed to be very close to some of the kinds of things that MacIntyre had been intending to say, while his analysis of the official statistics problem held out the possibility that his forthcoming book would leave very little more to say on the matter. At that stage all that could be done was to send for a microfilm of the thesis (Douglas 1965) on which the book (Douglas 1967) was to be based, and a preliminary reading served only to confirm the view that my own research had reached the end of the line. Fortunately, MacIntyre was less pessimistic, and I was slowly persuaded that there were still enough gaps in what Douglas had to say for the project to continue. The initially unnerving feeling of having been completely upstaged by the prior arrival of someone else was gradually replaced by the comforting knowledge that I was not, after all, working alone in a vacuum. Not only were there others in the sociology of deviance who were seriously interested in the official statistics problem, but here was someone else actually applying similar ideas specifically to suicide. Perhaps the problem was a significant one, in which case it might even be important enough for more than one researcher to work on it. And if nothing else, I could always justify my own research by pointing out that I was exploring established ideas in a British context.

At around the same time, another important event occurred when MacIntyre suggested that it was about time I wrote something, and he asked me to prepare a research proposal on the basis of what I had been reading. In it I attempted to formulate the problem in vaguely interactionist terms, arguing that there were a number of crucial stages involved in the process whereby deaths became officially registered as suicides. The importance of 'societal reactions' to threats and warnings before any suicidal act had taken place, both after an attempt and after death, were stressed, and the proposal was made that the research would attempt to investigate these various stages in the process. MacIntyre's response was very encouraging, and he gave me the go-ahead to get on with doing the empirical research, although I was still mystified as to where I could possibly start and what I could possibly do. One way of clarifying matters was to seek the help of other more experienced people in the department, and I therefore volunteered to present a revised version of the research proposal as a paper at one of a series of research workshops which were held at Essex University in those days for precisely this kind of discussion. This was to be my first experience of putting my head on the academic block, and I nervously circulated the paper in advance, in the hope that those who thought it to be nonsense would stay away from the seminar. As a further precaution I stayed away from the department until the appointed day when, having got to my room without being seen, I locked myself in to prepare for the ordeal. But it was not long before I had to open it for the leading methodologist in the department who, to my amazement, had come to say some quite complimentary things about the paper and to apologise for not being able to attend the meeting. This generally favourable response continued throughout the day, by the end of which one or two people had actually suggested that I should send the paper off to a journal. As a result the first publication on the research appeared a few months later (Atkinson 1968).

Lest it seem that all this detail is redundant, it may be as well to explain at this point that the acceptance of that paper had important implications for the way the research developed and for the eventual writing up of the whole project as a thesis. For one thing, it outlined a programme of further research which could never have been followed through in practice, and hence it deserved to be relegated along with so much other sociology to the dustbin of empty promises. At the same time, the fact that it was published, and even reprinted (in Giddens 1971), committed me to doing a certain kind of work notwithstanding that I was not at all clear as to the precise shape such work should or could take. A temporary solution involved an attempt to apply some of its ideas to a specific case: namely, student suicides. This led to a further publication (Atkinson 1969), but this, like the earlier one, failed to repudiate fully some of the positivistic assumptions that had been involved at the start of the research. Thus, both papers were still concerned with the problem of the *accuracy* of the statistics and hence had retained the notion that there was an empirically warrantable distinction to be made between *official* and *real* suicide rates. Similarly, both held out the hope of arriving at some kind of explanation of suicide *per se*, even though the emphasis on processes and social meanings provided a different slant from the more traditional concern with structural explanations. These, then, were some of the legacies of positivism that were to linger on during the next main phase of the research.

THE INTERACTIONIST PHASE AND THE PROBLEM OF MEANING

While it may seem that too much attention is being given to these early papers, it may also be noted that the way in which publications can affect the course of the research on which they report is something which is seldom referred to in research manuals and reports. Yet in the present case they seemed to have sufficiently important implications for the progress of the work, both positive and negative, for the subject to deserve further comment. One word of caution, however, is that it may have been a special case because of the subject matter in question. For the fact that most sociologists profess at least some interest in suicide meant that the first exploratory paper came to be fairly widely read, and it even began to appear on reading lists and to be used as a teaching resource in some institutions. The luxury of being able to forget and to rely on others to forget (or not to have read) one's earliest efforts, then, was something I could not take for granted, and whether I liked it or not I had already become associated with a style of work which created specific expectations about the kind of thing that might follow. This personal experience of being labelled as some kind of interactionist hastened my commitment to an interactionist 'career', which in turn strengthened my faith in the validity of labelling theory.

Some of the positive advantages of publication had rather negative effects on the empirical research. The subsequent jobs which they presumably helped me to get made the research an even more part-time venture than it had been at the start. And I became increasingly involved in giving visiting lectures, conference presentations and the like, events which tend to stimulate the proliferation of premature and inadequately formulated papers. Time which could otherwise have been spent in the field was diverted to the preparation of papers and talks about the research I should like to have been getting on with if only I did not have to keep writing about the research I should like to have been getting on with. Indeed, this present essay can itself be regarded as yet another instance of the kind of obstacle that keeps one from doing empirical work. Such complaints, of course, may seem hollow given how easily they can be overcome by the simple refusal of invitations. But this solution is likely to involve a long period of non-productivity while the research is being done, and there does seem to be quite a serious problem as to how the possible risks associated with this (e.g. failing to write it up or to get it published) are to be balanced against the instant gratifications sometimes involved in accepting invitations, and the deferred gratification that might eventually result from continual small additions to a curriculum vitae.

On the more positive side, a first publication serves a ritual integrative function similar to being blooded during a fox hunt, and this was particularly important in the Essex University context at that time. Research assistants in university departments tend to be marginal persons *par excellence* in that they are neither 'proper' staff nor 'proper' students, one effect of which is that there are few structured opportunities for them to benefit from the 'brushing with better minds' that is supposed to be a routine part of the university experience. This situation was aggravated at Essex University in those days both because it was a big department and because of a pervading self-consciousness about its status as a centre of sociological excellence. This meant that the staff were extremely busy doing the kinds of things which have to be done to sustain such a reputation, most of which involve various forms of disappearance. That there were several leading figures in different fields meant further that there was a high degree of specialisation, so that a researcher who did not happen to share in any of the available interests might have little to offer and little to gain in discussions with staff. In this respect I was one of the fortunate ones, and it was as a result of writing the first paper that I found and became friendly with someone who was at the frontiers of the relevant specialism. Dorothy Smith, it emerged, not only was working on mental illness, but also had done research at the University of California and actually knew personally many of the giants of interactionism. A small underground group of interactionists subsequently began to evolve around her, and the subcultural support and encouragement this provided were crucial factors in building up the confidence necessary to venture into what was still a rather new domain as far as British sociology was concerned.

Although this move towards the new perspective led to various changes of focus in the research, the way the problem had originally been formulated meant that only a slight alteration was necessary to continue without having to abandon the main theme. Certainly the idea that the alleged 'gap' between the official suicide rate and some purportedly 'real' rate could be measured was set aside, mainly on the grounds that it presupposed that there was some clearly defined objectified definition of suicide which could be applied in some unproblematic way to achieve such an end. But the interactionist literature on deviance, and particularly Douglas's work on suicide (1965, 1966, 1967), regarded the way in which activities were defined as deviant as involving complex social processes which were themselves worthy of study in their own right. Thus, the question of how some deaths get defined as suicide could remain as a central focus without being inconsistent with the ideas of the new perspective. Whereas originally it had been intended that the investigation would lead to more rigorous ways of doing Durkheimian positivism, it now came to be directed to questions about the different available definitions of suicidal situations and about the social meanings of suicide.

The general change in orientation did not, however, provide any immediate solution to the problem of what kind of empirical research should now be done, which is probably one reason why parts of the positivist legacy survived for so long. Another might have had to do with the very obvious difficulties involved in using participant observation to study suicidal phenomena. But I also retained doubts about the vagueness and apparent sloppiness which seemed to characterise some of the research strategies adopted by interactionists: a funny story here, an apt quote from a 'subject' there, a few extracts from a newspaper or television. Indeed, it sometimes seemed that anything one happened to stumble across would do, so long as it seemed relevant in some way to the arguments being presented. This was very different from the ordered way in which survey research could be carried out, and it was not easy to make the decision to forget so many hard-learned principles and exchange them for so vaguely specified an alternative. I therefore began to try ways of organising the research which would be both 'systematic' and relevant to my new-found interests. In examining press reports of suicide, for example, the newspaper would be held constant by looking at different issues of the same one over a fixed period of time. Coding was used to collect data from coroners' records, IBM cards were punched, and reasonably large samples were still considered a necessity.

While these variously positivistic methods were being deployed in the pursuit of answers to interactionist questions, other 'qualitative' data were steadily and unknowlingly being collected. I had obtained access to a coroner's records as a result of an offer from the Essex County Coroner to make them available to anyone in the newly established local university who had a serious research interest in suicide. Taking advantage of such an offer obviously involved meetings, but on the several occasions when I had lengthy discussions with him neither of us was aware that a 'research interview' was taking place. At about the same time I had been reading about the coroner system, and I had discovered that it was organised in a way which was ideally suited to examination by a lone researcher with virtually no financial resources and that this examination could be done without having to make the kinds of methodological sacrifices that typically have to be made under such circumstances. The idea was to interview coroners about the way they worked, how they dealt with equivocal cases, and so on, partly in person and partly by mail. The full-time coroners dealt with about one-third of all sudden deaths in England and Wales, and there were few enough of them for it to be, in principle, perfectly manageable to see them all. A mailed questionnaire asking similar questions could then be sent to the remaining part-time coroners so that, with luck, it would be possible to base the findings on the total universe of coroners and to forget about sampling problems. But this positivist dream of perfection was not to be, partly because I failed to get the official permission of the Coroners' Society to proceed, and partly because during the process of trying to obtain permission I had collected more 'qualitative' data which had given me other ideas. In short, the history of the first publication was about to repeat itself.

The interactionist underground had not been confined to Essex University; it had thrived elsewhere to the extent that a group of similarly inclined people had started a series of regular meetings on the sociology of deviance. Before the 'deviancy symposia' mushroomed into the National Deviancy Conference, the atmosphere was generally favourable towards labelling theory and the attendances were still small enough for working papers on research in progress to comprise a major part of the proceedings. When I presented mine, publication was again suggested, only this time a definite slot was being offered in the forthcoming Penguin book, *Images of Deviance* (Cohen 1971). The earlier experience had made me wary about publishing yet another 'exploratory' paper, and the positivist in me was worried that it rested so heavily on so few unstructured conversations with a handful of haphazardly sampled coroners. There was also the possibility that premature publication would finally put an end to any remaining hope of persuading the coroners that it would be a good idea to let me interview them. But the prospect of a certain publication, alas, proved too much of a temptation to delay until the project was nearer to reaching the newly promised goal.

Perhaps because of the wide circulation of Penguins, the paper (Atkinson 1971c) had an even more profound effect on the research than the earlier ones. It was more widely read, and news began to filter back that it was being regarded by some as a more authoritative statement than the first. Even though it had been meant to be exploratory and full of disclaimers about the tentative nature of the analysis, it seemed that some of the conclusions were already being cited as more or less definite and, apart from writing a more explicit disclaimer, it was difficult to see what could be done at this stage to reassert its exploratory character. Indeed, if people believed it already, the question arose as to whether it was worth doing more research or writing more papers along the same lines. Further work might lead to a public revelation that the earlier effort had been superficial and perhaps even wholly mistaken; or alternatively it might generate more and more data in support of a case that was apparently convincing enough to enough people already.

These, however, were not the only reasons why a new crisis was precipitated by the publication of the paper, and others arose from some of the points made in it. Briefly, the argument had been that, in the process of deciding how a death occurred, coroners looked for things that could be associated with a suicidal death and that these 'cues' suggested what kinds of further evidence it would be relevant to collect. The more suicidal cues that could be found, the more likely it would be that a death would be categorised as a suicide. It appeared that the officials worked with a model of the typically suicidal death, against which the actual cases were assessed. And, like sociologists and other suicidologists, they seemed to be collecting data in order to test hypotheses, and, to carry the parallel further, they appeared to be involved in explaining why people commit suicide. To find a cause or a motive for a suicide was evidently a crucial part of finding *that* a death was a suicide.

One implication of this, which was to become increasingly disturbing when I reflected on it, was that there appeared to be a convergence between commonsense and expert theorising about suicide, and that there were good reasons why the latter was in line with the former. For if coroners regarded evidence of, for example, depression or social isolation as strong indicators that a suicide had taken place, it was hardly surprising that statistical analyses based on their decisions would 'discover' such connections. It was still a puzzle as to what the import of this was for their practice of claiming that such correlations supported general explanatory theories, and the issue was ducked at that stage by attempting to incorporate the idea into a sort of a deviancy amplification model which claimed to show how such commonsense theories of suicide were disseminated and, by implication, how they might give rise to suicidal activities. In short, the positivist legacy was still evident in this continued concern to make causal statements about how it *really* is in the world: to replace one kind of determinism with another.

ETHNOMETHODOLOGY AND THE PROBLEM OF CATEGORISATION

At the heart of the final paradigmatic crisis in the research was the problem of what to make of the apparent convergence between commonsense and expert theorising about suicide, and in particular whether the implication of this was that the layman's charge against sociology to the effect that it was no more than commonsense was, after all, perfectly justified. When these doubts were at their height, however, subcultural factors again became important and led to a growing conviction that a way out of the dilemmas was provided by the ethnomethodologists. By this time, I had been at the University of Lancaster for a year when D. R. Watson, who had recently become interested in ethnomethodology and who was also actively engaged in suicide research (Watson 1975), joined the department. One immediate result of his arrival was that the pros and cons of the ethnomethodological programme became a constant topic of conversation, and another was a return to the writings of Garfinkel (1967) and Cicourel (1964, 1968) and the discovery of the work of Harvey Sacks (1963, 1966, 1972a, 1972b).

When Garfinkel's *Studies in Ethnomethodology* (1967) had first appeared, I had mistakenly concluded that it was in much the same vein as E. Goffman's studies (e.g. 1968), although much less clearly written. On rereading it, however, the methodological implications of Garfinkel's discussion of indexicality, reflexivity and practical sociological reasoning began to sink in, spurred on by the fact that a number of aspects of the studies seemed particularly relevant for precisely the kinds of problem that were causing the main difficulties in my own research. First, 'practical sociological reasoning' seemed to refer to the same type of process as the one which I had referred to as 'commonsense theorising' and, furthermore, Garfinkel had no inhibitions or doubts about the similarities between lay and professional practical reasoning. Thus, the central mistake of sociologists was held to be the failure to regard their own reliance on unexplicated interpretive procedures for making sense of a potentially senseless world as a matter for serious study. A second attraction was that the book includes an analysis of the problem coroners face when confronted with an 'equivocal death', although I initially received this with mixed feelings because there is one paragraph in which Garfinkel seems to say as much or more than everything I had written to that point (pp. 17–18), a discovery which brought back memories of the first reading of Jack Douglas's work on suicide (1966). A third relevant feature was that the problem of categorisation and description was regarded by Garfinkel as an issue worthy of analysis *in its own right*; such analyses had already begun to show rich dividends in the work of Harvey Sacks (1972a, 1972b) and E. Schegloff (1972). In one sense, this provided some justification for continuing with the main theme of my own research, although an important difference was that attempts to do something more than explore the categorisation procedures – like, for example, inventing quasi-causal models such as the one referred to earlier – could now be abandoned.

While all this suggested a way forward for the research without altering the general focus on the ways in which sudden deaths are categorised, the transition to ethnomethodology was rather more painful than the earlier change of perspective. For not only did it involve discarding some of the most deeply entrenched traditional rationales for doing sociology (e.g. to construct decontextualised descriptions and theories of social action which are different from and better than the situated practical descriptions and theories of members), but in addition the new analytic interest was to be in the topic of descriptive procedures rather than in suicide *per se*. Data on suicidal phenomena thus became no more and no less appropriate than data on any other topic describable by members, which meant that the earlier hopes of eventually being able to make some more or less definitive set of statements about the actual topic of suicide also had to be abandoned. There were compensations, however, as the new focus did provide a sort of definite solution to the central question of how sudden deaths get categorised: namely, in much the same way as anything else gets categorised. And if this seemed somewhat unsatisfactory after so much effort, it did at least entail a further compensation in the greater fascination of the new domain of inquiry implied by such a reorientation.

The foregoing, however, is very much a retrospective gloss of what was going on during the transitional period. During this time, for example, some other research in which I had become involved had provided me with excellent access to a police force (Atkinson 1974b), one consequence of which was that I was able to engage in a period of participant observation with a coroner's officer. And while this allowed for the development of some of the themes set up earlier in the research, it also led to an increasing scepticism about the potential of observational methods both for traditional sociology (including interactionism) and for ethnomethodology. Later I was to discover that this was the first sign that the history of my experiences in sociology, as related so far, had begun to repeat itself, for it increasingly became apparent that there were competing perspectives and choices to be made even *within* ethnomethodology. Thus, the highly technical conversational analyses pioneered by Sacks, Schegloff and Jefferson (1974) contrasted markedly with the ethnographic studies of people like Bittner (1967a, 1967b) and Sudnow (1965, 1967). But there was not enough time then (or now) to try out a selection of the available styles. Any description, as Sacks (1963) elaborates so succinctly, can be indefinitely extended and will always require an *et cetera* clause to draw it to a close. For the practical purpose of meeting the PhD thesis deadline (and the length limitation on this chapter), therefore, all that could be done was to tell a story of the journey through the perspectives up to the point where a new one through the varieties of ethnomethodology was just beginning (Atkinson 1973b).

2

Reflections on the Banbury Restudy

COLIN BELL

It is essential to stress that this is a personal account. This chapter has, however, been greatly improved by comments that I received on an earlier version from my former colleagues on the Banbury restudy: Margaret Stacey, Eric Batstone and Anne Murcott. This does not, however, imply that they approve or endorse this chapter. On the contrary, there remains a regrettable gulf between us, and it would be quite impossible to agree an account now. While each of us would produce a personally valid account, each account would be very different.

BEGINNINGS

Power, Persistence and Change: A Second Study of Banbury (Stacey *et al.* 1975) was finally published almost ten years after Margaret Stacey and I had begun to make specific preparations for restudying the town. Margaret Stacey's interest in Banbury had, of course, lasted longer. From 1944 to 1951 she had worked for the adult education movement in Banbury and, during that time, had collected with Charles Kimber and Cyril Smith the data that were the basis for *Tradition and Change: A Study of Banbury* (Stacey 1960).

I first knew that Banbury was the subject of a community study as well as a nursery rhyme when I was a final year undergraduate (at the University of Keele) sometime in 1963–4 when I came across *Tradition and Change* in the bibliography of *A West Country Village* (Williams 1963). I did not read it until the next year when I was a postgraduate student at Swansea being supervised by Bill Williams. During that year I also bought a copy of *Tradition and Change*, but without any interest or intention of doing a restudy. I was at that time doing the research that resulted in *Middle Class Families* (Bell 1968).

I remember that one particularly wet day in Swansea, during the summer of 1965, I discussed with Margaret Stacey certain difficulties I was facing in writing up my then current research. I complained to her about the desperate homogeneity in lifestyle and social position of the families whose social and geographical mobility patterns I was analysing. They were so similar; if only I had some working class families by way of comparison or was doing a proper community study with a wider range of population, then I believed that the writing up would be so much easier. Just how wrong I was will emerge from this account. Nevertheless the final chapter of *Middle Class Families* contains a typology of mobility patterns which I said (on p. 167) 'would require a considerable sample, e.g. a Banbury' to explore.[1] It was from that conversation that my involvement in what was to become the Banbury restudy began. In terms of how I then visualised the study it is important to know that I was particularly impressed by a diagram called 'Summary Social Structure' in *Tradition and Change* (p. 173). It divides the population of Banbury four ways: into traditional and non-traditional, manual and non-manual. I supposed that what we might do was to find out how the proportions that fell into each quarter might have changed in the intervening years.

Margaret Stacey had from the time of the first Banbury study thought that there should be a restudy, but she saw little hope of returning to Banbury herself. Now, however, we contemplated doing at least what Robert Lynd did when he returned to Middletown, or what Oscar Lewis did in Tepoztlan, or what Art Gallaher Jr did in Plainville (see Lynd and Lynd 1937; Lewis 1951; Gallaher 1961). That these were vastly different enterprises we were dimly aware, yet that was not fully thought through at that stage – though they were all mentioned in our original application for funds to the Nuffield Foundation. We spent a lot of time in the autumn of 1965 drafting our research proposal. We said that in particular our objectives were:

(i) (a) to assess the social systems present in Banbury, particularly those associated with class and tradition and
    (b) to assess the social changes which have taken place in these systems since 1950 when the previous study was made. Specifically the object would be to test certain predictions that were made in that study about likely future changes.
(ii) to observe the new immigration which is now taking place and which will continue for the next few years.

We said that our methods would be:

(i) By examination of documents, interviews with officials, town leaders and others, to gain some knowledge of the social developments of the period 1950–1966.
(ii) By participant observation by a number of research workers, who would be required to be resident in the Banbury area. Each would par-

ticipate in different aspects of the life of the town, their pooled data providing a qualitative assessment of the way the social system works.

(iii) By sample schedule to ascertain certain social characteristics of the population, where this is necessary to supplement the census. Place of origin, length of residence, place of work, whether in or outside Banbury, associational allegiances, kin connections, are examples of the information likely to be needed. This data would give some estimate of the size of the social systems isolated.

(iv) By examination of the local press and by interview of key informants to plot the leadership of the town's associations, in particular to ascertain the extent to which these overlap and cluster, thus providing indicators of the social system.

(v) By interview of selected sub-samples to analyze the relationships within the extended family, which vary with membership of different social systems, particularly between the locally-based and those which are not locally based.

Early in 1966 we were awarded £20,000 (which was £3,000 less than we had asked for) to start the research in October 1966. I was so eager to start in Banbury that I began hastily to write up my Swansea research, submitting it for an MSc Econ. rather than a PhD as I was not prepared to meet the University of Wales's nine-term residence requirements. Our grant was for three years to 1969, yet we did not publish until 1975. Some of the delay was due to publishing problems; some was due to my taking a lectureship at the University of Essex after two years of working on the restudy; the rest was due to the inordinate and really totally unforeseen difficulties we discovered in writing up and in working together. For while my research on middle class families may have suffered from a lack of comparative data, at least I alone had made most of the decisions about what to write about them – and I alone had done *all* the fieldwork.[2] Many of the lessons to be learned from the Banbury restudy emerge from having four people working together and from our failure to face, let alone solve, the organisational and authority problems involved.

As Anne Murcott, one of the research assistants on the restudy has pointed out to me, my view of the Banbury restudy is very much that of the foreman, and indeed I was often cast in that role by the other researchers. What is more, I suspect that I often gladly embraced that role in order to be more certain about what I should have done in the field. Some of the discomfort that is displayed in the following account probably derives from my feelings of being jammed between the boss and the workers. Of course, the foreman role is not easily compatible with the notion of colleagueship – a style of working that we also adopted when it suited us. This means that retrospective interpretations of what went on during the research depend on which of these two competing and almost incompatible models are now seen as the most appropriate. The reactions of my former colleagues to earlier versions of this chapter used both models almost interchangeably, and I too am not always easily able to keep them apart. I am somewhat heartened to discover that Jennifer Platt (1976) suggests that projects with three levels of hierarchy – like the Banbury restudy – are generally the most conflict-ridden.

DISTANCES

Banbury is about 200 miles from Swansea. It was always envisaged that whatever other methods we were to use the study would involve *fieldwork* – that is to say, living in Banbury. We never envisaged that Margaret Stacey would be more than marginally involved in the actual fieldwork, nor was she, though she visited us frequently to supervise the project. It seemed natural at the time that both I and the research assistants would live there. I moved to Banbury with my family in September 1966. Eric Batstone, just graduated from Cambridge, moved there with his wife earlier that summer and worked there for a couple of months before joining the project. Anne Murcott, just graduated from Edinburgh, moved there slightly later than us, with her husband and two young children. All three families bought houses in the town – in itself a fairly extraordinary thing to do for what was known in advance to be a limited stay. So in some ways we were very much more than the usual transient fieldworkers, and we certainly discovered a great deal in detail about the local housing market. The results of our very localised fieldwork in the neighbourhood in which we lived can be found in *Power, Persistence and Change* (ch. 7).

Locating the project physically in Banbury meant that we only *visited* the Swansea department (of which Anne Murcott and Eric Batstone could be forgiven for hardly feeling members), rather than visited Banbury to do occasional fieldwork – which was what Margaret Stacey was to do. Eric Batstone and Anne Murcott also registered for higher degrees with the University of Wales, both from choice and from the policy of Bill Williams, the head of the Swansea Sociology and Social Anthropology Department, who held that *all* research assistants should so register. This trivial point was to become very important in the organisational structure of the project, for while my responsibility was to see that the fieldwork was done I quite explicitly had no responsibility for supervising Eric Batstone and Anne Murcott. They therefore had two masters and split loyalties: me/Margaret Stacey/the project *as a whole* on the one hand, and their thesis/their supervisor on the other; or the project and their personal careers. The situation was actually considerably more complicated by the facts that Margaret Stacey was also their supervisor and that their theses (based as they were at least in part on subsamples from the main survey) depended on the project as a whole. In the selection of topics for their theses the research assistants were 'encouraged' to work in areas that would contribute to the project as a whole, but the demands of the project were not always compatible with producing a doctorate. It was a structure that could be manipulated by all concerned to maximise whatever end any individual chose to pursue at any one time. The research assistants' perceptions are that I failed to give them the day-to-day support and direction that they required. Yet there was an inbuilt organisational problem which was never satisfactorily solved. Eric Batstone's interpretation, for example, was that he and Anne were unhappy 'about the fact that we as raw graduates were given virtually no guidance as to what we did and how'. This organisational ambiguity meant that delays in thesis preparation could be blamed on the demands of the project; what seemed to me to be tardiness on the part of the research assistants or their unwillingness to do certain tasks could be justified by reference to the needs of thesis writing. I now realise that there was always a very serious authority problem built into the organisation of the project, a problem made worse by the kind of people we all were – and, what is more, became during the fieldwork.

Whatever were the original intentions of Margaret Stacey, myself, Eric Batstone, Anne Murcott, or for that matter the Nuffield Foundation, authority and responsibility within the project were always ambiguous, frequently changing and often uncertain. They were open to misunderstanding, reinterpretations and sometimes veiled, sometimes open conflict between the members of the research team. It is significant that the three fieldworkers were very inexperienced; I had only graduated two years earlier and Eric Batstone and Anne Murcott were straight from university. And though we were a long way from Swansea and had therefore to fend for ourselves from day to day – like any fieldworkers – we had neither the consolation of continual support nor the freedom that came from isolation. It was not a happy mean.

I kept a very detailed diary for the first three months of the fieldwork; when I reread it now it still conveys to me the mixture of excitement and boredom we faced. I still recall those months as some of the most interesting of my life. Yet the diary also records a lot of the trivial irritations. It was clearly seen to be my responsibility to find the research assistants something to do and to provide directions, but my diary records that we were far from sure in what direction to point or look. A great deal of fieldwork obviously does consist of just sitting around, which may well be the right and proper thing to do in Bongo-Bongo Land where occasionally, if the accounts are to be believed, the fieldworker may actually have something to observe. It was not entirely clear where we should sit or what we should observe in Banbury.

LOCATIONS

Or rather it was clear where we sat. This is a very important point about the fieldwork. We always realised that we would need an office in Banbury. On an early visit to the town, in the spring of 1966 before the fieldwork began,

Margaret Stacey and I called on a key informant of hers (a trade union official, Alderman and ex-Mayor, i.e. part of the local Labour Party establishment) and among other things asked about office space. We were recommended to approach a friend of his, also a Labour activist, who owned a large warehouse. On being approached by us he promptly offered us space, and what we eventually got was a huge (and impossible to heat adequately) room garishly painted, the previous tenants having been a pop group who used it as a rehearsal room.[3] So our first days as fieldworkers were spent as painters and decorators producing white walls. We very quickly became very close to the Labour Party who occupied offices upstairs; indeed later we exchanged our one large room for two of their smaller ones that were more suited to our needs. The point that needs emphasising here is that Margaret Stacey had fed us instantly (and very well) into her old Labour Party network — and this could now be seen as foreclosing on certain sorts of restudy that could have been contemplated, despite the conscious attempts of all of us, including Margaret, to keep all our options open.

Whatever the talents needed to be an excellent fieldworker actually are, they are not necessarily the same as those required to run a research team or manage an office. I was quickly (and my diary records sharply) reminded by the research assistants that if the office was cold or dirty it was my responsibility to do something about it. Certainly we started the fieldwork from an office that we variously viewed as interesting, quaint or a slum. Indeed sometimes we felt forced out of it (by each other and the need to restore our circulation) to stride the streets like some latter-day Robert Park. I was very conscious of the Chicago model of fieldwork and emulated Park not only by doing a lot of walking. We also produced together very early on in the fieldwork the ecological map that was the basis for that printed on p. 11 of *Power, Persistence and Change*. It was derived from several industrious days in the council offices looking at rate books.

Our office's location close to the offices of the Labour Party meant that very quickly we knew an enormous amount about them — far more than we were ever to know about the Conservative Party though most of the Tory activists were also eventually interviewed. Labour activists frequently dropped in, both on their agent *and* on us. We spent hours in their company. I am sure that there was at the very least some element of capture here — but we could also claim that we saw the local scene as one locally important group did, which was something some fieldworkers never achieve. The first weeks in the field, then, consisted of a fair amount of sitting in the office gossiping with Labour Party activists, interviewing more formally political activists from all three parties in their homes, and attending all and any attendable meetings that we could discover were going on. We also collected, Eric especially, employment statistics and began interviewing religious leaders.

We also spent a lot of time thinking about the whole nature of restudies and replications. For instance, I gave a seminar on the problems involved at the University of Kent in the autumn of 1966. I concentrated at that seminar on some of the difficulties of replication when the central notions of the first study are as tricky as 'tradition'. I also suspected (and still do) that there were some important lessons to be learned from Oscar Lewis's criticisms of Robert Redfield.[4] However, at that stage we were working well within what still seems to me to be a positivistic paradigm; before Christmas 1966 we collectively produced a list entitled 'Hypotheses to be tested', which was derived from *Tradition and Change* and which extended to nineteen foolscap pages of single-spaced typing. They varied from no. 2: 'Some immigrants found it unsociable', through no. 79: 'The function of the immediate family to pass on the ways of behaviour, manners and attitudes of the parents to the children is made easier by the differentiation of housing', to no. 178 (lastly): 'Few non-traditionalists have rejected every traditional value and traditionalists are not entirely closed to new ideas. Traditional society is capable of absorbing new ideas. What is non-traditional today may well be traditional tomorrow and this new tradition itself open to the challenge of fresh change'. It was at this time that I copied out the following footnote from *On Theoretical Sociology*:

'John Dollard's "Caste and Class in a Southern Town" teems with suggestiveness, but it is an enormous task for the reader to work out explicitly the theoretical problems which are being attacked, the interpretative variables, and the implicit assumptions of the interpretations. Yet all this needs to be done if a sequence of studies building upon Dollard's work is proposed.' (Merton 1967, fn. 30, p. 154)

Underneath it I queried, 'Applicability to *Tradition and Change*?'

QUESTIONNAIRE CONSTRUCTIONS

Towards Christmas 1966 we also began to work steadily towards producing the 'main survey'. It was originally assumed that eventually it would be from this main survey that various strategic groups would be drawn as subsamples that would form the basis of Eric Batstone and Anne Murcott's theses, though some alternative strategies were considered. In the end both research assistants added a considerable amount of observational data and some data based on samples they derived themselves. The main survey was the source of most of the head-counting data in *Power, Persistence and Change*. It was, however, based on what I now see to be a ludicrously overdetermined questionnaire. At the very least we should have asked fewer people more questions. The large sample size – we set out to interview 6% of the Banbury area (see app. 1, pp. 136–40 of *Power, Persistence and Change* for the details) – was, we believed, in order to get enough cases in each 'box'. Remember the influence of Margaret Stacey's diagram on p. 173 of

Tradition and Change? So, our reasoning went, if we were interested in, say, upwardly mobile, middle-class, Banburian-born women, then how many people in all would we need to interview to get enough such women? And so on and so on. Also we were overdetermined by both our knowledge of, and the then existing development of, data-handling technology. I was familiar with punch cards and counter-sorters but not with computing. Incredible as it must now seem, we set out to get all our basic data on *one* punch card only. That ambition determined how many questions were asked. At the time it did not quite seem the restriction that it now does, for we limited ourselves virtually to collecting what are normally used as 'face-sheet variables'. Margaret Stacey was adamantly opposed to asking what she always referred to (slightly contemptuously) as 'attitude questions' on surveys, and in this she was strongly supported by the Swansea Department at seminars. For instance, after much argument we did not even ask 'self-rated class' on the main survey – an interest in which would have seemed to be consistent with the main themes of *Tradition and Change* as perceived by most commentators. Eric Batstone suffered particularly here as he wanted 'class imagery' questions from which to draw his subsamples (see Batstone 1975). We, the fieldworkers, conceded far too easily to the retorts that we would not know what the answers meant. So our questionnaire was a short sharp instrument administered to a large number of people (1,449 with 220 non-contacts).

The administration of this research instrument and the analysis of the data it produced dominated much of the remainder of the project. Clearly there was no other way of systematically collecting so much information about so many individuals, yet David and Judith Willer's strictures on systematic empiricism (1973) could have had the Banbury survey in mind. We did not do much more than replicate the 1966 sample census. The survey caused us all a great deal of aggravation, but at least it gave us a *raison d'etre*. Somewhat oddly we called ourselves the Banbury Social Survey on our notepaper and on our noticeboard by our office entrance (with University College, Swansea in very small letters). This was done without a great deal of thought but seemed the simplest way at the time of telling Banbury what we were up to.

The survey itself was a lot of work, cost a lot of money (it was the biggest item on our budget after our salaries) and was very time-consuming. And as the bitter recriminations later showed, it was extraordinarily difficult to do well. It was easy to make mistakes in transcribing, coding and punching. Despite the fact that we had gone to the computing centre for advice before drafting the questionnaire, the staff there were not able to be as helpful as we would have liked. This was, of course, before the days of data analysis programs like SPSS. We once calculated that we could have produced all the tabulations we wanted on the old counter-sorter not only more quickly accurately and comprehensibly, but also more cheaply – even if we had stayed in the most expensive hotel in Swansea for the month we thought that it would have taken us to do the job. Eventually the research assistants and Margaret Stacey were saddled with the excruciating task of data analysis for several months. The sheer frustration of doing this kind of work, as those who have ever done it will know, can make one become very bitter and search for scapegoats. We were no different.

RECRIMINATIONS

Naturally a great deal of the data analysis took place in the last formal year of the project, 1968–9, by which time I was at the University of Essex. My move to the best sociology department in Britain brought to a head a number of the tensions and conflicts within the project as a whole. It would be true to say that the three of us in the field were never welded into a team; whether that was ever possible it is now impossible to say. Certainly Margaret Stacey's increasing intervention is now seen as a *consequence* of my lack of direction and co-ordination, though I saw it at the time, and certainly see it now, as one *cause* of my increasing detachment and eventual decision to take a teaching job. Anyway, by 1968 Margaret Stacey was much more heavily involved in running the project than either of us had initially anticipated. After I was at the University of Essex she took full and overt responsibility, and to that extent my departure rationalised the authority structure of the project. In the summer of 1968 Anne Murcott and Eric Batstone went to Swansea and I went to Colchester. By that time we had all had more than enough both of each other and of Banbury. This was not the happiest situation in which to start writing up a major community study, especially when one adds the data-handling problems mentioned above. That *Power, Persistence and Change* was written up at all owes more to the determination and endless energy of Margaret Stacey than to anything or anybody else. Left to ourselves I strongly suspect that we would have individually abandoned the data and the project. Yet to illustrate how bad personal relationships were at this stage, it was eighteen months after leaving the project before I was allowed to have the punch cards at Essex, largely because of the suspicion in Swansea that I would in some way 'run off' with the data and publish separately. There was also an unresolved disparity between the survey-generated data and that produced by our more general fieldwork activity. The closest approximation I know of a description of what I was doing is a phrase in William F. Whyte's *Street Corner Society* (1955). He based his sociology on 'observed interpersonal events'. I was familiar with that phrase while I was still in the field, yet I was never clear how my small-scale fieldwork observations were to fit with data from the survey.

Margaret Stacey and the anonymous reader of the typescript of *Power, Persistence and Change*, after it had first been offered to Oxford University Press, were more responsible for the final shape of the book than were Anne Murcott, Eric Batstone or myself. We also had an acrimonious meeting in the summer of 1970 that centred on the right (or not) of each of us as individuals to publish material we had individually collected.[5] It seemed that, as theses were by legal fiat declared to be independent pieces of work, the research assistants could publish independently but I could not. Fossilised in *Power, Persistence and Change* are some of my original aims, though they have been changed by all the upheavals that the project experienced since the summer of 1968.

Take, for example, the chapter on the expansion decision (ch. 6). I was much taken, while still a postgraduate student, with the approach to the analysis of social structure that some social anthropologists had used – in particular the analysis of dramatic occurrences.[6] Further, I had just reviewed Frankenberg's *Communities in Britain* (1966) which advocated such an approach to 'advanced' or more complex societies. I was very keen that such an approach should at least be attempted in Banbury if an opportunity presented itself. Banbury was facing the decision as to whether or not it should become an Expanded Town. I argued that an account and analysis of the parts played in this decision would allow a more dynamic approach to the social structure than the more conventional structural analysis. Whether such a direct application of a technique developed in very different societies was wise is another matter, yet that was my aim. I also thought that such an analysis would be compatible with the methodological prescriptions of the pluralist side of the community power debate (see Bell and Newby 1972, ch. 7). This is to say that issue analysis is the way to get at local community power; in particular we should be concerned with who gains and who loses from individual decisions. In fact the advocated intuitive cost benefit analysis is diabolically hard and open to all sorts of objections.

My original notion was to work through such an analysis and then 'out' in some way to the social structure of Banbury. I believed that a detailed account of a particular event or happening could be used as a limited area of transparency of the otherwise opaque surface of regular, uneventful social life.[7] In fact it did not work out like that; however, the discussion of the expansion decision is still in many ways the centre of *Power, Persistence and Change*, and the fact that so much space is devoted to it, in a relatively short monograph, was due originally to these methodological notions. The pluralist/elitist disputes over community power widened our interest to the issue as a whole – rather than one meeting or 'event' on which it had been my original intention to focus. For such an analysis I wanted to use actual observation of the public meeting called to discuss expansion. In fact our observations were crude and primitive (we did not tape, let alone videotape). So, despite the eventual widening to the expansion issue as a whole, perhaps it was always inevitable that such an event could not bear the explanatory weight and descriptive purpose that I sought to place on it.

PUBLICITIES

Our role as observers at such meetings raises the crucial problems of access that we frequently faced – access not just to individual meetings but to Banbury 'as a whole'. The Nuffield Foundation made it a condition of awarding the grant that there should be evidence that the study would be welcome in the town; so we had, in effect, to ask permission in some way from Banbury to do the research. This was a very difficult condition to meet really, not because it was in any way wrong to ask us to assure ourselves (and the Foundation) that we were going to be welcome, but because it was not altogether clear whom we should ask. What we did was to write to the town clerk, and he referred it to the borough council. This had some unfortunate consequences. A motion was put by the Labour members welcoming the study and offering it every assistance. They were, however, just a minority on the council, and a Conservative moved an amendment merely noting that the study was going to occur and making no objection. Council politics in Banbury were then going through a fairly rancorous period with a fair number of disputes over patronage and committee composition. It was unreasonable to think that a council which was divided on many matters would suddenly express consensus over us.

It was, we thought, going to be very difficult to do fieldwork on both sides of the political divide. Margaret Stacey had been aware of the 'Labour bias' accusations about *Tradition and Change*. Therefore, from the outset of the restudy she insisted that the fieldworkers should be divided between the political parties. So I took responsibility for the Labour Party, Eric Batstone for the Conservatives and Anne Murcott for the Liberals. This led to a leading Conservative ringing our office and asking whether he was speaking to the Labour or Tory one (we discovered much later that he too told this as a joke). I suspect now, on reflection, that we overestimated how difficult working with both sides would be, and this was because we were overidentifying with those whom we were studying. We were *too* friendly and *too* involved and were not exploiting the creative tension between the fieldworker as stranger and fieldworker as friend. There were, though, some advantages that followed from this overidentification. Arguments that were taking place in the locality also took place in our office between us. For instance, over the expansion issue Eric Batstone and I would argue from opposing Labour and Conservative positions with what appeared to be a considerable degree of genuine personal involvement. To a degree that even then seemed reckless, especially if all those notions about detachment and objectivity were remembered, we really cared about the expansion issue. I shared the deep depression of the Labour Party group on the council when expansion was rejected.

It should be realised that we rapidly knew more about local politics than did most Banburians. I, at least, was at times guilty of not realising that most, if not all, Banburians did not share my obsessive interest in their town, its politics and its social life.

GHOSTS

Just as Art Gallaher Jr (1964) records that he came across the ghost of James West in Plainville, the ghost of Margaret Stacey appeared in the council chamber the night we were debated. Not just were many of her old informants still around, but also she was well remembered by many (on both sides) as a Labour Party activist. It would be overstating the case to say that *Tradition and Change* was merely regarded as a socialist tract by local Conservatives, but there was a strong element of this in their reaction. This was despite the fact that Margaret Stacey had gone out of her way to smooth the project's path with influential Conservatives as well. We always strongly suspected that many Banburians, including town councillors, derived their knowledge of the contents of *Tradition and Change* from the national press reviews rather than the monograph itself. In particular, Kenneth Allsop referred to Banbury as 'a place pulsating with snobbery and riddled with class distinction'. *Tradition and Change* does say a lot about class divisions, and the bulk of the general population do confuse sociology with socialism, so perhaps we should not have been surprised at the reaction of a number of town councillors.

We had always planned to have a public meeting to 'tell' Banbury that we were there and what we were up to. This was greeted by the *Oxford Mail* with the headline 'New Probe Into "Snob Town"'. Most of the press coverage we received, though, was considerably more helpful and enthusiastic. We felt that through this public meeting and through the local press we were going some way towards meeting the Nuffield Foundation's request. Our meeting was eventually held in March 1967, in the Town Hall, and was chaired by the Mayor. It was attended by about 100 people, including half the Borough Council and many of Margaret Stacey's old acquaintances. The audience was swollen by some of the ladies we had already recruited to interview for us and members of an adult education class I was running in the town.[8] Bill Williams and Margaret Stacey came up from Swansea for the meeting, and they and I spoke from the platform.

Of course, however, the bulk of the local population were never asked and remained more or less unaware of our presence – although feature articles in the local press won us a slight local celebrity status. Throughout we had more contact with official bodies, organised groups and voluntary associations. However, as *Power, Persistence and Change* amply demonstrates, their membership and, even more, their leadership are hardly representative of the population as a whole, being overly male, middle class and middle-aged. Most of the time we, the three fieldworkers, had to negotiate our own individual way into local groups and gatherings. There were, as far as I know, no wilful attempts to mislead those we were studying, but there must have been many sins of omission. Our project was large and complex, we were studying many things, and even to ourselves it should be admitted that our precise aims were frequently anything but clear. It was not possible always to publicise what we were doing; if overt research in relatively open systems requires publicity, as I have argued elsewhere (see Bell 1969b), clearly we often failed. You just cannot keep uttering some sociological equivalent of the familiar police caution, like 'Anything you say or do may be taken down and used as data...'.

Many clubs and societies knew originally why we were interested in them, yet later seemed to forget. Frequently, the Labour Party treated us as activists. At Labour Party caucus meetings, to which I was lucky enough to be admitted as an observer, not only was my opinion asked occasionally, but also a couple of times I was expected to vote! But much social activity did not take place in closed settings at all. In the neighbourhoods in which we lived, for instance, all our immediate neighbours 'knew' (vaguely) what we were doing *in the town*, but nobody knew that we were also writing *them* up too. I was systematically collecting gossip, so successfully that by the end of two years living there I could give a socio-economic breakdown of the neighbourhood and supply, in addition, accounts of pieces of social action that articulated the division in the street. Similarly, while I went fairly regularly to watch Banbury Town football club (masochism has no bounds in fieldwork), I think nobody was aware that I used to 'age/sex/social status' the crowd too. I could hardly have had an announcement made over the loudspeaker.

STRAINS

Fieldwork bears heavily on the families of those who do it. I must emphasise again that we were all living there with our families – I, for instance, participantly observed as an expectant father in the maternity wing of Banbury's hospital. We shopped, used pubs, went to parties, movies and so on as ordinary, if hyperactive, inhabitants. The *structural* strain of fieldwork between fieldworker as friend and fieldworker as stranger resulted in great *personal* strain. We lived with this for two years at considerable personal cost. Fieldwork, let it be emphasised, never stops. We could not disentangle work from non-work. A good example of this that led to some irritation was that it was impossible to separate our everyday living expenses from those of the project; for example, when should we get a mileage allowance for running our cars, and when should we claim for entertaining in our homes an informant who may or may not also have been a friend? This was desperately important to us then; I was paid just over £1,000 a year while I was in Banbury, and the research assistants were paid £850. It may now sound very trivial, but it was the stuff of the day-to-day tensions and frequently increased our irritations with each other and the project. Doing fieldwork is like being continually on stage. On my arrival at the University of Essex one of the first things that we did as a family was to go and sit on the beach at Clacton in blissful anonymity among the crowds and take very little notice of our surroundings. It celebrated for us the end of the fieldwork.

Just as our differential involvement in local politics brought local conflicts into our office, there were further indications that strains (or contradictions?) that were exhibited in the locality were to be found within the research team too. The most important instance of this was the sex division of the fieldworkers. Margaret Stacey had always strongly argued for the appointment of a woman to the research team, saying, totally correctly, that if this had not happened there would have been all sorts of activity from which we, as men, would have been barred. At its simplest this was an argument based on the fact that, say, women's groups and associations were going to be more easily observed by a woman. Yet then as now (as in Margaret Stacey's period in Banbury), society, Banbury and us were all ambiguous about working wives who had young children. Sections of Banbury were overtly hostile, yet Anne Murcott could have had a reasonable expectation that we on the team would not be – after all, we had appointed her. Yet I do not think we were sufficiently sensitive (and here I mean Eric Batstone and myself most importantly) to her problems as mother, spouse and fieldworker. It was all very well for Margaret Stacey to tell me that she saw Anne Murcott's role as that of 'anthropological mum' when I wanted bits of questionnaires drafted. Hence the tensions and contradictions present in society as a whole over the employment of married women with young children were present in the research team also. My subsequent insensitivity doubtless added to the general tensions, conflicts, animosities, jealousies and later recriminations. Yet this I now see as structurally determined by the peculiarly exploited position of working mothers in contemporary British society, rather than by the individuals involved.

LESSONS

I have tried on several occasions since 1968 to try to systematise what in fact we were doing during the Banbury fieldwork. It was not always possible to disentangle the original object of study, Banbury, from the account of it, *Tradition and Change*. We certainly possessed a view of Banbury through *Tradition and Change*, especially that pervasive two-way diagram on p. 173. The diagram below gives some indication of what was involved.

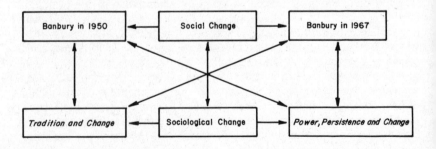

Clearly, Banbury of 1950 had become the Banbury we lived in from 1966 to 1968; that is, there had been some *social* changes, and it was to study these that the Nuffield Foundation had given us the grant, I believed. Yet most of what we knew of the Banbury of 1950 came from the *account* of it, and this altered our perception of Banbury in 1966–8 (hence the arrow between *Tradition and Change* and Banbury in 1967). There had also been a considerable development in *sociology* between 1950 and 1967, and so *sociological* change also helped determine the restudy. I take it as axiomatic that there was at least some relationship between the social and the sociological changes over this period. We also did some original research into Banbury of 1950 and so were not totally influenced by the first study (hence the arrow between Banbury 1950 and *Power, Persistence and Change*). What this all suggests is that before sociologists can replicate or before they embark on a restudy they need at the very least a theory of social change and some epistemological sensitivity to the relationship between knowledge and the social structure. Further, sociologists ought to be more aware of the social construction of accounts of reality. Nobody who produced *Power, Persistence and Change* was very interested at that time in that kind of thing. Let me conclude these remarks with a trite statement that has some obvious implications: it is impossible to replicate without some theory of social change. *Tradition and Change* had the rudiments of such a theory; the work that produced *Power, Persistence and Change* destroyed that theory.

Banbury will forever be the social system with which I compare all else; it is my Nuerland and my Tikopia. The project gave me a comparatively wide empirical sociological experience that was immediately valuable – and has continued to be valuable – in many teaching situations. Frequently I find that I do seem to know all sorts of details about stratification, politics, religion, deviance, housing, education and so on that derive from having had to become the sociological jack-of-all-trades that doing a community study requires. No doubt too many of my students think I know nowhere else! I find that even in Australia I still now use Banbury for comparisons in teaching. Also, the Banbury project will forever be the research activity to which I compare all others. It taught me many useful and painful lessons, some of which I have revealed here. Happily I have since discovered that team research can be quite free of the difficulties faced in Banbury – indeed it can be a creative and joyful experience. Nothing would have convinced me of that in 1968. The intellectual gain of trying to make sense of the experience led directly to my current concerns in epistemology and indeed to this book.

NOTES

1 An attempt to do this was in fact made on the basis of a subsample in Banbury, some data from which appear in a rather emasculated form in chapter 8, 'Women and the family', of

Power, Persistence and Change. A more direct link between *Middle Class Families* (Bell 1968) and the Banbury research is to be found in my article, 'Occupational career, family cycle and extended family relations' (Bell 1971). That article contains two case studies from *Banbury* to illustrate some general points raised by a letter I received (reprinted in the article) in response to a previous article, 'The middle class tribe' (Bell 1969a) based on *Swansea* material.

2 I think that it is significant that it was not until I started the Banbury fieldwork that I had found it necessary to keep a personal appointments diary; my life for the first time became closely inter-related with that of others. This is a sociological point of some importance and reflects, apart from anything else, the bureaucratisation of my research life.

3 Could it have been, I wonder now, Gary Glitter in an earlier manifestation? G. G. is arguably one of Banbury's most famous products.

4 Some of the fruits of these cogitations can be found later in this chapter and in my paper, 'Replication and reality' (Bell 1974).

5 Like my article cited in note 2 (Bell 1971). It was particularly ironic that there was by bizarre chance a misprint in that article that made me refer to 'any' rather than 'my' Banbury colleagues.

6 For an example and further references, see Bell (1968, ch. 7).

7 The phrase is V. W. Turner's (1957, p. 93).

8 *Tradition and Change* was linked with an adult education class Margaret Stacey ran. Indeed that was why she had been in Banbury in the first place – as an employee of the Oxford University Extra-Mural Delegacy. It was always thought to be important, therefore, that such a class should be associated with the restudy.

Appendix: Editorial Note

HOWARD NEWBY

'The conflicting reports indicate a lack of neutrality; sides have been taken, and however multiple and shifting these may be, loyalty no doubt forbids dispassion. It is not − and this should be clear − that anyone can be said to be lying. When an atmosphere grows thick enough with justifications, explanations, rationalizations, postures and regrets, not to omit occasional hostilities, untruth disappears just as surely as truth does. What remains is a series of viewpoints, none of which can be taken as proof of anything more than the state of mind of whoever expresses them, always speaking sincerely enough, beyond question, but not precisely with the cool, calm voice of historical accuracy.' (Sayre 1975, p. 118)

The above quotation may serve as an epitaph to the lengthy and often frustrating attempts to obtain publication of Colin Bell's account of the Banbury restudy *as it now seems to him*. In the light of these problems it is both necessary and appropriate to add a note which may help the reader's interpretation of this chapter.

Certainly none of the former participants in the Banbury restudy would deny that there is an interesting tale to be told of how the outcome of that research − and even, in some cases, the substantive findings − were crucially affected by the nature of the personal and organisational relationships between the researchers themselves. Clearly, then, an account of this is well within the ambit of this book and bears directly upon many of the issues raised in the Introduction. Unfortunately, insofar as these relationships became − and have, from time to time, remained − acrimonious, then 'sides have been taken'. Consequently there is simply no single account of the restudy upon which all four participants could agree and which at the same time would include precisely those ingredients that, by the stated criteria of this book, are important and relevant. Any editor of a book like this is therefore faced by a dilemma. The only account which would be agreeable to all the parties concerned would be one which was anodyne, evasive and thus *misleading*. It would be little more than the smooth, methodological appendix customarily found in most research monographs, which hides more than it reveals and to replace which this book was expressly conceived. The most obvious way to overcome this would be to invite each of the researchers to publish his or her own personal account – and indeed had this book been four times its present length this undoubtedly would have been a preferred solution. However, our publisher's understandable desire to produce a book at a saleable price has placed the current limitations on length and number of contributors. To include four accounts of the Banbury restudy in a book of this size – however laudable that might be from an academic standpoint – would completely destroy its balance. In anticipation of these problems, therefore, Colin Bell wrote this chapter on his own rather than considering a joint piece.

This is a dilemma which is unique to the Banbury restudy among the other accounts in this book. For Colin Bell's account is the only one which addresses itself in detail to the problems of doing sociological teamwork and to how, in this case, the partial failure to weld a team affected the eventual outcome. Under these circumstances an attempt by one of the parties to give a frank, albeit personal, interpretation of what occurred is unlikely to contain 'the cool, calm voice of historical accuracy' nor to be enthusiastically welcomed by former colleagues. Yet it is the *raison d'etre* of this book that such accounts of the entanglement of personal and professional life among sociologists, however self-justificatory and biased it may appear to others to be, are important, if not essential, for a more valid discussion of the methodology of doing sociological research. Hence this chapter appears in this book. It is not, and does not pretend to be, an objective account of the Banbury restudy. Neither is it an account with which Margaret Stacey, Eric Batstone and Anne Murcott agree or concur. Nevertheless to have removed this chapter from the book on these grounds would have been to undermine the whole basis upon which intellectuals communicate with one another and grow through mutual criticism in something like complete frankness.

Complete frankness is, of course, limited by the British libel laws (on which the editors have more to say in the Epilogue). When invited to do so, Margaret Stacey, Eric Batstone and Anne Murcott understandably declined to waive the rights which they have under the law and which might have enabled a more personally authentic, but also more vituperative and offensive, account to be published. It seems necessary to state, then, that the published account is both less frank – but, some might agree, less inaccurate – than the original draft. What has emerged is something less direct, less pointed, less explicit, less passionate, and thus less offensive, than the author may have originally intended. In consciously leaning over backwards to avoid the risk of a writ, what has been written may in some respects be regarded as too vague and diffuse. Nevertheless some important lessons can be learned for the future conduct of team research.

The nature of these lessons has clearly been very different for Colin Bell than for the other members of the Banbury research team. This is hardly surprising, given that the experiences of each of the four were in many important respects very different; for example, the 'lessons' learned by Margaret Stacey were obviously those of a research director, those learned by Eric Batstone and Anne Murcott were those of research assistants at the bottom of the organisational hierarchy, and so on. For this reason it is relevant to convey briefly a summary of their principal disagreements with Colin Bell's account, not at the relatively trivial level of minor factual disagreement, but at a more fundamental analytical level. Briefly summarised they were as follows:

(1) There was a general view that the chapter is more a rationalisation or an attempt 'to get something off his chest' than a serious organisational analysis.

There was a general agreement that there is indeed a serious problem about authority in research teams, but that this cannot be seen in isolation from the research process more generally. While the chapter concentrates on the am- biguities in the authority structure from above, it was felt that more attention should have been devoted to what the research assistants regarded as equally ambiguous guidelines as far as they were concerned. They were more conscious of a lack of day-to-day support and direction, a confusion between a total per- missiveness over the collection of data (on which the need to collect data for theses also impinged) and the requirements of the project *qua* restudy. This con- fusion often resulted in certain *lacunae* in the data or in data which was not collected in a systematic and comparable form by each of the fieldworkers. This in turn leads to a consideration of whether there is an inherent conflict between a hierarchical model of research organisation and the 'myth' of an academic community. The organisational implications of this myth as far as research is concerned are not entirely clear, but one aspect may be a more democratic structure where, at least to the point of irreconcilable conflict, decisions are the result of debate. However, it was felt, such debates are rarely mentioned in the chapter – and certainly nowhere are such debates discussed in relation to the research assistants.

(2) The account reveals a broader range of problems which derive, not so much from organisational and authority structures, as from the overarching range of conceptions of sociological work *within* which the organisational and authority structures are located. What emerges is a position which reveals an am- bivalence, a tension between a 'for sociology' and an 'off sociology' stance; a position which, it was felt, cried out for reflexive analysis *explicitly* in terms of the intersection of history, biography and social structure. Hence what comes over extremely strongly in the chapter is an account of the felt discomfort of a foreman – the research fellow – in an intercalary position, jammed between boss and workers, a tension reinforced by that revealed in the chapter between a conception of the research as a job on the one hand, and as a commitment on the other. This major tension between sociology as a job and sociology as a commitment has to be seen as a continuing problematic. This reflection on research in Banbury could have provided a case study of this problematic, but, it was felt, the chapter reveals too few glimpses of it, without analysis or com- ment, and points a very partial picture as a result.

(3) There is a failure to appreciate fully the implications and consequences of Colin Bell's departure from the project and his move to Essex before the commence- ment of the data analysis. It was originally envisaged that Margaret Stacey's role would be a more minor one than was eventually the case. It was to her sorrow that what was revealed in Banbury was an inability to weld a team and to share work and ideas. The subsequent lack of direction and co-ordination led her to intervene more than she had intended, and Colin Bell's departure gave her little option other than to take over the role of research fellow. Many of the features mentioned in the chapter were solutions (poor ones) to a problem which this departure created. Moreover, the research assistants felt deserted in Swansea and were bitter that the research fellow had not, like the captain of a ship, stayed on to see the whole thing through, whatever the difficulties.

It should be emphasised that these three points do not exhaust the objections offered, in terms of either content or method of presentation. In addition, they represent my summary of these objections, and the other members of the Banbury research team may prefer a different form of expression or emphasis. Nevertheless these issues are important; the reader is invited to ponder on them.

3
Talking about Prison Blues

STANLEY COHEN and LAURIE TAYLOR

INTRODUCTION

'Could you give me some ideas for my research project?' is the standard opening question from students of the sociology of deviance. 'What are you interested in?' is the immediate reply, and somehow or other a list of possible subjects emerges: the gay liberation movement, prisons, drugs. But what can realistically be 'done' about these research topics? After putting the student off yet another review of the literature, or a demonstration that labelling theory neglects power, structure and history, we find ourselves supporting any project which sounds vaguely like getting the student out of the library and into contact with people in the world out there. Arming him with romantic Chicago school injunctions about capturing reality in his notebook, with all the West Coast methods texts which tell him that soft qualitative research is as valid as anything else, and with a commitment to naturalism, appreciation and being on the side of the deviant, we send him into the world to 'tell it how it is'. This is all to be achieved with the aid of that most simple and accessible of research technologies: talk.

But typically we expect that there will come a time when the talking has to stop, the time when we feel that simple conversation with the deviant should take a more structured form, the moment when a questionnaire is designed or an interview schedule is prepared. And now ordinary talking becomes an adjunct to the real business. We may talk to the subject (people only become 'subjects' or 'respondents' as the talk takes on such structured forms as questioning or interviewing) about our intentions, and even talk a little after those intentions have been realised. But then too much talk can be disconcerting; we may even complain that the real research business is becoming difficult to complete because of the subject's readiness to talk too much. One of our graduate students once plaintively observed: 'They seem to think you've really come for a talk and get annoyed when you try to get away after the interview.'

When we ourselves look back at the research that we have tried to carry out with long-term prisoners over the last decade, it is apparent that questions about the nature and significance of talk occupy a central place.

Our first relations with the prisoners located talk firmly within a pedagogic frame: we lectured, they listened and finally we discussed. Gradually, for reasons we shall describe, this shifted: firstly into talk, then into structured conversation, and finally it was almost transformed into interviewing, questioning and measuring. These shifts in our style of intervention were sometimes occasioned by our own sociological self-conceptions, by ideas about the necessity to report back to our academic community in an acceptable manner. They were, however, also powerfully influenced by external pressures, by the strong views held by prison officers, governors and Home Office officials about the ways in which their captive population should be studied by outsiders.

We stumbled – by chance – upon an interesting group of human beings who were locked up in an exceptional environment.[1] We wanted to talk to them about themselves, their situation and, perhaps, the implications of this for others like them. And we wanted to do that for a long time – for at least the length of their very considerable sentences. This chapter records the failure of those intentions – a failure which was occasioned not just by the concrete restrictions imposed upon talking by officialdom, but also by our own restricted views of what constituted a sociological investigation. This chapter describes, then, how we managed to talk to some prisoners and how this talk was transformed into a research plan and was finally sabotaged in this transformation.[2]

STARTING TO TALK

Our research story started in 1967, when we began classes on sociology in the maximum security wing of Durham prison. At first we stuck fairly closely to our academic roles, running through our old lecture notes on the sociology of deviance and introducing a few digressions on such topics as surrealism, dadaism and hippies. The classes were more stimulating than those we took at the university; the men actually read the recommended books and had plenty of practical examples with which to refute our crasser generalisations. But for much of the time it was very like any other extramural class. Both the prisoners and ourselves had some interest in maintaining an academic atmosphere. It helped us because it distracted our attention from the most evident features of the situation: namely, the predicaments which our students faced, the conditions in the wing and the prospect of spending up to twenty years of one's life in such circumstances. And from their point of view, such an academic ethos was a welcome relief from the usual relationships which they encountered within the prison: the vulgar authoritarianism of the 'screws' (i.e. prison officers) and the patronising condescension of social workers, psychiatrists and chaplains.

We began to *talk* rather than to lecture when we ran out of material. At university it was easy enough to stretch a course on the sociology of deviance over three terms. There were plenty of topics and books to be covered. But the prison experience brought home to us the irrelevance of much of our usual material. Was there really any point in getting these students to read their way through Eysenck's *Crime and Personality* (1970) or Trasler's *The Explanation of Criminality* (1962)? After all, such an exercise only provided a platform from which we could launch our standard lecture on the inadequacies of behaviourism. And what validity had this, when the men's own self-conscious analysis of the nature of criminal activities already provided a trenchant critique of such an approach?

Our first real conversations were rather wary exchanges about culture and lifestyles, about the absurdities of academic life, the posturing of professionals, the hypocrisy of administrators. Their stories about mad screws and demon governors were traded for our tales of eccentric professors and militant students. Our own contributions became more intimate as we recognised the peculiar confidentiality of the situation; they could hardly lay their own emotional lives on the line for they sat alongside the only people they would know really well for the immediate future. But we were away from friends and relations; there was no chance of any incestuous feedback; we could be more honest than in most social situations. There was therefore something indulgent and artificial about the manner in which we established intimate relationships. The men became drafted into a sort of reference group role; we began to regard them as a stable and sympathetic audience for our accounts of the personal, domestic and occupational difficulties we experienced in everyday life. We later described the perpetuation of this relationship as follows:

'Over the years, as we pass through different periods in our lives, we are highly conscious of the men's continuing situation. As we send them picture postcards of our holidays, accounts of concerts, news of friends, we wonder how such fragments are received within the wings, about how they are related by the men to the individuals they knew during the period of the research. For these men ... know more about our obsessions and anxieties than most other people. When we move our homes, or change our jobs, their letters have a habit of undermining our newly manifested sense of purpose by recalling our old cynicisms; they cast doubt upon the reality of our new romances by recalling our earlier fervours. Unlike our present friends they do not know our new rationalizations well enough to condone our apparent inconsistencies. They compare the relative simplicity of their world with the cultural hustle of our own, hope that we are well and apologise for taking up our time with their letters.' (Cohen and Taylor 1972)

An opportunity for this imbalance to be corrected was provided by the arrival in the prison of a team of Home Office researchers who had come to inquire about the effects of long-term imprisonment. In their many years of experience of the penal system, the men had built up a cynical attitude towards research in general and psychological research in particular. Psychologists 'come in and use you for other things they are doing outside', as one of them remarked. It was not therefore surprising to us that these researchers were met by a partial boycott; one member of the class was apparently delegated to inform them as politely as possible that the approach they were adopting did not meet with the approval of most of the men and would they therefore please try to find some other subject.

The attitude of the prisoners to the Home Office research team prompted considerable discussion in the class. We shared most of their criticism of the standard psychological approach; we were no more convinced than they about the value of investigating the effects of long-term imprisonment by considering such matters as changes in reaction times, or shifts along such personality dimensions as extra-introversion. (The subsequent publication of the results of the Home Office research has reinforced fully, rather than dispelled, such doubts.) We were less ready to agree, however, about the inadequacies of all social science research. And with the hope of proving our point we suggested that we should start a collaborative research project on exactly the same topic as the Home Office researchers: the effects of long-term imprisonment. All we would have to do was structure our general conversation a little more, so as to concentrate upon their life in prison, their ways of adapting, their hopes, fantasies and frustrations.

We had drifted into a research project. The sociological studies of prison life which we had so glibly been lecturing about took on a new light. At the time we believed our insights (such as they were) to be wholly inductive. We now recognise that the salience of certain dimensions was determined as much by their appearance in the literature as by the men's concentration upon them in discussion. So, for example, we concentrated on the passage and marking of time, as these were constant themes in other autobiographical accounts of prison life. And, similarly, we stressed the significance of the inmate subculture and the nature of inmate solidarity, as an acknowledgement of the attention these had received in traditional sociological studies of the prison community.

In any event, we decided that our emphasis was to be on the subjective experience of imprisonment rather than on the more standard sociological features of the prison world. This is not the place to describe the theoretical basis for such an approach. We have discussed this elsewhere, and in any case the particular perspective we adopted is now considerably better known and accepted than it was in 1968. However, in view of the latter research difficulties we encountered it is worthwhile emphasising one or two general points about the overall nature of the investigation.

We have never been very happy to describe our work as 'prison research', although this definition has been forced on us from time to time. For we were primarily examining the way in which a particular group of people responded to a set of special psychological and environmental circumstances. It was not so much the 'prison' or the 'prison subculture' which concerned us as rather one particular enclave: the maximum security wing and the effects it produced. This meant that our research had more affinities with social psychological research on extreme situations than with traditional penological investigations.

However, our research did not look at a specially constituted experimental environment – like the McGill coffin or the Ames room – but looked rather at a natural one which had been assembled in the real social and political world for a set of specific purposes over a long period of time. The environment, unlike its standard experimental counterpart, was already rich in symbolism, it had a known history and a foreseeable future. In all these respects, and others, it was unique. Therefore some of the assertions by official critics that the research said little about what was the case for all prisoners, or even all long-term prisoners, or that it did not take into account the different circumstances pertaining at another security wing, were largely irrelevant. Neither was it appropriate that we include a control group in our research design, as was repeatedly suggested to us by the Home Office. We were describing the *specific* reactions of *specific* men to *specific* circumstances. This did not mean that there was no comparative element in the work. But the comparison was not between different kinds of prisoners, or different kinds of prisons, but rather between the taken-for-granted ways in which people outside prison coped with their daily problems of living, and the adaptations to these taken-for-granted ways which were demanded of individuals placed in special circumstances. How did this unique environment render problematic such everyday matters as time, friendship, privacy, identity, self-consciousness and physical and psychological deterioration?

Our enthusiasm for finding these answers stemmed from the sense of intimacy that we now felt we enjoyed with many of the prisoners in the maximum security wing. It was still a little unilateral – they talked more about us than about themselves – but it seemed only a matter of time before a more balanced and equally intimate discussion could take place. For several months we more or less let the talk ramble along; we only prodded it back in the direction of prison experience when a digression threatened to absorb the whole evening's talk.

But we gradually realised that some formal constraints were necessary. Up to that point we had been behaving like naive inductionists, hoping that patterns, and recognisable themes and dimensions of experience, would somehow emerge if we talked for long enough. However, it became clear that our notes on the conversations resisted any such structuring; the range of topics was too great, the levels of analysis were too varied, the differences within even so apparently homogeneous a group were impossible to comprehend.

We were accordingly drawn into adopting certain methodological devices in order to bring some order to our material. In a way, these methods were nothing much more than techniques for encouraging talk on certain topics, for constraining the level of analysis at which that conversation took place, and for prompting specific considerations of certain key dimensions. (Such dimensions had been referred to at times by the men, but they achieved their 'key' position chiefly by virtue of their recurrent appearance in the literature on extreme environments, e.g. time, privacy and deterioration.)

Often such dimensions could be explored by 'unstructured interviews', by allowing the men to respond at length to certain specific questions. More personal and elaborated accounts emerged from the stories, essays and poems which we encouraged them to produce on particular topics. A technique which we have rather pretentiously referred to as 'literary identification' enabled us to investigate, in an apparently impersonal way, some of the more intimate features of the men's experience. The following provides an example of this approach:

'A particular problem – say masturbation – would be concentrated upon in a discussion of Freud. This would lead easily into a general discussion of masturbation, in which techniques, fears and notably performances would be discussed. The actual feelings of the men about the subject could however then be further elaborated by reference, for example, to Genet's *Our Lady of the Flowers* or Roth's *Portnoy's Complaint*. This would enable them to select one or other literary contribution as most accurate or honest and thus provide us with a more sensitive indication of the significance of the behaviour than would have been obtained from a general discussion of a topic such as masturbation.' (Cohen and Taylor 1972)

Our only other 'research technique' was the collaborative writing up of the work. As soon as we had produced a rough description of a particular feature of life in the wing, we would read it to the men and ask for factual and theoretical comments. This exercise also promoted talk in that the men recognised that they were now involved in producing a version of their world which would be transmitted to an outside audience.

SOME PROBLEMS OF RESEARCH TALK

Although we find it pretentious to talk about the above strategies as our 'methodology', and although we have not the slightest evangelical desire to persuade other sociologists to abandon their perfectly sensible methods and follow our stumbling path, we nevertheless become defensive when our approach is attacked as being so intuitive and *ad hoc* as to be useless. Given our interests in dimensions of experience, there was no alternative but to promote the maximum amount of talk. The techniques that we used were only variants of those which are commonly employed to prompt discussion, e.g. in seminars or at parties and social gatherings. But such everyday usage does not in any way disqualify them as research methods. Indeed, we would regard the circumscription of talk which is imposed by more structured methods (e.g. the use of questionnaires and personality inventories) as essentially more intuitive, in that it necessarily involves the researcher's assuming that his questions are salient to the dimensions he explores and that the answers can be read as 'complete' responses.

Our apparent promotion of talk as a research method must sound as naive as a recommendation to urban man to give up electricity in favour of candlelight on the grounds that the former is too complicated. We are not, of course, advancing a blanket argument against other more formal techniques in prisons or any other research setting. And structured talk of the sort we were indulging in is not without its own problems.

For one thing, we soon became aware of the subtle and not so subtle ways in which the researcher influences his data by telling the subject enough to produce the definitions of reality he wants to hear about anyway. This is, after all, a feature of most structured talk; when a friend comes to 'talk his problems over' with us, we pick up enough clues to know what sort of response is wanted: sympathy, advice or a sharing of our own problems. In the last decade, social psychologists have produced compelling evidence on how so-called 'demand characteristics' or 'observer effects' substantially transform the 'findings' of standard experiments and laboratory situations (see, for example, Rosenthal and Rosnow 1970). Subjects monitor their performance in such settings, and their comments after the experiment such as 'How did I do?' and 'Did I blow it?' are only comprehensible by understanding the sensitisation which occurs to what the researcher actually wants to hear.

These effects were compounded by our methods. For once the answers had come back to us, we then went on to do what is unusual in research but commonplace in ordinary talk: namely, interpret the answer and then hand such interpretation and meta comments back to our partners for inspection. It did not take long for us to see some unintended consequences of this interchange. For when a sustaining philosophy, a way of maintaining one's symbolic universe intact, is given back, attenuated, formalised and disguised with the conceptual baggage of sociology, then this makes it, more self-evidently, one among many others. It is open to inspection: delusions may be pierced, fictions become manifest, survival ideologies become relativised too much by self-consciousness.[3] Our relative ignorance of how the prisoners did in fact keep themselves psychologically alive meant that we had no clear authority to offer one interpretation rather than another. As we wrote:

'We have not just transcribed philosophies, ideologies and views of the world: we have played some part in creating them and our commitments are such as to make us wonder whether certain ideologies can be allowed to go unchallenged when they first appear. We recognize our concern for example in trying to keep the men in a rational frame of mind, although we know full well that the rationality we seek to encourage may only be championed by us so assiduously because it more or less works for us in the outside world and fits best with our own working theories of human behaviour.' (Cohen and Taylor 1972)

As we were later to realise, passages like this, which did little more than record an uneasiness and uncertainty about what effect our talk was having, were to be cited as evidence against us on the grounds that we were 'just putting words into the prisoners' mouths' – A curious charge, if it carries with it the implication that questionnaires, formal interviews and other structural methods somehow give subjects *more* chance of being uninfluenced by the researcher. Our answer to these charges is primarily empirical and pragmatic: if the subject recognises himself in the sociologists' accounts, then, in a sense, the findings are 'better' than those in which the subject disappears – irrespective of what method is used.

This still leaves open the weird possibility that the field disappears altogether. That is to say, we are told by the subjects that our initial definition is false, fortuitous or really explained by something else. It is true that this is more likely to happen with unstructured talk than with a more formal design where, although negative findings or confirmation of null hypotheses might be reported, the researcher will hardly admit that he has totally misconceived the problem. By the same token, this 'mistake' is more easily rectified in unstructured talk; one just carries on talking. As critics have correctly pointed out though, one distortion that resulted from our pursuing this strategy was a reliance on the comments of the more articulate members of the group – those who were better talkers – to tell us what the field was like for everyone else. This is a frequent error made by inexperienced fieldworkers.

We don't believe we have got anywhere near solving the 'handing back' problem implicit in conducting any sort of research talk. Simply to be self-conscious about it does not get one out of the by-now familiar critique of 'positivist' sociological research, well summarised by Cicourel (1964): 'Researchers in the social sciences are faced with a unique methodological problem: the very conditions of their research constitute an important and complex variable for what passes as the findings of their investigation'. What we learned the hard way was that bargaining about these conditions' is part of a political game to decide what research can get done at all.

The sociological profession is not too helpful in playing this game and is often evasive about the duties we have to our subjects when we start any structured talk. In a spirited defence of the sociologist's 'right to know', Horowitz (1970), for example, makes the strangely defensive claim that 'Sociologists are not interested in directly affecting the lives of particular people they study'; they are interested more in abstract categories: all prisoners, all homosexuals or whatever. It was partly this 'professional' response which led us further away from our subjects and our original interest in them.

SELF CONTROL ON OUR TALK

A literary critic has suggested that the odd lines we remember from poems and popular songs we once knew, are not merely arbitrary selections; they may often be the very lines with which the poet or song writer began the construction of his complex work. We remember them because they are especially vivid, imaginative or honest.

This observation becomes salient to us when we reread the report of our research at Durham: *Psychological Survival: The Experience of Long-Term Imprisonment* (Cohen and Taylor 1972). Some paragraphs still seem fresh and honest, while others appear almost to have been inserted by some unknown person, an alien being, quite hostile to our aims and intentions.

The sections which still retain some meaning for us – which actually recall the prisoners and prison – are those in which we concentrate upon reporting and analysing the structured talk in which we participated. Even here, we can see that much of the structuring was imposed by ourselves outside the actual talk, rather than being realised within it. But despite such *post facto* tinkering – our occasional concentration upon certain 'key' dimensions which were not necessarily so regarded by the prisoners, and our continuous use of 'outside sources' to reinforce the validity of our reported talk – the passages recall the talk.

This is certainly not true of those sections in which we jump hither and thither in order that we may somehow land for at least a brief period upon the sociological mainland. When we talked to the men, we concentrated upon the comparison between their life and life outside. The central feature of our talk was the contrast between the relatively unproblematic nature of such dimensions as time, friendship and deterioration in ordinary life, and the sudden salience of them in the maximum security wing. But in *Psychological Survival* we became embarrassed by our lack of conceptual clothes – was it really enough to say that life in prison was different from life outside? – and bolted for sociological cover. Long-term prisoners, we said, are like explorers, migrants or the victims of disasters. Well, so they are, but not in enough ways to make the comparison illuminating. This was comparison for comparison's sake, a sociological fetish about generalisation at the expense of differentiation.

But even more disturbing in retrospect is our eagerness in another section to make use of traditional etiological and predictive models of human behaviour. Suddenly we were no longer interpreting talk; we were into the game of classifying prisoners into distinctive groups, and then using this classification as some sort of baseline from which to predict their behaviour within the prison. Nobody pushed us; we just fell that way back into the arms of some of our sociological colleagues. Of course we weren't just 'talking' to the prisoners; we were getting something of sociological value out of that talk, something which could not be discovered by the actual talkers but only by the trained analyst who brought his interpretations to bear upon the material once the talking had stopped.

SOCIAL CONTROL OF TALK

So far, the problems of talking and knowing what to make of this talk could be seen as generic to all sociology. Our preconceptions were those of the discipline as a whole and would have emerged if we had been doing research on, say, a school, a factory or a political movement. But the project was really sabotaged by the fact that talk in the particular setting of the prison was subject to unique controls, taboos and restrictions. The second part of this chapter describes how the power exerted by the Home Office in defining what talk is allowed in prisons led us to collude unwittingly in our own downfall.

This power is only one example of how talk is the subject of control in our society. Talk can be deviant – 'Careless talk costs lives' was the familiar slogan in wartime Britain – and controlling the right to talk is a tool for protecting the powerful. Large organisations have intricate hierarchies for regulating talk; some people have more right to be heard than others, and this right may be even more finely defined in terms of whether the communication may take the form of memos, circulars or actual face-to-face conversation. The powerless are supplicants, sure that their problems will be solved 'if only they could talk to X', and in settings like schools and armies may be subject to rituals like having to ask in a prescribed way: 'Permission to talk, sir?'

We should not be surprised, then, that an organisation as hierarchical as the prison, which in turn is located in a hierarchy such as the Prison Department at the Home Office, should have firm controls on talk. Indeed the depersonalisation effect, so often remarked upon by students and inmates of total institutions, appears in its extreme form as a definition of the inmate as being ineligible for any talk at all. Enshrined in prison history are the rules laying down silence as a means for ensuring conformity and protecting the prisoners from evil influences.

Criminals who find themselves in institutions like prisons become in a real sense the 'property' of the Home Office; when a prisoner enters through the gates, the prison officer in charge signs a paper certifying that he has 'received the body of the prisoner'. The degree of control that is exercised over these bodies is well documented in standard journalistic, sociological and autobiographical accounts of prison life. Less clearly understood is the control exercised over the access of others to these bodies: friends, relatives, journalists, politicians, lawyers and researchers. The researcher is trapped in a complex web of social and political restrictions. Each of the standard textbook problems – access, sponsorship, financing, setting up relationships to obtain data, what can be published – poses unique difficulties when the agency in control of the subject is an official one like the Home Office. In

Britain this authority is able to exercise a high degree of control of research through forces which we shall first list in general; then we shall describe how they were used, successfully, against us.

(1) *Centralisation of power*   The Prison Department of the Home Office retains a degree of central control quite unique among the prison systems we know.[4] Unlike, say, in the United States, Governors or others concerned in day-to-day management have little discretion in varying the conditions of access for research. Whether or not and how one may talk to prisoners is always a decision for the Prison Department of the Home Office.

(2) *Legalisation of secrecy*   Again, unlike in most social democratic systems, the need to maintain organisational secrets is protected by powerful legal devices. The most formidable of these is the Official Secrets Act, a blanket provision for criminalising any openness about prison life. Teachers from outsiders, all ranks of prison staff themselves and, of course, researchers are required to sign the clause of the Act which prohibits the publication of anything discovered in the course of prison talk or observation.

(3) *Standardisation of research*   The Home Office, and particularly the Prison Department, has used its obvious and legitimate identification with correctional aims to develop a highly circumscribed system for deciding what constitutes proper research. Either by carrying out its own research – through such bodies as the Home Office Research Unit – or simply by using its definition of proper research to exclude outsiders, it has created a virtual monopoly of research on its own workings. This monopolistic power consists in being able to say when talk is not research.

(4) *Mystifying the decision structure*   Few organisations whose co-operation sociologists are likely to require are simple, and most are 'bureaucratic' in the non-perjorative sense of the term. Most sociological research involves difficult invisible work, and it is naive as well as self-serving to complain about having to attend meetings, submit documents or carry out political negotiations. But the notorious in-penetrability of civil service decisions, when supplemented by the special aura of secrecy associated with prisons, makes it peculiarly difficult for researchers who have not moved in such circles to know exactly how decisions are reached. We were not clear at the time and are no clearer now about the precise step in the hierarchy at which particular decisions are made. We never knew and still doubt, for example, whether it would have been better to go over the heads of civil servants and deal with politicians.

(5) *Appealing to the public interest*   Even if legal controls are weak or in practice only likely to be used as a last resort, there is a more fundamental moral pressure which can be used by officials: the appeal to public

interests. Even if we never got as far as being explicitly warned that 'careless talk costs lives', there was a veiled threat that hung over most negotiations, to the effect that the authorities, as custodians of the public interest, knew that some of the things sociologists might get up to in talking to prisoners would be against the public interest.

We shall now describe how these powers from outside, and the earlier problems of talk we have discussed, led to the curtailment of the research. These modes of exercising power could and have been applied to other research. In our case, they were particularly effective because our methods left us so vulnerable.

We have no wish to present ourselves in this chronicle as figures of moral and academic rectitude. At times we resorted to methods which we knew would arouse official antagonism – in particular, the publication of material without formal clearance. But such tactics were only adopted after long and frustrating debates, and at the time they seemed the only way to enlist some support from others.

From the beginning, those in charge of the maximum security wing knew more or less what we were doing and respected our motives. In May 1969 we outlined to the Governor the ways in which we were proceeding, and informed him of our intention to publish an article in a journal such as *New Society* and of our concern to respect the normal conventions regarding security and anonymity. We concluded by thanking him for his co-operation.

The Prison Department of the Home Office were less enthusiastic. In July 1969 they outlined their first objections to our proposals: a set of reservations which contained in embryo most of the problems which eventually destroyed the whole project. Their letter complained, without expansion, that our type of research 'would lead to a concentration upon the lurid aspects of long-term imprisonment'. The perspective we had described was referred to as 'falling somewhere between research and journalism'. Six years later, a member of a Home Office-sponsored research team wrote to *New Society* denouncing our work as 'journalistic rubbish'. Presumably the Home Office's original and subsequent perjorative references to journalism conveyed a concern not only about the journalist's emphasis on people and happenings (rather than findings and conclusions), but also about his unfortunate tendency to be able to communicate to an audience wider than academic specialists. Research is usually safe when presented in technical language in a journal with a circulation of a few hundred academics.

In any event, the Home Office letter ignored our interest in the ways in which a particular group of men coped with a unique environment and urged us to expand the project into a comparative study. And finally, despite the Governor's assurances to the contrary, we were told that our work would involve 'interfering with facilities on which the Durham team's project ought to have first call'.

Faced with the Home Office's apparent misunderstanding of our proposal and local interest in the project, we continued to take classes and collect material, leaving it to the Prison Department to decide whether what we were doing constituted research. In December 1970 we published an article in *New Society* (Cohen and Taylor 1970) to clear some of the ambiguity of the previous two years. We hoped it would demonstrate the seriousness of our interest in aspects of penal policy and the viability of our methods. We were anxious to give evidence of our respectability; we were doing more than just 'talking'. This meant that the article had to be, by most standards, an 'academic' piece; we took care to anonymise the prisoners and even the prison (referred to as 'Endtown') and discussed fairly abstract problems about the experience and structuring of time. In no way was this a sensational, exposé job on the prison. Without, we hope, sounding too self-righteous, we stress that then and any time since we could have used our privileged knowledge in all sorts of less academic ways. We have continually, for example, had journalists from the tabloids breathing down our necks for revelations about train robbers, torture gangs and child murderers.

The Home Office response to the article was unfavourable. They objected to our failure to obtain official clearance and repeated their previous concerns about the nature of the research. Not only did they complain again about our concentration upon a 'small minority', but now they also declared that our research distorted the nature of official policy on long-term imprisonment by suggesting that the inmates were destined to spend most of their lives being shunted from one maximum security wing to another. The value of our work was described as lessened 'by a subjective approach in some parts and by the fact that it seemed to base so much on a regime that will have a limited life'. Grudgingly, we wrote back and conceded that our predictions about the future life of the prisoners were based on our present knowledge of the operation of the wings; we admitted that we must withdraw our comment if circumstances were indeed changing. We had already encountered Technique Number One: 'this is not proper research', and this was our first taste of Technique Number Two: 'things are changing anyway'. This second technique is as obstructive as the first to inquiry into the operation of the penal system. Since that time we have heard of many examples of its use from journalists and researchers. Anyone who describes unsatisfactory conditions in a prison is quietly informed that it would be inappropriate to include such material in his copy for matters are about to change. We could hardly have been given a more effective example of the duplicity inherent in this type of 'anticipatory' censorship, than over the case of maximum security wings.

At first glance the Home Office position seemed perfectly tenable. How could we continue to write about the continuing existence of security wings, when in 1966 the Mountbatten Committee had condemned conditions in the wings as 'such as no country with a record for civilised behaviour ought to tolerate any longer than is absolutely necessary as a stop-gap measure?' And in 1968, the Advisory Council on the Penal System had noted that, although improvements in the wings had been made, 'no-one regards the containment of prisoners in such small confined units as anything other than a temporary and most undesirable expedient'. Hadn't we also read the Home Office publication, *People in Prisons*, which in 1969 gave us the news that 'it remains undesirable that men should be detained for very long periods in such confined conditions'? Our readiness to accept Home Office assurances about such matters was only undermined in 1972, by a newspaper letter from the Director General of the Prison Service in which he admitted that two out of the four security wings were not yet closed but would be run down in 'due course'. Today we look back upon all the promises we read and heard with total cynicism. Many of our original Durham sample remain (after ten years) in much the same conditions that we originally described. The security wing principle still remains a feature of the prison system. (Two final ironical comments on the situation were provided: by the Control Units which in 1974 introduced a punitive and isolated regime undreamed of even at the peak of the security tightening-up in the mid-1960s; and by the news that our old 'anachronism', E-Wing at Durham, had been reopened to hold 'high-risk' women prisoners.)

Nevertheless, the original E-Wing did close in June 1971, and this provided the Prison Department with an obvious way to block any further work on our project. We were simply refused permission to visit the men in the prisons to which they were transferred (even during official visiting hours), and our letters to them were censored or sent back on the grounds that they were not 'normal' or 'personal' correspondence and could have been used 'for the furtherance of our research'.

At a last-ditch meeting to save things (at the end of 1971) we were still being presented with the familiar objections ('this is not proper research' and 'things are changing anyway'), plus a new one that figured prominently in later negotiations: the Home Office's concern for our safety. Not only could we be seized as hostages, but also we were too immature to understand the dangers of being corrupted, exploited and conned by groups of ruthless gangsters. We persisted with our arguments and after a wait of two months received the starkest of replies: 'I am afraid that we cannot see our way to allowing you the facilities you want to study this particular group of long-term prisoners.' The 'facilities' we were requesting at that stage were minimal: the right to correspond with and visit a handful of prisoners.

We had more or less abandoned any hope of convincing the Home Office of the validity of studying the reactions of a small group of men to a special environment. In June 1972 they were still referring to 'the very narrow issue of the handful of prisoners in the old security wings. Special wings are almost phased out of the system . . . we think that it is pointless and harmful to continue to concentrate attention (as your revised proposal still would) on the small untypical part of the long-term population and on a form of treatment that is now almost a dead letter.'

One straw was held out, the one on which we were to base our ill-fated 'follow-up' project, i.e. the possibility of replacing our sample with a more 'representative' group of long-termers. But we insisted that this should not be a straight replacement; we would broaden the study, but if we couldn't see the old Durham group as well how could the study be described as either 'follow-up' or 'longitudinal'? We therefore proposed a division of our application into two separate categories: permission to have access to the original group, and facilities for carrying out a new project into the wider problems of long-term imprisonment. This concession seemed to provide the only way in which we might continue to make any sort of contact with our original sample. It was not enough. The Home Office rejected any request to see the original group and we informed them that we therefore had no alternative but to publish the admittedly incomplete data that we had obtained up to that point. This appeared in *Psychological Survival.*

The book was inevitably weakened by the fact that it covered only four years of the prisoners' lives; the theoretical edifice, as we implied earlier, was too heavy for the empirical material derived from talks and observation. There were many questions which we left hanging in the air. 'It is possible', wrote the reviewer in the *Times Literary Supplement*, 'that there are some in the Prison Department who may cherish the hope that this little Penguin will waddle off into obscurity.' Certainly, an official silence was maintained, although we heard informally that the book had been described in the Home Office as 'setting back sociological prison research by twenty years'. A strange remark, for since T. Morris and P. Morris's (1962) study of Penton-ville ten years before, there had been *no* empirical study of a prison regime. (And the Morrises had also been told that their work similarly set research back *twenty* years; at this rate of regression, research was already back to 1942 and on the way to the only previous twentieth-century study, Brockway and Hobhouse's *English Prison Today*, 1922.)

The first informed reaction from the official prison world pleased us more than any academic review. The *Prison Service Journal* published a review by J. A. Green, then Head of Development Training at the Staff College, but formerly Assistant Governor at Durham, and in charge of the maximum security wing during most of the research. He acknowledged the possibility of this type of research as 'novel but realistic' and at the same time com-mented constructively on its problems, particularly the lack of attention to the staff perspective. He concluded that, despite this imbalance and other methodological problems, 'the work represents a step towards the involve-ment of men who are going to spend a large part of their lives in prison in an examination of their predicament'. The picture we presented should be 'recognised and its implication examined'. Even this muted recognition must have been too much for the editors of the *Prison Service Journal*. They took the unusual step of following Green's review with a 'methodological note' which repeated the ritualistic attack on our methods and declare that if future researchers or teachers encountered problems of access 'it would be clear where the responsibility lies'.

With the beginning of 1973, we embarked on a series of political manoeuvres in the faint hope of resuming some contact with the prisoners. This was the beginning of nearly two years of negotiation, by the end of which time we had not got anywhere near going into a single prison or talking to a single prisoner.

These were talks about talking, and each successive meeting at Eccleston Square, the headquarters of the Home Office Prison Department, was prefaced and terminated with the ritualistic language of diplomacy and industrial dispute: both sides were at least 'round the table', much 'groundwork' remained, there was 'mutual goodwill', earlier 'misunderstandings' or 'breakdowns in communication' should not be harped upon, each side would obviously have to do some 'hard thinking', a compromise was 'in sight'.

Mystified by this rhetoric, we lost sight of our crucial weakness in the negotiations: that we had no bargaining counters at all. Much as the prisoners were sympathetic to our project and appeared to regret the severance of our contacts, we could hardly expect them to leap on the rooftops or go on hunger strike to demand their own friendly researchers. And if we seemed stubborn or made unreasonable-sounding demands, then we would only be confirming our irresponsible attitudes.

The weapons, then, were clearly on their side, and the major one they exploited was the 'closed awareness context' which surrounded us at the meetings. We were totally dependent on them for information about such matters as the removal of men from one prison to another or policy changes on long-term imprisonment. And if we were told that something had to be altered in our design because of 'security reasons', we had no way of contradicting this rationale, an explanation of which, of course, could not be given for 'security reasons'.

Whether this was intentional or not, we were further bewildered by the contradictory messages emanating from the officials. Mr C. visited us privately to assure us that the 'research people' were very interested in the project, and that if only we could present it in the form of a properly argued research plan we would get the go-ahead. If we produced such a document, he would speak on our behalf at the next meeting. We accordingly produced the document, and at the next meeting Mr C. remained completely silent throughout the three hours. Earlier on we had been visited by Mr G.; the *real* problem, he hinted, was our involvement in radical prisoners' groups such as PROP. If we continued to do such things as handing out inflammatory leaflets to prisoners' relatives or speaking on the same platform as notorious ex-convicts, how could we be expected to gain the confidence of the prison authorities?

Returning now to the chronology of the negotiations, the first move in the final round was to write to the Minister of State at the Home Office describing how the project had been destroyed along with any chance of informed public debate about the policy of long-term imprisonment. This letter was acknowledged but never replied to. We sought through a distinguished academic intermediary, Nigel Walker, to reopen direct negotiations with the Prison Department.

This last move eventually led to Mark Two: a completely revised proposal which included the concession we mentioned earlier, i.e. the inclusion of other long-termers in the inquiry. We proposed to follow through the original Durham group until they moved towards the end of their sentences and to extend the analysis – using more conventional questionnaire and interview methods – to include cohorts of about 150 other prisoners at different stages of very long sentences. Our earlier tactical manoeuvres to obtain access were now beginning to transform the whole project.

By the middle of 1973 we had obtained agreement in principle to this proposal. We were elated at the prospect of at last being able to pick up the threads of the original research. For reasons we have never been quite sure of, a civil servant's version of a gentleman's agreement had been struck. We would 'submerge' the notorious Durham group in the larger sample, we would accept all reasonable requests about security, confidentiality, publication, etc., and in return we would be let in again. Both parties agreed to regret the 'misunderstanding' of the past. During the next eighteen months periodic references were to be made to the old days when things had mysteriously 'gone wrong'.

Meetings, letters, research proposals and timetables followed fast. We applied for, and eventually obtained, a grant of some £11,000 from the Social Science Research Council (SSRC), to cover research costs (mainly recording equipment, travelling and secretarial help) for a five-year project into the effects of long-term imprisonment. By December 1973 our Christmas cards to the ex-Durham prisoners informed them that we would be seeing them soon.

A few months later, though, there appeared the first of the doubts that were to precipitate our abandonment of the research. Despite the agreement in principle about the research and despite the fact that we had spent nearly a year talking only about practical arrangements (such as sampling and interviewing procedures), we were now informed that the Prison Officers' Association were objecting to the research and had been told that 'approval has not been given'. In addition, there was opposition from the Governors which threatened the whole project. Our anxieties were quelled by reminders that we knew all along that 'all would not be plain sailing'. After a series of meetings with the various staff groups concerned, we were once again shown the green light.

But now what were typically referred to as the 'nuts and bolts' of the project, the details that just needed 'sewing up' before we could actually enter a prison, began to look very different. While negotiating at this practical level, we were being drawn into a series of compromises which far from being just technical added up to a principled threat to the whole project for which we had obtained the SSRC grant. Firstly, our tenuous attempt to retain some contact with the ex-Durham men (the only way of carrying out a genuine follow-up) was being undermined. For 'operational reasons' access to certain key informants was not guaranteed: X would be in a prison outside the sample, Y raised special problems. We were also being steered away from certain prisons – one on the grounds that it was already overused for research, despite the Governor's denial that this was so.

But most critical were the conditions under which we could actually talk to the prisoners and what would happen to information we collected. It was now insisted that a prison officer be physically present during all discussions and interviews, not just within reach (as was the Durham practice) but actually supervising the conversation. As if this was not enough control (the reason later given to us was not, of course, 'control' but our physical safety), *all* these interviews and discussions were to be tape-recorded. The Governor or another member of the prison staff would then seal the tapes in an 'envopak' which would be sent to P2, the security division in the Prison Department headquarters in Eccleston Square, London. A secretary (employed at our expense) would then transcribe the tapes in a room at Eccleston Square. After transcription and any 'necessary editing' of objectionable material, the tapes would be retained by the Prison Department until needed.

This extraordinary procedure originated from our own request to have *certain* material tape-recorded, because of the obvious technical benefits that tapes have over written records. Subtly, the Prison Department used their concession on this (we were constantly told how we were the first prison researchers to be allowed the privilege of having talk tape-recorded) as a new and almost total form of control over what we would be doing for five years.

We stress that we were quite prepared to sign the Official Secrets Act and had every intention to abide by the normal requirements about security and to submit all material for clearance before publication. But to allow this degree of control over how we talked at the initial stage seemed intolerable. How could we reasonably expect the information we were interested in to be communicated under these conditions?

The final catalyst came with the revelations in the press in October 1974 about the existence of the new Control Units. During the very period of our regular meetings, the Units were being set up. We were given no information about them despite the fact that they were located in two of the prisons in our sample and were part of an innovative policy clearly relevant to our whole research interests. It was not difficult to predict that such developments would occur in the British penal system (Cohen 1974b), and the point was not that their actual existence impeded the research. As we later wrote to the Prison Department, 'no researcher stops doing his work because he disagrees with some aspect of the organisation he is doing research on'. The point was rather that their silence about this change seemed indicative that this was information with which we could not be trusted.[5]

Restricted access, intolerable delays, censorship of basic material, and then the Control Units – it seemed impossible to continue taking public money for a research project under these conditions. Accordingly we wrote to the SSRC announcing that we would have to terminate the research and return the grant.

When, as a first frustrated reaction to this ending and to the years of wasted time, we published a bitter chronology of our dealing with the Home Office, we were accused several times of naivety. We have to acknowledge a degree of such naivety; we simply did not understand the Pandora's box of problems we had opened. At times, though, all this was a calculated and disingenuous response. We wanted to ask, and kept repeating, why it was not possible simply to talk to a group of long-term prisoners about their lives and to report what they said. Our real naivety lay in the belief that we could somehow stand aside from the roles insisted upon by our colleagues and by the Home Office. It was only as sociologists, after all, that we could be allowed to enter the prison – and once there we were expected to behave according to traditional research guidelines. And when we started using such guidelines we were clearly acting in bad faith by trying to draw around us a cloak of professional integrity in order to protect an activity which was, by most sociological standards, a piece of 'unprofessional' activity. But equally, the Home Office acted in 'bad faith' by ever pretending that they would relax their controls to such an extent as to allow critics of their policy and apparent 'sympathisers' with the prisoners to conduct a form of research which lay outside normal conventions.

There were some exceptions to this hostility. Throughout these years we have had many sympathetic contacts with Governors, Assistant Governors and prison psychologists. But this local support has counted for little. Such individuals are unable to give any public indication of their approval or disapproval; they may not even enter into public debate about prison life. This blanket of silence (invariably justified by reference to the all-embracing Official Secrets Act) immunises the system from criticism and positively encourages the type of 'Sensational revelation – Official denial' sequence which characterises public information on our penal institutions.

Our research plans were a small and unimportant casualty of this policy of secrecy at all costs in the name of security. There was nothing particularly radical about our work (as some colleagues never cease to inform us), but the consternation it aroused within the prison administration, if nothing else, at least demonstrated the ways in which even the most innocuous attacks upon this silent institutional sphere are thought to justify concentrated and sustained resistance. The decision to abandon our research was not an easy one to take. But to have continued would, we believe, have provided implicit support for the present Home Office policy on research. That policy remains a serious impediment to independent sociological inquiry; we can only hope that our decision will strengthen rather than weaken the determination of other researchers who are faced with unacceptable denials of access or censorship of basic research data. More particularly, we hope that in some small way it will alert grant-giving bodies and professional associations to the difficulties which researchers face within British penal institutions. The most immediate way to resolve some of these difficulties would be the abolition of section 2 of the Official Secrets Act. It is this highly ambiguous regulation (already heavily criticised by the Franks Committee) which more than anything else gave officialdom the powerful argument for denial of access and for application of censorship during the long and convoluted campaign that we have described.

NOTES

1 There has been some heavyweight sociological criticism recently against those of us who regard the criterion of 'interesting' as being worth remembering. Presumably these critics would want sociologists to write about uninteresting things. For a discussion of how theories are seen as interesting, see Davis (1971).

2 More details about the methods we describe in the first part of this chapter (and particularly the method of mutual interpretation of the data) may be found in the book we eventually and prematurely wrote (Cohen and Taylor 1972). The second part of this chapter appeared in a slightly different form in a later article (Cohen and Taylor 1975), and we wish to acknowledge permission from the editor of *New Society* to reproduce part of that article.

3 For discussion of the paradoxes of self-consciousness (which owes a great deal to the prison research) see Cohen and Taylor (1976, ch. 2).

4 See Morris (1975) for some views on how this system has worked.

5 A few months after we terminated the research, a newspaper published details of new policy on long-term prisoners which would have affected our whole research design had we known about it. The plans were made during our negotiations and by the very same officials we had been meeting.

4
Becoming a Sociologist in Sparkbrook

ROBERT MOORE

PERSONAL BACKGROUND TO THE STUDY

When we were finishing *Race, Community and Conflict* (Rex and Moore 1967), John Rex and I often remarked how we should each write our Sparkbrook novel. This was not because either of us had lost faith in sociology; it was rather an expression of our need to communicate something of our response to Sparkbrook as a human situation, filled with humour, conflict, hardship and affection.

It is difficult to reflect upon this without sounding sentimental or romanticising two years' hard work. I was a new graduate facing the opportunity to 'do' sociology and very unsure how 'it' ought to be done. I discovered that full-time research is not a job; it is a way of life, and so one's life becomes woven into the research just as much as the research becomes part of one's life. For a year I ate, breathed and slept Sparkbrook. I made new friends, made and dissolved relationships, took sides in conflicts, had problems with my landlady and went to parties. In a twelve-year retrospect it is these personal experiences that stand out and the technicalities of research that are most obscured by the passage of ideas.

To avoid sentimentality it is best only to indicate those personal experiences where biography and methodology may impinge upon one another. Some were very dramatic. For example, a building in which I was talking to an Irish political activist caught fire, and though he and I escaped a third man died. My own life was certainly saved by the failure of a fire extinguisher, which thwarted my attempt to rescue the third man; the smoke forced me back moments before an explosion destroyed the area I was trying to penetrate. This event might have brought the research to a premature end. Another time I was crouched under a hedge with bottles and bricks flying overhead as West Indians and tinkers fought a pitched battle. The police arrived in force, and I was moved on. What does the eager researcher do when moved on? I ran around the block, took my coat off and strolled innocently into the middle of the battle again.

The physical well-being of the research worker is also under threats of a different kind. For example, pints of very sweet and strong boiled tea destroy the digestion, and visiting Indian families puts one's stomach awash with it. The round of religious observances on Friday, Saturday and Sunday, interspersed with teetotal pub-crawling on Fridays and Saturdays, almost every week is physically debilitating and at times mentally numbing. Typing up notes on Monday morning becomes an ordeal. It is only in writing this that I now realise that I am owed my annual holiday from that year! How does this degree of physical involvement affect sociological judgement?

Demands on the emotions are certainly felt very acutely when one is working in the field of race relations. For example, it is very difficult to keep calm while listening to a bleary-eyed, unshaven Brummy, dribbling in his beer while holding forth on the way in which West Indians lower the tone of his locality. John Rex and I were amazed, irritated and later angered by a senior member of the local government who, in an elaborately stage-managed interview, attempted to mislead us about the local authority's race policies. But we remained polite, even deferential, throughout. The most beguiling interview was with a dim and amiable young prostitute who said as we parted that if I wanted to know any more about her work I could call at her place 'any time'.

The sociologist in a locality like Sparkbrook cannot remain isolated. He is a resource that individuals and groups within the locality try to mobilise on their own behalf. Tenants send for his help when being evicted (he is obviously some kind of social worker); landlords look for his aid in interpreting the housing law and dealing with tenants (he is obviously a man with influence); and officials, meanwhile, take him on one side to make sure he knows the 'real' housing problem (he is obviously a seeker after truth).

At a simpler level, families ask for help in understanding letters from the local education authority, or for advice on housing. Such simple aid cannot be refused; but then one is invited to state opinions and express support in local conflicts, which raises the question of how detached the sociologist should be thought to be. With the daily comings and goings of community life go friendship, and with friendship go invitations to meals and to meet families and friends. All these are good research opportunities, but they are also opportunities to become a participant non-observer in the life of the community.

In Sparkbrook, the problem of involvement and detachment was most acute on election day in 1964. A personal friend had gone to work in the Conservative Party ward committee room to observe activities there. Late in the afternoon a consignment of 'Nigger for a Neighbour' leaflets arrived. The old ladies who formed the core of the local party were eager to distribute the leaflets, but the Young Conservatives who had come into the ward to help were liberal antiracists. The conflict over the leaflet eventually emptied the office except for the friend. Had she not stayed at her post the

Conservative Party effort in the ward would have collapsed. She could have left, observations of conflict completed, but we would then, I believe, have been guilty of unethical behaviour, because her help had been accepted in good faith by the Party. I doubt if any sociologist today would carry out covert observations of this kind.

These personal observations can be concluded by saying that the year in Sparkbrook and political events in 1965 changed my political life and destroyed the liberal optimism that characterised many activists at the time. We had been encouraged by the events of the 'freedom summer' of 1964 in the USA, and this liberal optimism was to die a slow death – but for me it was a quick death in 1964–5.

Perhaps nothing said so far is unique; it is the everyday story of sociologists. Nevertheless it is sometimes hard to believe, reading the monographs, that sociologists are ever *there* at all. Neither John Rex nor I achieved the distinction of A. Vidich and J. Bensman (1958) in being burnt in effigy – but we were there. It was our involvement in personal and human terms that prompted us to discuss our novels.

POLITICAL BACKGROUND TO THE STUDY

But let us return to the presociological beginning. How was it that sociologists were to be found in Sparkbrook in 1964? The study of Sparkbrook was one of a number financed by the Survey of Race Relations, which had been set up by the Institute of Race Relations to spend a grant of £99,500 from the Nuffield Foundation. The Institute was founded in 1952, largely, it seems, to study the implications of nationalism and political freedom in the colonial world for businessmen and the military.

The Institute never tried to become a lobby or a pressure group. This remained true when from 1957 onwards the Institute began to take a greater interest in domestic race relations. The dominant attitude was one of liberal detachment: to seek the facts and to reason with the men of affairs who influence events. The Institute thus sought to whisper in the corridors of power rather than to debate in public places. Naturally enough the Institute had little effect on the development of policies, always finding itself in a position of accommodating to bad decisions rather than campaigning to prevent them. Thus even the 1965 White Paper, while regretted, was seen as providing 'the first systematic review of policy and attempt to define remedies'. This silver lining to the cloud proved to be base metal in 1968.

In 1971 and 1972 the Institute's Council moved into a clear political position in attempting to suppress questioning and criticism of its work from its own employees. It was also strongly opposed to the more penetrating discussion of *racism* and its relation to capitalism that was developing among blacks. The whole issue came to a head with multiple threats to academic freedom by the Council. The membership voted the Council down on this question, and its conservative members resigned – a number of them appearing later on the governing body of the Runnymede Trust. I played a part in mobilising academics against the Council, and the materials I collected during this period will perhaps form the basis of a future book. These events are worth mentioning because they draw attention to a question that has become increasingly salient in British sociology: namely, the funding of research and the control of research funds. But they also point to a fact that I believe has been borne out by both our work and that of others: that it is possible to do good research even with 'tainted' funds. At the time, we knew virtually nothing of what we know today about the then Institute. In fairness it should be said that our freedom to publish was never limited in any way. While sociologists should not seek out dubious sources of money, fear of the hidden hand of bourgeois interests, the state or the CIA should not deter them from seeking any funds at all.

So much for the personal and political background to the study. The remainder of this chapter will be devoted to methodological questions and practical problems. It will conclude with a discussion of the public response to the publication of *Race, Community and Conflict* and with some final reflections.

METHODOLOGICAL CONSIDERATIONS

The methodological basis of our work is argued in detail in the Introduction to *Race, Community and Conflict*. This Introduction was written in outline at the beginning of the project as a result of the first meeting between John Rex and myself. As an undergraduate I had read *Key Problems of Sociological Theory* (Rex 1961) and thought how much I should like to work with the author. I wrote to him and later had a telephone call to say that he had some money for race relations research, and to ask was I interested. We met at the Bamboo cafe under the railway at Golders Green, and John Rex outlined his project. He spoke largely in terms of 'doing a survey'. This puzzled me; how did all this connect with the issues raised by *Key Problems*? The question must have appeared legitimate because the chapter that finally became the Introduction was begun in direct response to it.

We rejected a functionalist approach to the study of Sparkbrook (pp. 3–4). We recognised that there was some degree of more or less integrated 'order' about the city (pp. 6–7) and that a measure of consensus about, for example, social status might be found (p. 7). But order and consensus were treated as themselves problematic and as the outcome of domination and subordination or of truce in conflict. Order and consensus are not given, they have to be discovered and explained, not used as the basis for explanation. We began therefore from an action frame of reference: 'considering the goals of typical actors representing the various host and immigrant groups, the various politico-economic classes and more specifically what we have called "housing classes" ... It is out of the clash of interests, the conflicts and the truces between these groups that Birmingham society emerges' (p. 6).

In studying one zone of the city our task seemed clear: 'We must find out who lives there, what primary community ties they have, what their housing situation, economic position and status aspirations are, what associations they form, how these associations interact and how far the various groups are incorporated into urban society as citizens' (p. 11). It was my task as the fieldworker to find out these things by whatever methods were appropriate.

Sparkbrook was not chosen at random for study. It was an area in which 'race problems' were beginning to manifest themselves. The level of coloured immigration was emerging as an important political issue nationally, and in part this was an expression of the anxieties of cities like Birmingham and districts like Sparkbrook. Neither the city government nor the local residents knew whether immigration was a good or bad thing, but they did observe overcrowding among coloured immigrants and the physical deterioration of the areas in which they lived. There is a rich store of racist beliefs through which to interpret such observations, rather than attributing overcrowding, for example, to white discrimination. Race therefore was becoming an issue in Birmingham, and this was reflected in the press and in the growth of a demand for an immigration colour bar. Locally it was becoming an issue too; it was proposed to one time that an immigrant candidate should run in the local elections. Meanwhile, under the general slogan 'Something must be done', the Sparkbrook Association was set up to meet the individual social needs of the population and to create a 'fuller and happier life' for the whole community.

The current explanations of the race relations situation were then either heavily psychological, in terms of *prejudice*, or semi-sociological, in terms of the *stranger hypothesis*. This latter notion assumed that, because immigrants were strangers to the British and found Britain strange, a period of learning and adjustment was necessary; the problem would be solved when immigrants had assimilated or *integrated*.

Such a framework as the stranger hypothesis takes the culture and values of British society as non-contradictory, homogeneous and static; the changes required for assimilation are to be made mainly by the immigrants. Consistent with our 'action' (as opposed to 'functional') framework, we treated the host society, as already indicated, as a complex of competing groups. We also recognised that, far from 'assimilating', the immigrant might change the host society and that between them they might create something quite new culturally. By contrast, the immigrants might live in a more or less self-contained colony and only engage with the wider society in a very limited way (e.g. in the labour market).

Our general sociological perspective and our views on urban society and race relations mutually reinforced one another. It would have been difficult to stress conflict and then make consensual assumptions in adopting an assimilationist approach to race relations. Our task in studying immigrants was no different from studying Birmingham society in general. We had to discover 'what kinds of primary community immigrants form in order to obtain some sort of social and cultural bearings in the new society and also what relationships exist between their community structure as a whole and the complex system of class conflict and status which we refer to as "the host society" ' (p. 14).

In looking at the *development* of immigrant–host community relationships, we thought that one likely development was 'the incorporation of the immigrant into the society as a legal citizen having the social rights of the citizen' (p. 15). The word 'citizen' was important in our analysis because, following T. H. Marshall (1965), we recognised the significant body of legal, political and social rights that the term subsumes. These rights go some way to modify the unbridled operation of the market and the use of naked force in human relationships. What has, in fact, happened since 1964 is that these rights have gradually been stripped from the Commonwealth citizen by successive governments until his status is now worse than that of an alien 'migrant worker'. This is a point to which I shall return in the conclusions to this chapter.

In both the quotations defining the research task (pp. 11 and 14) we used the term 'primary community'. This was important to us because we accepted the simple psychological notion that the individual needs group ties to ensure emotional security and personal stability. The group that provides this security and stability is the 'primary community'. The family is usually such a primary community. In the transitional zones of a city, typified by Sparkbrook, one can expect to find many people who have broken with or lost their primary community in a temporary or permanent way. One such person was Alec, and Estonian alcoholic who haunted the Sparkbrook Association. Truly a lost soul, sinking in despair and self-pity, he would cry and talk about his past and his lack of a future. He tried to find friends and company in the Association, and he did so. At times we even saw him happy. He tried to show his gratitude by cleaning the windows and doing other jobs, but he could not manage the ladder because of the alcohol. His inability to reciprocate the friendship he received reduced him again to tears. Alec is now dead, though I do not know the manner of his passing; he could well have walked into the road under a bus.

One man who coped more adequately was in the process of creating a new primary community and became a key figure in our methodological thinking, though we met him only once. He would have formed the basis of a chapter on 'The functions of associations' had the publishers not thought it too advanced for their readers. The man in the Brewers Arms was an old Brummy, born and bred in Sparkbrook. His parents were dead and he had not married to form a new family of his own. None of his old neighbours remained. The really important group with which he had identified was his regiment in the war, but now that was disbanded and there was not even a British Legion in Sparkbrook to compensate. So the man sat drinking in the

Brewers Arms, he engaged in a market relationship to obtain alcohol, which maybe reduced the pain of isolation.

The walls of the Brewers Arms were decorated with holiday postcards, details of darts matches, notices of outings, etc.; clearly it was not solely a marketplace. Our man entered into these more affective relations firstly by being bought a drink and then by being allowed to buy drinks – a form of reciprocity which modifies the callous cash nexus. The barmaid meanwhile doled out homespun wisdom, providing a form of pastoral care in telling men when they had had enough and ought to go home to their wives. Here then we saw the Brewers Arms taking on some primary community functions and providing pastoral care. But there was more to it than this. There was a lot of expressive activity also, largely comprising the singing of Irish songs about mother or the old country. In order to enter fully into the life of the company our old man had learned Irish songs and could sing them in some sort of Irish accent. Thus our long and rambling discussion with him was frequently interrupted as he made his way unsteadily to the microphone to take his turn to sing; he was almost invariably beaten to it by another singer.

Life in the Brewers Arms did not really lead anywhere except to hangovers, but it provided some sort of minimal community and gave life some sort of meaning to our man. The churches, the Labour Party, the Sparkbrook Association all provided cameraderie and mutual aid, pastoral care and opportunities to express beliefs and values. In addition they offered objectives, goals to be achieved by action. It seemed very clear to us after the night in the Brewers Arms that when we observed associations in Sparkbrook we would have to understand them at least as performing these four functions: mutual support, pastoral care, expressive activity and achievement of goals. These 'functions' are not necessarily non-contradictory; the Labour Party, for example, had developed mutual support and expressive activity around the Labour Club bar. There was virtually a 'no politics' rule in the Club, and the leadership centred on the habitué's of the bar; the Party was not equipped to win elections thereby.

Experiences in the Brewers Arms proved intellectually stimulating, and our friend Alec was a sociologically very important type. Given that everything seemed likely to be so interesting, a framework was clearly needed if data were to be selected and organised.

PRACTICAL CONSIDERATIONS

The day-to-day task of doing research has to be broken down according to some kind of division of labour. The methodological insights have to be turned into *jobs* for sociologists to do. Our division of labour was broadly threefold. Firstly, Alan Shuttleworth worked through the back numbers of the local newspapers and wrote a sociological narrative of the developments surrounding race and housing policy in Birmingham. The choice of housing as an issue was dictated by events; there was no shortage of jobs, and the main resource for which people competed was housing. Questions of urban decay more or less associated with the arrival of black immigrants were the major public issue for the press and politicians.

Secondly, John Rex made a series of visits to Birmingham during which we collaborated in interviewing key actors at the city level. In other words we studied the organised development of policies and conflicts. We were especially concerned to discover the definitions of the housing situation given by the Labour Party leadership, planning and housing officials, public health authorities, etc. One important aspect of working together was to have two witnesses to some of the statements made, in case they were later denied. Unfortunately John Rex interviewed alone when a senior official responsible for 'integration' described Pakistanis as 'a bunch of frustrated, shrivelled up little bastards', so the comment never appeared in the book.

John Rex and I also worked together on the Commonwealth Property Owners' Association (CPOA). This was an organisation of landlords formed mainly to represent their interests against the local authority, especially the health department which was seen as pursuing hostile policies. In fact the policies were only hostile insofar as the law did not favour landlords who overcrowded their premises according to public health definitions. The CPOA was a citywide organisation.

This division of the work seems fairly clear. I was not solely responsible for dealing with citywide questions and the articulation of Sparkbrook interest groups with city policy and politics. The division was sensible as the interviews were of limited number and could be handled jointly during visits to the city; also, John Rex had a longer experience of politics in Birmingham.

The third part of the work was entirely my own. This entailed working in Sparkbrook and establishing the 'typical' actors and groups to be found in the locality and the extent to which they constituted anything recognisable as a 'community'.

I knew what was meant by Sparkbrook, but it seemed important at an early stage to define the locality quite specifically, if only to provide an arbitrary cut-off for where I should visit people, go to church and visit pubs. Such working definitions are especially necessary if sampling techniques are to be used. The definitions, however, could not be rigidly adhered to, e.g. the main West Indian Pentecostal church was outside the locality. Students at the School of Architecture had previously carried out a land and building use survey in Sparkbrook, which was too good an opportunity to miss. Their study provided a map of all the buildings, showing multi-occupations and non-residential uses, and their outer boundaries also coincided with census enumeration districts. So the students' map was adopted. It was a wise decision, because in the event there was no one social entity called Sparkbrook (we wrote of 'The three Sparkbrooks' in our second chapter), although the area chosen was widely recognised by natives as being the essential Sparkbrook.

Perhaps as a result of my time at sea and familiarity with charts and concern with spatial relations, my mind works very geographically. I always buy a map when I arrive in a town and have an almost photographic memory for its details at a glance; I always know which way north is and notice slight changes in wind direction during the day; I never get lost in town or country. So inevitably I worked for a week or so on maps of Sparkbrook, eventually locating nearly all the multi-occupied houses (and hence a substantial proportion of immigrant dwellings) from the Rating and Valuation lists. These too were then transferred to the maps. We were later able to add data from the 1961 Census to these maps at the Enumeration District level.

My first foray into Sparkbrook underlined the difference between geography and sociology. I knew exactly who I was, but I was lost. I was standing outside the houses when what I wanted to know was probably happening inside.

In the event I made my base in the Sparkbrook Association. I ate in the cafes, did my shopping in the shops and drank ginger beer in the pubs. Like the man in the Brewers Arms I made contacts. I talked about Sparkbrook and its problems, about the Irish countryside or problems of Islam, depending on whom I was eating or drinking with. I was told 'I ought to see' so and so, and armed with my informant's name I would make a visit. The Sparkbrook Association also provided a list of organisations in the locality, and I then called upon the officers of these organisations. From this activity flowed further information and invitations, and soon, in addition to mapping the formal organisation of Sparkbrook, I found myself with opportunities to visit private homes to meet and talk with 'unimportant' people.

In trying to understand any organisation, in the first instance I adopted a commonsense approach in seeking an answer to a series of obvious questions. What are the objectives of this organisation? Who are its officers and members? What are their activities? What services do members receive?

This is really quite a simple operation: the information comes from officers or members of the organisation; their objectives might be written down or embodied in statements that are repeated again and again; the membership can be checked against lists or observations at meetings. Not all objectives are clear however; to state that the function of a church is to save its members tells us very little about practical policies and short-term goals. Similarly 'pastoral' care may not be all it seems; the help offered by the CPOA was often based on traditional patron–client relationships between men engaged in a complex pattern of social obligations having its origin far beyond Sparkbrook.

Organisations also have 'latent' purposes; some were very obvious, like the way in which West Indian football teams created a warm community life for their supporters with dances and fund-raising activities. It was not difficult either to discern the racial implications of the interest the Barber Trust Residents' Association took in 'maintaining standards' in their area (p. 72).

One of the most surprising discoveries we made concerned religion. We thought religion would be fairly marginal to the life of Sparkbrook. It soon became clear that religion had an important function for incomers from Ireland and further afield. Through religion the immigrants were reminded that the same God watched over them as at home and that the same moral demands were made of them here; 'No drink, no loose women' was the message in church, chapel and temple. Additionally, religious organisations provided pastoral support and sought to preserve the home culture while equipping immigrants to cope with the new world of Birmingham. I was very impressed also with the ways in which the Jamaican churches seemed to give expression to the frustrations of a low-status group.

Even more remarkably, it seemed that some of the older and more marginal members of the native society found opportunities to celebrate the past and express their present resentments through religion. This could be heard in their public prayers, the sermons and the conversations at the end of the services. As far as I know, there are no textbooks which tell the sociologist how to interpret expressive behaviour. He has to listen to what people are saying, decide what they mean and make a judgement. Hearing what people mean *rather* than what they say involves a use of the sociological imagination that lies close to skills in literary criticism. But it also entails that elusive factor of empathy, of being able to see the world through the eyes of specific others.

One prime method of investigating associations was to take part in their activities. In the case of the Sparkbrook Association, for example, it was essential to see how the 'fuller and happier life' was to be turned into concrete policy objectives. Immediately and obviously, the organisation's problems were encountered; for example, the social work ethos that motivated many connected with the Association led then to define goals in terms of the needs of families. In any objective sense the main need for social work activity was in providing support for men living alone. Here we see the values that actors hold leading them into quite specific courses of action that can be understood in terms of these values and beliefs.

The Association was widely representative of the whole Sparkbrook locality, thus, in theory, equipping it to tackle the community's major problems effectively. The inability of the Association to do so underlined the problematic nature of the concept 'community'. There was no single entity whose interests the Association could serve, because the locality contained competing and conflicting groups. By being representative the Association incorporated the conflicts of interest. Thus on questions like housing they had no policy, because landlord, tenant and local authority representatives could never agree. The Association was at its best on 'non-controversial' issues on which there was unanimous agreement at public meetings and at the private deliberations of the governing body, like the need for social work, street lighting and refuse collection. Here it was possible, through my continuous exposure to the daily life of the Association and knowledge of its personnel and clients, not only to learn about the problems of such associations in themselves, but also to discover a fine illustration of 'the problem of community' that related back directly to the prime objectives of our research.

How specific conflicts of interest worked out could be discovered in case studies. I spoke to health inspectors about particular houses and then to the landlord and tenants. I went to court to hear the landlord defend his practices against the local authority and the local authority assert its right under the law to control the activities of landlords. I visited the scene of evictions, sometimes playing the role of mediator between landlord and tenant, hearing each explain his position and preventing them coming to blows. I attended public meetings, followed the press coverage, talked with anti-tinker activists and watched the development of local authority policies in response. Meanwhile I was trying to understand the economic role of tinkers in an industrial area like the West Midlands by talking to them about their work. Tinkers and Pakistani landlords were typically pariahs: people doing necessary jobs to which low esteem, shame and punishment attach.

In talking to individual migrants and native Brummies I tried to discover specific data in an informal way. These included: where they lived and their housing status; how long they had lived there and what their previous movements had been; what family they had or where their closest kin were located; what, if any, organisations they belonged to; what work they did and how they spent their free time. Opinions were usually expressed quite freely, but depending on the drift of the conversation I would ask what people thought about living in Sparkbrook, how did they get on with their landlord and where else would they like to live. In most cases this line of discussion elicited remarks about the ethnic minorities in Sparkbrook and a statement of position, usually in the form of a blanket condemnation followed by exceptions: 'All the blacks are dirty and shifty – but I like Jamaicans, they're different, real gentlemen.' If appropriate I asked why people had come to Sparkbrook and what their hopes were now that they were here. In the case of immigrants I would ask about their family at home and whether they intended to return home or to bring their family to Birmingham.

In addition to this kind of information I collected many details of biographical idiosyncrasy: anecdote, traveller's tale and religious homily. In turn I was questioned and had to talk about myself. A very small portion of this material is given in ch. 4 of *Race, Community and Conflict*, on 'The immigrants'.

The material collected in the ways so far described was recorded in rough notebooks. At meetings and where I had formally asked to meet officers of organisations I took longhand abbreviated notes on the spot. Sometimes I did this in the more informal setting of the home or a cafe; it was a question of personal judgement as to whether the respondent would be embarrassed or frightened by a notebook. For some the notebook was an incitement to eloquent speeches, interspersed with: 'And put this in your notebook ... have you got it down?' If it was inappropriate to show a notebook I would make mental notes and then write them up in my book before speaking to anyone else. This was done in a cafe of the Sparkbrook Association or sometimes under a street lamp. One quickly develops marvellous powers of retention providing no other encounter intervenes.

The early part of every morning was spent in my office at the University. Here I typed out fair copies of the notes, gave them reference numbers and maintained an index with cross-references for individuals, organisations and topics (e.g. housing, violence, family life). Typing the notes myself also provided an opportunity to review the information and to spot gaps in the notes. From this I could write brief instructions to myself for the day's work, or questions to ask if I met a particular informant again.

At meetings or church services there was little difficulty in making records. I always counted the numbers present and noted the age, sex and ethnic characteristics of the attenders, together with any significant spatial groupings within the meeting place. With experience it was also possible to say where people came from and who they were: English property owners from Gladstone Road, West Indian tenants from Claremont, etc. Notes were made of who spoke and what they said, of resolutions proposed and of the voting by those present. At church services I recorded the main points of prayers and sermons and also the hymns sung.

These skills are all basic tools of the trade for the sociologist, and they are only learned by practice; I doubt if my excellent teachers in undergraduate days could have taught me how to do this. Research seems to be out of fashion among young sociologists today, but when I have had postgraduates doing observational or unstructured interview work I have only found it possible to give the very roughest outline of techniques and warnings against obvious blunders. Beyond this one can only cross-examine the researcher when he returns and point to the data he needs. One cannot teach people to look and listen, beyond advocating commonsense.

In meeting the people of Sparkbrook and talking to them I was trying to find the 'typical' actors in the locality. In retrospect I think I was not entirely sure what this meant, especially as I had only really engaged in undergraduate discussions of what an ideal type might be. I tried to put the notion of 'statistically average' out of my mind and concentrate on building up character studies of Kitticians, Azad Kashmiris, Brummies, landlords, social workers, etc. who stood, as it were, for all people in these categories. A statistically average landlord or Irish teenager would be a lifeless and uninteresting construct. Methodologically, what was necessary was a hypothetical actor in terms of whose subjective meanings interests and actions could be understood. In practice we had real people who expressed their values and beliefs, who were explicit about their material interests, whose actions or lack of actions could be observed. I think this confused me personally, but it did not influence the research. I later saw that sociological explanations only need in theory to be reducible to statements about meaningful action by hypothetical ideal-type actors. When you have real actors you only have to explain what their actions mean in terms of the real meanings given.

In other words, a certain amount of methodological discussion had led me to believe that 'doing' sociology was more difficult and demanded more abstract skills than it really does. The relative unpopularity of research today may in part be accounted for by the daunting nature of the philosophical issues that have been discussed recently. I do not offer a philistine response to the serious methodological questions that surround problems of intersubjectivity and phenomenology. They are very knotty problems that we cannot ignore. Nonetheless, without solving these problems it is possible to say something significant about what goes on in society. Luckily the majority of the population are unaware that they have problems of intersubjectivity.

From the very beginning it was clear that a more formal survey of the locality was necessary. The data I was collecting were sociologically rich and socially colourful, and they could be used to make sense of what was happening in Sparkbrook. But my meetings with people were based on introductions from friends or relatives or were haphazard; I approached organisations through their officers. How typical, in the statistical sense, were the people I had met? How widely held were the views I had heard expressed in cafes, pubs and churches? Did my face or my manner invite particular kinds of meetings or evoke particular opinions? I felt that a more 'objective' survey would provide an important check on the rest of my work. At a more general level a survey was also important in terms of the public presentation of the research. It would be easier to reject our findings if it was held that I had only spoken to selected people and that no attempt had been made to sample opinions generally in Sparkbrook. In addition, a little money was available for a survey, so it seemed sensible to conduct a questionnaire survey of a sample of the Sparkbrook population.

There was one other rather compelling reason for surveying Sparkbrook. The population was so poorly enumerated and subject to so many estimates that in our research we could not really say how many people we were talking about. All we knew was that houses stood in the streets, so we sampled houses; I had hoped that this would provide something of a population census also. We were able to calculate the ethnic structure of Sparkbrook from our sample, but it was an estimate with a very low reliability. My original intention *both* to 'do a survey' and to enumerate the population was quite unrealistic, as these operations demanded quite different kinds of sample.

The questionnaire had to be administered in difficult circumstances: the population of Sparkbrook (especially 'Sparkbrook 1') was fluid, with tenants moving from house to house at quite short notice; many worked irregular hours; many spoke little or no English. In fact seventeen languages were regularly spoken in the houses of Sparkbrook people. We needed interviewers who were highly motivated and interpreters who could work with them and establish rapport with the respondents.

I decided to use student volunteers for the job, preferably sociology students who would have an appreciation of the objectives and problems of the research. It was difficult to train them as I had little experience myself. I gave them dummy runs interviewing me and then letting them listen to themselves on a tape recorder. I stressed the importance of trying to ask the same questions to all subjects and explained the reasoning behind each question. The hope was that if a question was misunderstood the interviewer could try again with different words. This seemed to break all the rules of interviewing or perhaps to establish a different set of rules for this kind of situation. Furthermore, I asked students to write down *anything* they wished about the interview, the respondent, his or her home, etc. This produced a lot of gratuitous information about religion, family planning, styles of interior decoration and 'social problems'. Again it seemed that only students could do this, given their interest in the topics of study.

None of the interviewers were paid, although the most committed would make up to six calls before finding their subject. John Rex asserted in public (albeit humorously) that I was a slave driver! From one or two incidents he observed on his visits I think he believed I spent all my time putting cold, exhausted and weeping girls back on the bus to Sparkbrook clutching bundles of questionnaires. Interviews were often slow; in the non-British households they often entailed spending the evening eating and drinking with the family. Single men who usually only came 'home' to sleep were extraordinarily difficult to contact. In the end we interviewed over half the individuals we believed to be in our sample of households and only failed to get some information on $2\frac{1}{2}$ per cent.

We piloted the questionnaire in Balsall Heath, an area with characteristics close to Sparkbrook, and this gave our first batch of student interviewers an opportunity to try out their own skills as well as to test the efficiency of the schedule. I then visited every house drawn in our main sample to establish the population and languages spoken by them. I thus visited 201 dwellings containing 382 households. On the basis of this 100 per cent scan of the sample, interviewers and interpreters were given their final instructions and sent to work. Population movements were so rapid that interviewers often arrived with the wrong interpreter. Many interviewers also had to spend much time convincing the respondents that the research was disinterested. Few immigrants could believe that we were not snooping with a view to passing information to the authorities.

I made one or two blunders during the interviews. For example, I went out myself to interview where there were special problems. In one case I tried to interview some non-English speaking Poles in Russian. Eventually a

Polish-speaking student called to reassure them about my visit, and, incidentally, he completed the questionnaire and culled much additional information about this unusual household of Polish peasants. On another occasion I took an Egyptian student as an interpreter to a Yemeni household. When we came to questions about money the Yemenis became very aggressive, and when one of them picked up an iron bar we fled the building. I was later told that these Yemenis had previously been harassed by the press who thought they were sending money home to be used against 'our boys' in Aden. I have become a more tactful sociologist since these incidents.

The results of our survey are embodied in *Race, Community and Conflict*. We did not regard this bit of the research as having any kind of scientific priority over anything else. It did give us a broader picture of the structure of the population, and we did achieve a fairly wide sampling of opinions on various issues. Whatever the statistical reliability of our work in this respect, we were able to establish two data that seem important in retrospect because events were soon to alter them: firstly, we discovered that many immigrants hoped to return home or cherished beliefs about a possible return home; secondly, we found that white attitudes to potential race questions were mixed and ambiguous. The subsequent raising of the colour bar created a more permanent coloured population, and the White Paper *Immigration from the Commonwealth* (1965) and the discussion surrounding its publication moved British opinion towards a more overtly racist definition of the immigration situation.

I have not read a book before or since my time in Sparkbrook that describes a survey similar to mine. Indeed I have never done one like it myself again. My most recent experience was with a postgraduate student surveying other students. She achieved an 84 per cent response rate with a postal questionnaire and one reminder; having expected a 40 per cent response rate she found herself with more coding and analysis than she had anticipated, and she thought this created problems for her. But I am sure this student still does not know how unhelpful handbooks of research techniques can be. I cannot believe that sociologists do not get into at least some of my difficulties. They seem not to write about it, however.

PUBLIC RESPONSE TO THE STUDY

Race, Community and Conflict was written under great pressure from our publishers and sponsors in the 1965 long vacation. Publication was then delayed until 1967. The book was launched with a lunch for top people at the Café Royal and everyone said what a good job we had done.

The immediate response to the book was political; we had expected this but nonetheless found it disappointing that the work was not seen as a serious piece of sociology for some time.

The local press had serialised parts of the book, and a debate about Sparkbrook was under way, by the time the book appeared in the bookshops. Locals wrote letters to say that Sparkbrook people were very respectable, in spite of what we had said, and that there were many worse areas in Birmingham. But on 16 February 1967 the national press joined in. A leader in *The Times* squared the circle by arguing that our book showed the need for rigorous immigration control. It added that perhaps the rules could be altered to make sure that Commonwealth whites 'who bring nothing but benefits to British life' were not excluded. The general contention was denied by none less than the Archbishop of Canterbury in a letter to *The Times*. *The Times* was for calling a spade a spade and making no bones about the colour bar. This position was not fully embodied in policy until 1972.

This leader also set out what was to become the rhetorical basis of future race policies: 'the most rigorous restriction on coloured immigration that is permitted by humanity and common sense ... generous and imaginative treatment of those coloured people who are here'. These were, and still are, incompatible objectives. An immigration colour bar is not good for race relations; the British immigration colour bar has not been good for British race relations. Nonetheless what *The Times* stated in 1967 has become a taken-for-granted basis for all discussion since. The doctrine is no less odious.

In opposing the doctrine of *The Times* in 1967 one could still be called a liberal; in objecting to this same doctrine today one is a 'woolly-headed idealist'. Many who say this still believe themselves to be liberals. The political spectrum has so shifted this issue that to maintain the same liberal stance is to appear to be moving towards an unrealistically humanitarian or idealist position. One sociologist went so far as to describe me, in 1975, as almost 'anti-law, anti-British and anti-white'.

It was only in 1974–5 that I was able to devote the time for research and writing to show that 'the most rigorous restriction' precludes both humanity and commonsense in the administration of immigration law. I did this in my third book on race relations, *Slamming the Door: The Administration of Immigration Control* (Moore 1975b, with Tina Wallace). The fact that I have produced three books on race (see also Moore 1975a) may indicate the effect the Sparkbrook study had on my subsequent career.

The answer to the contention of *The Times* was underlined by *The Economist*, which noted that the 1966 Birmingham Housing Act enabled the city to exacerbate the social problems that were blamed on immigrants by confining lodging houses and their tenants to their existing zones. Hugo Young in the *Observer* (Young 1967) made a related point in a sympathetic review, drawing attention to the defects of Birmingham city's policies. He repeated our observation that the 'intolerable strain' which it was claimed taxed Birmingham's social resources had grown in a period when the city's population had fallen.

Such subtle points were lost on Enoch Powell in his review for the *Daily Telegraph*. Most of the article was an exposition of his views on the need for immigration control. He said that we had made no integrated proposals for countering the trend towards segregation and the development of punitive policies towards the inhabitants of the segregated areas. He was soon to begin a more vociferous advocacy of the policies we had warned against, so he presumably wrote tongue-in-cheek. What he meant by not being able to recognise integrated proposals was that he did not like our proposals 1–11 on pp. 270–1.

The *Guardian*, the *Listener*, *The Economist* all noted that centrality of housing policy to the development of districts like Sparkbrook. But no perceptible policy changes followed. The Labour Government had given Birmingham the Act it needed to restrict the lodging houses. Wolverhampton later asserted for a very long period that it would resist the Race Relations Act as it affected their council house allocation policy. The main response from Birmingham was to try to find who had informed us about discrimination in housing allocation. They also found a self-appointed champion in the Bishop's Chaplain to Coloured People who, by leaping to the public defence of the Coloured Peoples' Liaison Officer (an ex-colonial policeman), saved the local authority from having to comment. I later called to see the Chaplain to point out to him the implications of his action. He subsequently became Bishop of Mashonaland and was not conspicuous for his opposition to the illegal Smith regime either.

Television also responded to the publication of our book, and John Rex and I broadcast on both television and radio in connection with it. But one incident was especially revealing. We were approached by 'This Week' programme with a view to doing a broadcast on the book; we were consulted by telephone and expected, in due course, to be called to appear in a programme. We never appeared. Instead there was a programme featuring Roy Hattersley, the Sparkbrook MP. Our book was on the table in the background of the introductory sequences, and it was said that 'some people' alleged Sparkbrook to be a scene of seething discontent and conflict. Hattersley then interviewed a smiling West Indian and asked him if he was happy. The answer was in the affirmative, and thus we were refuted.

We wrote a letter to the *Listener* to explain how we had been treated, but the letter, which was factual and inoffensive, was rejected on the extraordinary grounds that it might contravene the Race Relations Act. We were subsequently told that Birmingham Council had made it quite clear that, if either John Rex or I appeared in a programme, none of them would. The producer bowed to this pressure and thus excluded the authors of a book that was, by implication, the subject of discussion. We thus never appeared on television in the Midlands.

The city fathers of Birmingham were clearly very angry. It may therefore have been fortunate that I had moved to Durham to join John Rex by the time the book was published. A colleague in Birmingham had made the very simple observation in 1963 or 1964 that Birmingham had no planning policy beyond the central redevelopment areas. This too angered the city, and the colleague was reprimanded by the Vice-Chancellor of the University for publishing the comment.

On the publication of *Race, Community and Conflict* an attempt was made by both the city fathers and the National Association of Local Government Officers in Birmingham to have us reveal one particular source of information. It was quite clear that our informant would have been punished in some way. So when we were publicly challenged on the details of the practice of discrimination in council housing allocation we could only assert that our information was reliable and not back the contention with the kind of hard evidence that was needed.

Some time later our informant was asked to appear on a nationally networked television documentary programme. Given the opportunity to give his evidence to such a wide audience he agreed to appear, expecting this to cost him his career in local government. In the event the interview never went out, although the programme did. The explanation of this contains a mixture of farce and more serious events. The programme was to be compered by a television 'personality' who plainly thought of himself as one whose name was a household word; he still appears and plainly still regards himself as a very important personage. Our informant had no television set and had never heard of his interlocutor. When he asked to be introduced to the latter – who was in fact in the room already – the interviewer had what our informant described as a tantrum. When the tantrum was over the interview began, and our informant (a very upright and scrupulously honest member of a puritanical Protestant denomination) answered the questions put to him in a way that drew an unequivocal picture of housing discrimination in Birmingham. The interview completed, the interviewer said they would record it again with the same questions, but this time he wanted the following answers . . .; he then proceeded to dictate a series of responses that would have presented an entirely different picture. Our informant refused to deviate from the truth, so his interview was never used.

The academic response was not so immediate, but when it came it was soon clear that the notion of 'housing classes' was of central interest. It would not be appropriate for me to review the debate about this in this chapter, nor to comment on the general discussion of our book which has also continued. Suffice it to say that we seem to have achieved such a permanent place in the literature that hardly a book is written on race relations in Britain without citing *Race, Community and Conflict*.

There was an interesting response from students. John Rex and I were in great demand to speak at meetings organised by students. I found that College of Education students were particularly responsive to the book, because it spoke to situations which they had encountered in teaching practice but for which their training did nothing to equip them. With the help of the Student Christian Movement students organised a conference in Worcester, at which we spent much time trying to hammer out just what it was they needed in their courses to help them cope. Some of these students are now teachers with as much as eight years' experience behind them; some, I am sure, chose to go into challenging Sparkbrook-type situations. It is a sobering thought to think that many went equipped with little more than a copy of *Race, Community and Conflict*. Did the book change the course of many of their careers?

Students in the University of Nice took a whole project to test '*l'hypothèse Rex et Moore*' in various European cities. Collectively they produced a cyclostyled volume, four inches thick, dealing with towns and housing classes in both Eastern and Western Europe. I also have a small collection of carbon copies of student essays sent to me from various parts of the country by their authors. The flow of these essays stopped quite abruptly in about 1970; perhaps other works had caught student imaginations or perhaps they were writing essays on the impossibility of sociology instead.

It certainly did my self-esteem no harm for me to 'pass into the literature' so early in my career, and it remains both flattering and embarrassing when someone at a conference says in a loud voice, 'Oh, you're *the* Robert Moore.' I have no way of knowing if others experience this – perhaps they do – but I suspect John Rex and I have been widely read outside the profession and by people who later come into sociology. So we are likely to be 'known' rather better than some of our much more distinguished colleagues.

FINAL REFLECTIONS

On reflection, the main reason why *Race, Community and Conflict* has lasted so well is probably because it made a theoretical contribution to the study of the city and of race relations that transcended the particulars of time and place in Sparkbrook.

We never intended to say that housing classes in any way replaced any other kind of social classes. But undoubtedly this idea has been attributed to us, especially at a more rhetorical level by those who believe class in the Marxist sense to have a teleological primacy. Class in the sense of relationship to the means of production is clearly related to housing classes, but the connection is not simple and unambiguous.

What we said was that there was conflict over the ownership and control of urban resources, and that in this conflict one could therefore discern classes and interests related to ownership of, say, domestic property. Furthermore, it is possible to see this conflict as having a life of its own, to be understood in its own terms. Urban politics and urban administration is, after all, concerned with the distribution of a special set of resources which include housing, education, health and welfare. Urban politics is not the politics of the workplace, and the contenders are not labour and capital. The ways in which the two sets of conflicts relate raises a wide range of sociological issues worthy of systematic study. That the two sets of conflicts do not directly relate raises the important issue of the trade unions' failure to grapple with non-work-related, non-economic issues. I know of little work in this field. Similarly, the fact that most town dwellers, *qua* town dwellers, are the clients and dependents of large bureaucratic organisations like local authorities, building societies and insurance companies seems to have generated very little interest among sociologists. Is mass society *urban* society rather than just *industrial* society? These are all questions arising from the study of the city that can, for the purposes of inquiry, be separated from a discussion of work and community or work and stratification, class and family life, and so on.

I think that if we were starting research today on a district like Sparkbrook we might adopt a slightly different approach. This is because the whole emphasis in the study of race relations and the blacks' own understanding of their situation have shifted. We are now very much more conscious of the economic role of the migrant worker in the European economy, and legislation has now changed the status of the Commonwealth coloured citizen from that of potential immigrant to potential migrant worker. I think also that even in 1965 we were beginning to think of migrant workers as an exploited Third World resource. But only now are books being published in which this is spelled out. (Berger and Mohr 1975; Mitchell 1973; Paine 1974). But one crucial factor in the organised struggle by migrant workers against both employers and indigenous trade unions has been their ability to mobilise as a community. This was perhaps most sharply demonstrated in the Leicester Imperial Typewriters dispute (Moore 1975a). So one would quickly come back to a community study.

Our work in Sparkbrook was influenced by the Chicago School of Urban Sociology and by the public debate about peculiarly urban resources. We were certainly influenced by American discussion of the growth of the ghetto and the beginning of the ghetto explosion. The freedom summer of 1964 focused on desegregation of social facilities – not on economic issues. It was only after the question of segregation had been more or less dealt with that the underlying economic issues in American race relations became salient in any compelling way. However, I am trying not to *explain away* our approach, but rather to defend it as the right one and as an approach that has largely withstood the assaults of its wilder critics.

Today I would start from a discussion of the role of ethnic and national minorities in the economies of Europe. Housing is a vital issue in every country that has migrant workers. I would add to a Sparkbrook-style analysis a discussion of the importance of housing in controlling and ensuring the mobility of migrant labour (Moore 1976). I would widen the list of housing classes to include, for example, the inhabitants of bidonvilles – a special category of owner-occupier – and the workers living in company hostels in which employers control their private and political lives. Then I would turn to the peculiarities of the British city and welfare state to discuss the conflict of housing classes in the urban political arena. To this would have to be added the special race relations dimension. The black – whether he be full citizen or migrant worker – bears the objective and subjective stigma of race. If no attempt is made to understand the *racial* element (and John Rex's subsequent work has been much concerned to specify the peculiarities of a race relations situation), then there can be no real understanding at all. One very difficult issue that needs analysis in both the labour and the housing markets is the way in which race and class can become the same thing; in other words, one's labour market situation can become one's racial situation.

In policy discussions in 1964–7 I was an advocate of dispersal as a means of avoiding the growth of ghettos. My position today is the reverse. The rise of police and other violence against the black population, and the proven importance of community mobilisation in industrial conflicts in a recessional period, make it essential for immigrant communities to remain physically intact. This is not to condemn them to the physical deprivations of the urban twilight zone. The distribution of resources does not need to deprive such areas of adequate amenities, but neither should the act of providing resources be used as a means of dispersing the existing population. It also seems to me important that the black population needs to raise questions about the content and purposes of the education their children are receiving. This kind of issue is best raised in predominantly black schools where it cannot be shrugged off as minority demands. The predominantly black district, in all its cultural and political diversity, seems to me a better basis from which to formulate and press demands and defend interests than a population dispersed throughout white estates.

5

In the Field: Reflections on the Study of Suffolk Farm Workers

HOWARD NEWBY

INTRODUCTION

The initial problem with studying farm workers was that I had no problem – no theoretical problem, that is. Instead I had a personal sympathy with the plight of the farm worker, somewhat reminiscent of W. F. Whyte's concern for the inhabitants of Cornerville (1955, appendix), and I therefore spent several months 'doing the literature' in a systematic but aimless way not knowing quite what I was looking for. In an early encounter David Lockwood had confided that formulating one's problem was the most difficult stage in any research process, and although this provided something of a psychological prop I nevertheless felt inadequate. What I now realise, with the benefit of hindsight, is that the positivist paradigm of problem formulation, hypothesis, operationalisation and testing is not so much misleading as personally inoperable (cf. Fletcher 1974, p. 68). Had I not possessed the initial interest in farm workers, irrespective of a professional interest *qua* sociologist, then I would never have been able to devote five years of my life to studying their social situation with all the boredom, tedium, depression and sheer physical effort that it entailed (as well as the satisfaction and elation). I suspect that the graveyards of unfinished research projects are full of 'disinterested observers', and I would have joined them had I been investigating, say, bank clerks.

Nevertheless this is not how the methodology textbooks would have it, nor the smooth accounts that appear in the methods chapters of so many monographs. Consequently issues of this kind often appear as so many personal inadequacies to the individual researcher. Nowhere, it often seemed to me, had others before me encountered the problems with which I was confronted; therefore I felt that there must be something wrong with *me*. Reassurance is hard to come by. Doing sociological research on farm workers was in many respects unremarkable. There were no serious conflagrations which marred its progress, unlike the experiences of others – including some of those described elsewhere in this volume. Many of the problems are, I am convinced, familiar to many researchers, yet they are rarely discussed or given the weight they deserve. Consequently the feelings of inadequacy and insecurity often remain firmly entrenched in the mind of the individual research worker, particularly the graduate student embarking on his PhD thesis, which was my status when I began seriously to examine the social situation of the farm worker in 1970.

HOW IT ALL BEGAN

My interest in farm workers arose during the second year of my undergraduate course at the University of Essex in 1969. Then, as now, the degree scheme in sociology involved a minor research project which was to be undertaken during the summer vacation between the second and third years, financed, in those days, by one's local education authority. I decided that a 'community study' would provide me with six weeks' pleasant holiday at my LEA's expense. After vaguely considering Cornish fishing villages and Hebridean crofting communities, I settled upon Norfolk agricultural villages, since a student friend came from North Walsham and could provide me with local contacts. The village I chose to study was Trunch, four miles north of North Walsham, where, so it happened, my brother had (a number of years previously) spent several summers camping with other members of his Sunday School. Because of its strange name it had stuck in my mind, so I picked it out on no more rational grounds than that.

It did not take long to discover that to do a community study in six weeks was, to say the least, unrealistic. While I was casting around for what a journalist would call an 'angle', a local retired farm worker recounted to me the story of a strike which had taken place in the village in 1910. Trunch, it emerged, still possessed one of the largest branches of the agricultural workers' union in the country, so I decided to study the unionisation of agricultural workers. I hypothesised (the Essex course in those days was heavily oriented towards scientism) that those farm workers who joined the union were either relatively deprived or alienated. Then, purloining questions from Runciman (1966) and Blauner (1964), I interviewed a sample of workers in Trunch, together with others in a lowly unionised village, Stalham, situated on the edge of the Norfolk Broads. Unfortunately the 'hypotheses' proved incorrect – unionisation seeming to be related much more to the level of integration of the agricultural worker into the local village community – and the eventual dissertation consisted mainly of negative findings. Nevertheless it was well received and I was encouraged to consider postgraduate research.

Meanwhile my social conscience had been aroused concerning the deprived and exploited situation of the farm workers. They manifestly worked so hard and with such skill for such little material reward that I was quickly overtaken by a strong sense of injustice. They seemed to be the most deserving of the poor, as indeed they are. The problem is that, because anyone with political sensibilities to the left of Genghis Khan has supported an improvement of the farm worker's lot, demands made on his behalf typically become absorbed in a sponge-like swaith of inconsequential sympathy. This sympathy was even extended by many Norfolk farmers, who clearly displayed the wherewithal to raise farm wages but who pleaded an inability to do so because of the government's cheap food policy, stating that they would love to pay more but could not afford to – in spite of being among the most prosperous farmers in England. Had they argued that they were not charitable organisations but businessmen interested in profits and that this entailed reducing costs (including wages) as much as possible, I would have at least respected their position. I was not so idealistic as to believe that Norfolk farmers (of all people) would suddenly become converted to egalitarian values. However, I was incensed by their insistence on dressing up their economic rationality with phoney paternalism. I was able to build up a moralistic head of steam that was to keep me going through thick and thin for the next five years.

But I still needed a sociological excuse to conduct my moral exposé. I began with a vague notion of studying further the relationship between relative deprivation and unionisation, but my heart was not in it. I was personally convinced by the arguments put forward by Barry (1966), Urry (1971) and others (e.g. Burns 1967) on the tautological nature of the concept, and I wrote a working paper in which I persuaded myself that further explanation along these lines was futile. In the meantime I was spending several weeks in London, combing through agricultural statistics, back numbers of the farming press, and the academic literature in the libraries at the London School of Economics, at the headquarters of the National Union of Agricultural and Allied Workers (NUAAW) in Gray's Inn Road, and at the headquarters of the National Farmers' Union in Knightsbridge. I was amazed by how much work I could do when there were no distractions (at the London School of Economics even the tea and food were so execrable that there was nothing to do but return to work as quickly as possible). Looking back, I realise that these weeks provided a bedrock of knowledge that was to serve me well during future years. I had read virtually anything and everything that was related, however tangentially, to the social situation of agricultural workers that had been written since 1906 (the year the NUAAW was founded and my initial cut-off point for the literature).

I soon discovered that the sociological literature on agricultural workers was virtually non-existent, apart from fleeting references in a few rural community studies. The only extensive body of literature, apart from an interminable series of books on rural reminiscences and cameos of village life, was that written by agricultural economists on farm labour, some of it verging on a sociological abstracted empiricism akin to rural sociology in the United States. Much of this literature I found very useful in providing a factual basis, albeit an uneven one, on which to proceed. Since it was mostly atheoretical, however, it still did not help in my search for a theoretical problem to investigate. Nor did it help with what I was looking to agricultural economists to contribute: a political economy of modern British agriculture. A few scattered writings on what was normally referred to as 'policy' were the only offerings here. This absence of a serious consideration of political economy suggested an inability on the part of most agricultural economists to distance themselves from their object of study. This seemed to me to manifest itself particularly in their consideration of the determination of the earnings of agricultural workers. The low wages of farm workers were regarded by a number of writers as being part of the problem of low factor returns to agriculture generally in industrialising societies. Having had a sociologist's training, I was naturally puzzled by this. Why must agricultural workers inevitably carry the can for the low income problems of farmers? This was contingent on the power of the farmer in the local labour market, not on the market for his farm produce. It seemed odd that economists, of all people, should not have recognised this. In East Anglia, for example, farmers were among the most prosperous, yet farm workers among the most poorly paid, in the country. Since the war arable farming had not been noted for its low returns.

It occurred to me that the economists' arguments were perpetuating the myths put about by many farmers about farm wages. Stripped of its academic jargon, the economists were concurring with the view that farm wages were low because farmers could not afford to pay any more. My moral outrage came bubbling up to the surface of my mind again. Here there seemed to be a group of academics to whom farm workers and their representatives ought to be able to look for independent judgement but who had been captured by their main informants (and, as I was later to judge, main clients): namely, the farmers' lobby. I looked upon them as tied economists. Once more incensed, I sat down and wrote a paper on the low earnings of agricultural workers, which criticised the economists' model and offered a tentative sociological alternative. It was a *cri de coeur*, strident and shrill with the argument overstated. I sent it to the *Journal of Agricultural Economics* and the editor, correctly, asked me in so many words to 'cool it' and resubmit. Fortunately, having got it off my chest, my mood had mellowed and I agreed to his suggestions. The paper was published (Newby 1972a), and as a result I established a wider range of contacts with agricultural economists interested in farm labour. Although I still believe that many agricultural economists are too intimately connected with the industry for the good of their own independence and integrity, I would be the first to admit that my initial feelings were an over-reaction.

This episode had two fortunate consequences: I was now immortalised in print in a reputable journal – a not inconsiderable factor when it came to future job prospects; and, more relevantly as far as the immediate needs of the research were concerned, writing the paper had acted as a safety valve. I had blown my top in an innocuous manner and hence was more prepared to contain my own feelings when it came to interviewing farmers and others with whose views I might be personally unsympathetic. Rightly or wrongly I was able to take a cooler and more detached view – or at least play that role – so that I in turn hoped to avoid the danger of 'going native', which was an accusation I had implicitly levelled at agricultural economists. I still hankered after the role of objective scientific observer and believed then that this was both possible and desirable. Such has been the force of the arguments against positivism in sociology over the intervening period that I am now less sure on both counts, but at the time this seemed to be a happy outcome.

THE PROBLEM EMERGES

After I had spent nearly a year compiling statistics, going through the literature and chatting to NUAAW officials, my research supervisor began to make suggestive noises about seeing more concrete results from all this apparent diligence. At about the same time I stumbled across my problem. While at the library at the London School of Economics I had come across P. Self and H. Storing's, *The State and the Farmer* (1962). I was immediately attracted by the book's detached (though not necessarily objective) view of British agriculture, by its faltering steps towards a political economy, by the clarity and thrust of its analysis and, not least, by its urbane wit and droll humour. Although now somewhat dated it was a book I admired, and I scoured London before tracking down a hardback copy, over ten years old, in the nether regions of Foyle's. In a lively chapter on the NUAAW, Self and Storing had drawn attention to the 'easy (which is not to say equal)' relationship between farmers and farm workers. From the back of my mind I recalled Runciman's (1966) observations about the 'deference vote' in rural areas. That was it; I would study agricultural workers as a case study of deferential workers. A perusal of the political science literature on working-class Toryism followed and then a literature which has strongly influenced me: the historical studies of American negro slavery, particularly Genovese's (1971) work on rebelliousness and docility among negro slaves. I then assembled a lot of secondary material into a working paper which could almost have been entitled, 'Why farm workers are worth studying'. Both my supervisor and graduate seminar at the University of Essex were appreciative; it was suggested that I submit it to a journal for publication. A shortened version was later published (Newby 1972b).

I now had two publications to my name before talking to a single farm worker (except for those interviewed in Norfolk), but I remained overawed by the problems of venturing out into the real world to follow up my ideas. It was here that the importance of subcultural support for the lone researcher, especially the raw and inexperienced graduate student whose marginal situation in academic life is well known, manifested itself. I was fortunate in that at Essex I was never made to feel isolated from the academic staff in the department. Despite its reputation as a cross between a hothouse and a bear pit, I was only aware, from 1970 onwards, of a lively intellectual environment and a surprising degree of *Gemeinschaft*. A brief spell as a research assistant in 1970, reanalysing data collected for the Roskill Commission on the siting of the third London Airport, had enabled me to establish a number of personal friendships with various members of staff. In addition, my relationship with my supervisor, Colin Bell, was not just the customary one of student protégé; it was that of co-author, friend and, eventually, colleague. The isolation which I suffered was not, then, the usual anomie of the graduate student, but rather an isolation from brands of sociology other than that followed at Essex. As an Essex 'product' I had internalised many of the department's taken-for-granted views without, at that time, recognising them for what they were.

Nevertheless, this cultural support seems to me to be more important than the nature of the individual relationship between a graduate student and his superior, which ostensibly appears more crucial. Within a very short period of time any graduate student worth his salt will acquire a greater knowledge of the minutiae of his topic than his supervisor. Hence the supervisor's role is mainly limited to winding the student up at the beginning, with a few preliminary references to the literature and some contacts with others working in adjacent areas, and then letting him go. Henceforth his function is to ensure that the student does not go wildly off the rails, to give the odd push or partial rewind and to cast a benevolent, but rather passive, eye over the subsequent proceedings. The continuing support and stimulus often come from a wider set of relationships, with either staff or fellow graduate students; they express interest in what one might otherwise consider rather banal findings, offer suggestions for reading or advice on methodology, and grant psychological support or a spirit of camaraderie when the going is tough. Thus the best work carried out by graduate students – and it is often overlooked just how many important contributions in Britain and the United States have been products of higher-degree research – has often emerged from situations where these conditions have been able to be met, the Chicago School being the most notable example (Faris 1967).

INTO THE FIELD

After due consideration, and in spite of doubts placed in my mind by a somewhat unnerving seminar which I gave at Swansea, I decided to use a survey method. I was distrustful of the impressionistic and unreliable nature of participant observation and the inability which it presented of talking to more than a handful of farm workers in what would inevitably be a somewhat arbitrarily selected location. But what really convinced me of the need to conduct a survey was the complete absence of any sociological data – in some cases of even the most elementary sociographic kind – which could present a backdrop to the kind of in-depth exploration which participant observation would entail. I therefore set about drawing up a sample for a survey and designing a questionnaire.

Very early in the research I had decided that my fieldwork, of whatever kind, would be carried out in Suffolk. My experiences in Norfolk in 1969 had taught me that farm workers there were very atypical of the country as a whole, particularly if I was to follow up my early interest in unionisation. As I had discovered, non-union workers were very hard to come by in Norfolk, and even when my interest moved to the study of deference Norfolk's radical traditions made it an inappropriate location. My sojourn in Trunch had also indicated that the nature of the local village social structure might be important, so I also desired an area where there was a reasonable spread of communities from genuine agricultural villages to villages which had been inundated by urban, middle-class newcomers (Pahl 1965; Bell and Newby 1973). This ruled out Essex, where few agricultural villages remained, so my attention was focused on Suffolk. North and West of Ipswich there was a good spread of villages, but farm workers in West Suffolk were organised mainly by the Transport and General Workers' Union, so I could not assess the degree of unionisation – my first and very crude index of possible radicalism (indeed, all I had to go on at this stage). East Suffolk, on the other hand, had a more representative rate of unionisation for the country as a whole. I collected detailed agricultural census data on all the parishes in East Suffolk, and on the basis of this alighted upon forty-four parishes around the market town of Framlingham, situated twenty miles north of Ipswich, which were reasonably representative in terms of farm size and unionisation. They were also in a block running north from the outskirts of Ipswich to a quite remote and isolated rural area, so they were subject, more or less, to progressive urbanisation the further north one travelled. These parishes became the locale for the survey. (This selection is described in more detail in Newby 1977.)

I do not wish to dwell on the technicalities of sampling and questionnaire design, since they can be found in the conventional methods cookbooks, whose recipes I largely followed. As such, they are concerns which lie outside the expressed purpose of this book. However, some problems not customarily referred to can be highlighted briefly. Farm workers represent a highly scattered population, isolated and often socially invisible. The logistics of doing a survey are thus formidable: problems of creating a correct sampling frame, problems of contact, problems of travel, problems of interviewing as a piece of social interaction, all pile on top of each other. All sociologists believe that their own respondents present more difficulties than everyone else's, so I do not wish to overstate this; I merely wish to point out that the temptation to take some short-cuts was irresistible. In particular I sampled farms rather than farm workers, since I believed I could obtain a reliable sampling frame of farms (mistakenly, since the Ministry of Agriculture refused to co-operate and I was forced back on to the Yellow

Pages) and then contact the workers via the employer. This was not only an administrative convenience, but probably also an administrative necessity. However, the result was that, in common with so many other sociological studies, I was taking the easy option of homing in on a captive set of respondents. So much sociological research takes place in an institutional setting – a factory, office, school, prison, hospital – whereby contact is made, especially with working-class respondents, via people in positions of authority over them. For despite our awareness of the 'Hawthorn effect' the practice continues, and we hope we can rectify any misconceptions of our purpose in the interview situation itself – but this in turn requires a careful and sensitive appraisal of the role required to obtain a sympathetic *rapport* with the respondent before data collection even commences.

Two important consequences follow from this. The first is that, following observations by Jack Douglas (1967) and A. V. Cicourel (1964), the method of obtaining the data is often valid sociological data in its own right. The necessity to approach farm workers via the farmer was already telling me something about the social situation of the workers I eventually interviewed: namely, that the majority *were* socially and geographically isolated, that they *were* socially invisible to many inhabitants in the locality, and that the employer *was* a significant other in their lives. In addition to this, by carefully considering the role I would need to adopt in order to obtain valid data from the agricultural workers I was to interview, I was already operating with an implicit theory of their social situation. In other words, theory and method were inseparably intertwined even at this relatively early stage in the data-collecting process. Thus the role that I quite consciously adopted was not that of researcher or investigator (which I believed ran the risk of inspiring either hostility of taciturnity), nor that of friend (which was patently inoperable), but rather that of student. I was not investigating rural society; I was studying it. Most farm workers were aware that nowadays young people do a lot of studying in order to 'get on' (seen as a good thing – data again!) and that this might involve the sort of activity I appeared to be doing. I needed no other justification than that it was necessary for my degree, which in turn would enable me to obtain a good job. Almost universally (my refusal rate was less than 3 per cent) farm workers were willing, indeed eager, to *help* bright young men 'get on'. Although I was worried about the ethics of unduly preying upon their good nature, this role had the advantage of being substantially correct and of not being perceived by the workers as a threat to themselves in any way. In turn I hoped that in the future I would be able to repay their kindness by doing what I could to campaign for an improvement in their conditions. There remained, of course, the danger that farm workers, in their eagerness to help, would feed me answers to my questions which they believed I wanted to hear. However, the role of student offered fewer risks of this than any other. I hoped that as an objective seeker-after-truth I would be perceived as having no particular axe to grind.

Despite all these precautions the problems of validity remained. I was aware of the frequently cited observation that surveys offer reliability at the expense of validity, while participant observation offers validity at the expense of reliability. I was also uncomfortably aware that somehow I was going to have to interpret my survey-generated data, and I was in danger of having created a set of statistics without knowing what they *meant*. Driving up from Essex University to conduct interviews, no matter how many of them, was not going to be very helpful. The contrast between the self-consciously cosmopolitan *avant garde* Essex experience, and the experience of the traditional, rural, working-class culture of Suffolk, was startling; it seemed like two completely different worlds, reminiscent of the journey between Harvard and Cornerville described by W. F. Whyte (1955, p. 331). I felt the need to cut my hair and wear a tie whenever I went to Suffolk — and suffered much ribaldry at Essex as a consequence. Again this was data — farm workers are, on the whole, very respectable members of the working class — but I was made aware of the very severe gap in culture and lifestyle and the problems that this could create, however sympathetic I might be personally. Somehow I had to get inside the farm worker's skin, to assume his *Gestalt*, if I were to make any valid sense of my data at all.

I decided that some participant observation was essential, in addition to the survey. It would enable me to make valid inferences from the survey data, while insights gained from the participant observation could be checked for representativeness against knowledge gained through the survey. If I could live and work with a farm worker while carrying out the survey I could overcome these interpretative problems. I contacted the NUAAW District Organiser, and he gave me three names and addresses of branch secretaries through whom I could possibly find somewhere to live. On the first I drew a blank; his wife was about to have a baby, and the last thing either wanted was an extra person to feed and look after. With the second I was more successful; the branch secretary and his wife were willing to put me up in the spare bedroom of their tied cottage — full board at the subsistence rates allowed by my Social Science Research Council grant was a most welcome addition to their housekeeping. Although I did not know it then, the arrangement was a piece of purest serendipity. Jack and Doreen Hector, with their two young children, Susan and Sally (the names are all pseudonyms, as I have no desire to destroy their anonymity), performed a crucial role in the successful outcome of the research. Between them, Jack and Mrs Hector played the famed role of Doc (Whyte 1955). They were wonderful key informants, with an encyclopaedic knowledge of the area, almost always accurate. They could give me the personal biography of half my sample, and through their extensive range of contacts I was able to talk to other interesting informants who lay outside the survey. We soon struck up a warm personal friendship (which still exists), I was made to feel instantly at home, and the quality and quantity of the food can be gauged by the fact that I put on nearly a stone in weight during the six months I lived with them from March 1972. My wife was encouraged to come and stay at weekends, and we still continue to make visits to each other's homes. It could all have been so different: a draconian landlady, indigestible food, a cold and damp room. As it was, the Hectors lifted a great deal of the psychological strain of doing fieldwork. I did not feel impelled to bolt for home as quickly and as often as possible, and I could relax with them between interviews. I also had the added bonus of two sensitive and intelligent informants. Often the first words on entering the house were, 'I heard something today which might interest you ...'. How many pieces of research, one wonders, have been made or broken by such strokes of fortune?

DOING FIELDWORK

Doing the survey was an experience that involved a number of sequential stages, familiar to most researchers. At the beginning the dominant emotion was one of elation that the real world seemed roughly to correspond to how one had envisaged it; one conveniently overlooked the unexpected but bored friends with anecdotes about how abstractly conceived ideas were unfolding before one's eyes. Then the novelty began to wear off. Respondents began to settle into a pattern, and interviewing became a routine. Eventually a certain tedium set in; enthusiasm could only be raised with an effort, and asking the same question for the two-hundredth time became a hard slog. One longed for an eccentric respondent to disrupt the established pattern. By the end I had interviewed 71 farmers and 233 farm workers, each interview lasting on average half an hour for the farmers and one and a half hours for the farm workers. It was an exhausting experience, both physically and emotionally. Wandering into people's homes and asking them a series of sometimes intimate questions was not something which I found came naturally to me. I would become quite nervous immediately before knocking on someone's door, and on the few occasions when it was slammed in my face or I was the object of abuse I became quite rattled and gripped by agonies of self-doubt. What right had I to ask all these questions anyway? What was it all for? Was it all worth it? Somehow Galtung and Blalock had not had all this trouble.

At the beginning each interview left me completely drained – a feeling not unlike that after having completed finals. So much in interviewing depends upon handling the particularistic nuances of the situation, so that it can be authoritatively defined in the manner conducive to one's intentions. With the farmers, this meant convincing them that I was a serious researcher, with the requisite stage props to prove it: briefcase, printed questionnaire, formal demeanour. Farmers were more difficult to handle than their employees. Some resolutely refused to be mere respondents but insisted on questioning my questions. I soon discovered that surveys demand a certain passivity; one does not *really* want one's questions challenged. In addition my own personal antipathy to the views of most farmers meant that I was much more consciously playing a role. This not only was more stressful but also resulted in ethical questions' lurking in the back of my mind. Did I not have a moral obligation to 'come clean' with my views? With the farm workers the ethical problem was slightly different: was I not exploiting them for my own ends? Here my main concern was to understate the accoutrements of professionalism: leave the briefcase in the car, appear casually to jot down notes on a piece of paper, laugh, crack jokes, adopt what I hoped would appear as an engaging earnestness. In both cases the reputation of sociology (= socialism) in general and Essex University students (= Angry Brigade, long-haired, drug-crazed layabouts) in particular did not help, but I found I could turn even this to my advantage by gaining their confidence through answering questions about it. However, there was again the danger of revealing my personal opinions – which would have antagonised nearly all farmers and most farm workers – from behind my deliberately anodyne and occasionally evasive replies. Constantly being on guard, weighing my words, controlling my gestures – these were the stuff of interviewing, on the whole a carefully contrived and executed performance, not daring to let the mask slip.

The ethics of this continue to concern me. No one was under any obligation to answer my questions, but I still found the whole business faintly distasteful. I was not telling outright lies, but I was engaging in systematic concealment. Perhaps I was over-reacting; all this careful affectation may have been totally unnecessary (though I doubted it). Perhaps my conscience is oversensitive: why should farmers need to know my political views? Whatever the answer, these questions must surely cross every researcher's mind although they are so rarely discussed. On the other hand, one assurance I readily made and was determined to keep – especially in a particularistic rural society – was a guarantee of total confidentiality. This seems to me to be the right of every respondent, and it had to be firmly adhered to despite occasional nudges and winks over cups of tea to pass on the replies of others to certain questions. In both cases, acting otherwise would probably have cut me off from any further sources of data, so my stance was largely governed by instrumental considerations. The confidentiality issue coincided with my moral stance, but on the exploitation issue I was not so sure. Surveys are research *instruments* and consequently involve using people in an instrumental way. By and large the researcher is only interested in each respondent, *as an individual*, for the information he can obtain from him. With participant observation one can at least create deeper emotional bonds, and although this also creates its own peculiar problems that of using people as statistical cyphers is not among them. In the end I salved my conscience by deciding that the farmers were quite capable of looking after themselves, economically and politically, without further help from me, while with the farm workers I hoped, against my better judgement, that the ends might justify the means.

Interviewing, then, was tiring, stressful, exhilarating, boring and interesting; in other words, it was virtually my life for six months. I was pleasantly surprised by the openness of most respondents. I had been led to believe that outsiders in rural society faced insurmountable barriers of non-communication, and my fears were confirmed when, shortly after sending out the first batch of letters to farmers asking for an interview, I learned that the local branch of the National Farmers' Union had met to discuss my request and that a proposal – fortunately rejected – to present a united refusal had been debated. This, however, was an isolated incident; in general, garrulousness was a greater problem than taciturnity. I concluded that the reputation of farm workers for being withdrawn and unsociable was largely a myth spread by popular writers on rural life who wished to demonstrate their status as *afficianados*, privy to the innermost secrets of the rural psyche. Certainly some workers were suspicious, but most of them soon unwound, aided perhaps by my non-threatening role of student; only five workers refused to give me details of their income, for example.

Interviewing also opened up a whole new world to me. I had undergone intensive training in the weeks before entering the field by diligently reading back numbers of the farming press. I felt I could inspire confidence by talking knowledgeably about the problems of rust on Joss Cambier barley (a current obsession), and indeed there were many occasions when I was subjected to a minor initiation ceremony when I was asked a few questions obviously designed to reveal my ignorance. Knowing the correct answers certainly helped. However, the knowledge gained from magazines was nothing beside that which I gained (often literally) in the fields. Farms, I discovered, were fascinating places, and farmers and farm workers alike were delighted to show me around them and explain everything to me. My personal interest in natural history also struck a sympathetic chord. Much of this was motivated by sheer curiosity on my part which went well beyond the bounds of professional interest. The same considerations applied to many of the houses I visited; I would be less than human if I were not occasionally touched by an unforgivable voyeurism. Some farmhouses were positively palatial – including a sprinkling of national monuments and stately homes – and a lifestyle I had never before seen, let alone experienced, was opened up to me. On the other hand, I observed scenes of almost Dickensian squalor, not the less so for being in a rural location, which were equally alien to my own experience. Travelling from one end of the British class structure to the other in the space of a few hundred yards was certainly unnerving.

Much of the experience I was gaining was new to me, and this freshness, I feel, sharpened up many of the impressions that I was gaining. For the first time in my life I was doing sociological research; for the first time I was also living in a rural area and on a farm. I discovered that a mixture of naivety and willingness to learn was a not altogether inappropriate fieldwork technique – provided I had either the knowledge or reliable informants to ensure that I was not being fooled. For the first time in my life also I conducted lengthy conversations with titled members of the English aristocracy and even entered their homes. I found myself – and hated myself for it –

being obsequious and deferential in their presence. Was this not a better way, I wondered, of studying deference – through my own personal experience – than asking farm workers about it?

My own personal experience and biography are clearly more relevant to the problems I encountered while participantly observing. Indeed, throughout the period of fieldwork the question I was most frequently asked was whether I came from a rural background – something which I judged to be indicative of the extent to which farmers and farm workers perceived themselves to be a distinctive breed, separate from the remainder of the population. I was gratified by the faint expressions of surprise which often greeted my negative reply, but I also realised that these feelings of distinctiveness, apart from a few epiphenomena, are objectively groundless despite their widespread adherence. In fact, I was born in Derby into a skilled and relatively affluent working-class family. I was a classic product of the Education Act 1944: my brother, who failed the eleven-plus, became an apprentice fitter with Rolls-Royce and later a draughtsman; I passed the eleven-plus and escaped from both Derby and Rolls-Royce to which undoubtedly I would otherwise have been destined. This background was to have important consequences when it came to studying farm workers. Being drawn from the 'respectable' end of the working class I fitted into the Hectors' lifestyle quite easily, since the Hectors were also 'respectable' (and had 'rough' neighbours as if to highlight the distinction) and had by 1972 reached a material standard of living with which I was familiar from my more affluent parents in Derby in the late 1950s. I was constantly overwhelmed by a sense of *deja vu*. I did not feel, although I undoubtedly was, a complete stranger; neither did they feel uncomfortable in my presence. Living with the Hectors was to have a profound effect upon the course of the research. In many respects Jack Hector corresponded to many of the stereotypes of the deferential worker, and through a close observation of his and his neighbours' patterns of interaction I was able to revise many of my original ideas on the subject. That is, both my conception and my theory of deference changed during the fieldwork period itself. In the light of this it is necessary to describe in some detail the social environment of the Hector family.

A CASE STUDY

The Hectors live in a semi-detached Victorian tied cottage, in a rather isolated situation two miles from the nearest village. The house was one of a dozen or so scattered farmhouses and tied cottages which formed a loosely knit hamlet called Littleover, which exemplifies what I have elsewhere called a farm-centred community (Bell and Newby 1973; Newby 1977, ch. 6). Directly across the lane from the Hectors' house lived a farmer, Mr Gemmill, who was not Jack Hector's employer but who employed four workers who lived nearby. The Hectors' neighbour on one side was a famous film director who had bought and restored a former tied cottage of Mr Gemmill's. The other neighbour, Jim Davies, worked with Jack Hector on the same farm. Three further farmhouses were within a hundred yards of the Hectors' house, as were several other tied houses occupied by the workers on the surrounding farms. All this enabled the Hectors to compare their own lifestyle with that of employees on other farms and to compare other employers with Jack Hector's 'guv'nor'. The isolation of Littleover also enforced a certain reciprocity. For example, there was a Sunday newspaper syndicate whereby households took it in turns to fetch and deliver the Sunday papers from the newsagent two miles away; there was also access to the Gemmills' telephone, while the other residents would in turn alert Mr Gemmill to straying cattle and help him to round them up. Many of the wives had young children, and walking down the lane twice a day to wait for the school bus afforded ample opportunity to chat and exchange gossip. In this way normative control was exerted, and it applied to both farmers' and farm workers' wives.

Jack Hector had worked on the same farm since 1941, for the first fifteen years with horses. The farmer was Colonel Todd, a retired army officer and colonial tobacco grower who had moved to Suffolk in 1939 to avoid the ravages of wartime London. He was an archetypal Grand Old Man, the stereotype of the English country squire, and in appearance and demeanour he completely filled the bill down to his clipped moustache and clipped accent. He was active in public affairs, being Chairman of the Board of Governors of the local school, a magistrate, a benefactor of local charities and agricultural shows, and also an active conservator of the countryside. He employed ten men, but the day-to-day running of the farm was in the hands of a manager. Colonel Todd therefore rarely gave orders *directly* to his workers. He lived in a 'big house' nearly a mile from the Hectors' cottage. Doreen Hector, Jack's wife, had worked for Mrs Todd as a domestic before she was married. Both her father and her two brothers worked for Colonel Todd, and they all lived in his tied houses nearby. The Hectors' network of friends and kin was almost entirely bounded by the houses which constituted Littleover. The only exceptions were Fred and Elsie, who ran a village post office near Beccles, and Bill and Kath, who lived in Felixstowe. Bill was an ex-farm worker who then worked as a docker. This, briefly, was the social network of the Hectors' which I invaded in March 1972.

It soon became apparent that Jack Hector thought the world of his employer and that, totally fortuitously, I was going to be able to observe 'deference in action' at first hand. The basis of this deference seemed to lie in the fact that Colonel Todd conformed to all that was required of the paternalist employer. A prerequisite was a certain level of wealth and modestly splendid lifestyle, but this was *only* a prerequisite. In many ways more important was his apparent lack of economic instrumentality: in his farming practice he was determined to retain as many trees and hedgerows as possible; as an employer he did not 'work his men to the bone'. However, it was individual acts of benevolence and consideration to his workers that most marked him out as a 'real gentleman'. However hierarchical the *structure* of the relationship might be, its *content* was one of affable sociability. He chatted to his workers at local shows and around the farm. Knowing each of them individually he made solicitous inquiries about wives and children. Mrs Todd frequently did the rounds of the tied houses with gifts in kind of pork, butter, etc., and at Christmas there were gifts for everyone of course. On the day of the Smithfield Show or the Suffolk Show each worker would be given a packet by the 'guv'nor' containing enough money for fares, admission, meals and a little over besides. The workers were unanimous: 'It's not everyone who'll do all that for you.'

My first inclination was to explore this comparative dimension in deference. It seemed that deference was an exchange for the benevolence of the employer that lay outside the employment contract. There was a good deal of evidence to support this view. Colonel Todd's removal from the day-to-day running of the farm gave him ample scope to play the role of patrician squire, which he did with consummate skill. This merely pointed up the contrast between the 'guv'nor' and Mr Gemmill in Jack Hector's mind. The Hectors' relations with the Gemmills were much more intimate, but also more ambivalent, summed up by Jack Hector's comment that 'Wally' Gemmill was 'a good neighbour, but a bad farmer. I shouldn't want to work for him but you can ask them for anything and they'll help you no matter what it is.' Mr Gemmill was a bad farmer because he lacked the benevolence of the 'guv'nor' to his workers. There were no perks or treats, and the relationship was a much more instrumental one. The Hectors and the Gemmills would, however, meet socially during the winter to play cards, and Mrs Hector and Mrs Gemmill were often popping in and out of each other's houses on small errands, while Jack Hector would often chat to 'Wally' when he was out digging his garden. But again attitudes were ambivalent. The Gemmills were in the *Farm Holiday Guide* and ran a thriving holiday bed-and-breakfast sideline. Comments about this often revealed Mrs Gemmill's snobbery; she would not take in 'workers' because they 'lowered the tone' of the place. My arrival across the road prompted the remark to Mrs Hector (*a propos* the University of Essex) that student unrest was what happens when you give the 'working class' too much education. Colonel Todd would never make comments like these to the Hectors and would thereby demonstrate, in contrast to the Gemmills, that he was not 'stuck up' and thus was a 'real gentleman'. This intrigued me: what was it about deference – which must of its very nature contain a notion of hierarchy – that was linked to the very *denial* of hierarchy in the way in which everyday relationships were conducted?

My puzzlement grew when I compared the Hector–Todd relationship not only with the Hector–Gemmill relationship, but also with the Hectors' relationship with a small farmer farther down the lane, George Bly. He made a living from just thirty acres of arable land, and as far as Jack Hector was concerned their relationship was certainly not a hierarchical one, since in terms of income and lifestyle they were virtually on a par. 'Captain' Bly, as Jack Hector mischievously referred to him, was looked upon as something of a joke. He had bought an antiquated combine harvester for £10 (I whimsically contemplated offering him £5 for it, thereby obtaining the most prestigious lawnmower in Essex) and a tractor that was so old that he dare not risk towing a trailer across a ten-acre field at harvest but instead made a two-mile detour around the more smoothly-surfaced country lanes in order to reach the farmyard safely. He was an appallingly bad farmer in terms of husbandry, his fields being so full of weeds that it seemed that wild oats were his main crop. He and Jack Hector were on Christian name terms and were able to exchange jokes about politics, a topic normally taboo between farmers and farm workers ('Is he still alive, then?' asked Jack Hector about the local Conservative MP). In no sense did Jack Hector defer to 'the Captain', yet neither was George Bly 'stuck up'. This demonstrated that a sense of hierarchy was a precursor of deference, whatever the affable sociability which often characterised the day-to-day content of deferential relationships.

Meanwhile I was also exploring what I took to be the comparative nature of deference by observing the relationship between the Hectors and their neighbours, the Davies family. The Davies' household was decidedly 'rough' compared with the respectability of the Hectors'. The house was much more sparsely and poorly furnished and considerably less clean and tidy. Jim Davies drank regularly in the local pubs and was besotted by snooker, which he played several evenings a week in a nearby club. This was the cause of frequent arguments with his wife, usually punctuated by shouts and the sound of crying children. The Davies family were treated rather disdainfully by the Hectors, especially by Mrs Hector, who constantly plied me with derogatory comments and allegations concerning the Davies' behaviour, despite that she hardly ever ventured across the threshhold of the Davies' house. Much of my first few days in the Hector household was spent listening to these and many other accounts, as though the Hectors were keen to enlist my support. For most of the time a kind of mutual armistice was maintained, Mrs Hector at least being very careful not to give grounds for further gossip or attack. The outcome was that virtually no neighbourly assistance took place between the Hectors' and Davies' households; instead the Hectors were drawn by their respectability towards the Gemmills. This merely reinforced the respectability syndrome of the Hectors and enabled the Davies family to be stereotyped – by no means all the allegations were true and those which approximated to the truth were usually exaggerated. Nevertheless, Jim Davies' disrespect for 'the guv'nor' and his refusal to play the role, either privately or publicly, of the deferential worker was regarded by Jack Hector as being merely part of his inferior status. One therefore deferred to 'the guv'nor' because to do otherwise would be to reduce oneself to the level of the Davies family.

By now I was groping, in a crude and mechanistic manner, towards a conception of how deference was built up out of a particular set of relationships. Before I had even begun fieldwork I had been aware that deference could not be regarded merely as a behavioural phenomenon; many farm workers were quite capable of behaving 'deferentially' without 'really' being deferential, i.e. holding deferential attitudes. Now I thought that I could see how these deferential attitudes arose from the social setting within which the deferential worker was embedded. Jack Hector's deference was 'genuine' to the extent that it was not a public act; indeed, on the one occasion when I observed Jack Hector touch his forelock and Mrs Hector bob a quick curtsey in the presence of Colonel Todd, it was with a good deal of embarrassed self-consciousness (perhaps because of my presence) and a realisation that such rituals were anachronistic in the 1970s. Their deference went considerably beyond this, and when Colonel Todd suffered a minor heart attack and was rushed into hospital in Ipswich the tears that were shed were undoubtedly genuine. And yet I was still uneasy. Somehow things did not add up. There was no doubt in my mind that Jack Hector deferred to Colonel Todd, in virtually any way in which deference has customarily been defined, but in other ways Jack Hector was decidedly undeferential. He voted Labour and was, after all, not only a trade union member but also a local branch secretary. However, he told me he would refuse to take part if the NUAAW called a strike; he could not let 'the guv'nor' down. He thought that many farmers were rogues or worse and favoured the miners when they were on strike, to the extent that the farm manager 'stamped his foot' at him for voicing his support. How did this square with the absolute and solid bedrock of his deference to 'the guv'nor'? My head started to buzz with confusion over what deference 'really' was and (ignoring for a moment the obvious reification) whether I would recognise 'it' if I 'saw' it. I was beginning to become worried. Supposing I had interviewed Jack Hector in the survey and asked him a question about the 1972 miners' strike. On the basis of his support for the miners I would have classified him as a radical, or at least non-deferential. Yet he *was* profoundly deferential towards his employer. In general I might call this somewhat divided consciousness 'ambivalence' – which is what I eventually did – but I was still not satisfied. The contradictions seemed obvious to *me*; why were they not so to Jack Hector?

These doubts and uncertainties reached a climax during a fieldwork set-piece that I had been looking forward to for weeks: a cricket match between Colonel Todd's XI and a Farm Workers' XI composed of his employees and their families. It was not many months since I had seen Joseph Losey's film of *The Go-Between*, in which a cricket match performs the role of a symbolic gladiatorial combat that unleashes the underlying conflicts of the situation. I confidently looked forward to many of the farm workers' taking a delight in hurling down short-pitched deliveries or hitting the opposition bowling out of the ground, but in this sense the match proved to be a disappointment, since the workers were playing against a team of infinitely better cricketers. The game was played in the grounds of a public school on a glorious day, amid an atmosphere I thought had disappeared from England after the First World War. Colonel Todd's XI turned out immaculately in blazers, creams and hooped cricket caps; the Farm Workers' XI were mostly in grey trousers tucked into their socks. Cries of 'Well shot, sir!' rang out from the pavilion where Colonel Todd's team and their wives were seated. At tea there were, of course, cucumber sandwiches. I sat on the boundary between the pavilion and the carpark with Mrs Hector and her children, trying not to laugh. I confess that the Edwardian public-school atmosphere was so authentic that I could see in it only parody. *They* could not be taking it seriously, surely?

Colonel Todd's three sons were all playing: 'Mister Jonathan', Mister Rodney' and 'Mister Harold', as Mrs Hector called them. They were all married with young children, and frequently either they or their wives would have to walk to their car, sometimes with a child and sometimes alone, to fetch or return some small item. Without exception they paused for a few moments in front of Mrs Hector and made smalltalk about the weather or the children. This was done in the most ritualised and stylised manner, and as Mrs Hector described the children's latest illnesses or the prospects for the summer holidays Colonel Todd's relatives would gaze around the field hardly listening to the replies. Social convention demanded that they acknowledge her presence, but they obviously had no interest whatsoever in the conversation. I found their demeanour condescending in the extreme and deeply offensive and only with difficulty refrained from commenting on their manner to Mrs Hector. It was as well that I remained quiet, for after we had returned home she gave a detailed and enthusiastic account of her encounters to her husband, finally commenting (to me): 'That's one thing about the guv'nor's children, they'll always stop and have a word with you.' I had found the Todds' behaviour faintly insulting, but to her it had reaffirmed her deference to them. The puzzle afforded by this manifest contradiction between my interpretation and Mrs Hector's was to linger in my mind for months to come. I did not feel that I could 'solve' the 'problem' of deference, to my own satisfaction, until I had successfully accounted for her interpretation in a manner that would make sense to me also.

THE PROBLEM RESOLVED?

The reconciliation, such as it was, took nearly six months and was achieved not by further data collection but by armchair reflection on my part. Some impetus was given to my thoughts by coming across E. Goffman's brilliant article on 'The nature of deference and demeanour' (1973) which helped me to visualise the importance of both ritualised interaction and interaction ritual in deference. However, I remained wedded to a very mechanistic attitudinal approach to deference, which still left me confused (see, for example, the discussion of the paper by Fryer and Martin in Bulmer (ed.) 1973).

Then three occurrences helped to relieve a certain amount of the confusion. First, in preparation for teaching a course in comparative sociology at the University of Essex I read Dumont's *Homo Hierarchicus* (1972), and his notion of fission and fusion in hierarchical relationships rang some bells in my mind. Secondly, while attending a conference at Durham organised by the SSRC (see Bulmer 1973) I had a chat in the bar with Margaret Stacey, during which she mentioned deferential voters in Banbury. In her view, she said, we needed to move away from talking about deference as though it were an *attribute* of people and instead to start talking about deferential *relationships*. This gratified me, for it was precisely the conclusion I had come to from my observation of the Hectors. Thirdly, I came via Dumont to Simmel, especially his essays on subordination (see Wolff 1950, pt III). Eventually – and here I must acknowledge the help and encouragement of Leonore Davidoff at Essex who was tussling with similar problems regarding deference and domestic servants – I fashioned an account (I hesitate to call it a theory) of deference which seemed to explain both what I had observed among Suffolk farm workers, especially the Hectors, and the conventional accounts of deference given by historians, political scientists and sociologists.

There is no need to labour this account here, since it is a complex argument and has been published elsewhere (Newby 1975), except to say that it was ironic that the theoretical end-product of, by that time, over three years' investigation was a slim paper which contained no empirical data and only an odd fleeting reference to agricultural workers. However, it is probably worthwhile making a few wider points. It is quite possible – and I would be the first to admit the possibility – that my period of reflection was aided by my withdrawal from the field and by subsequent cognitive dissonance on my part. Following the well-established pattern of post-fieldwork reflection set by anthropologists, I had indulged in what W. Baldamus (1972) calls 'double-fitting', i.e. altering the theory to fit the 'facts' and the 'facts' to fit the theory. In my case the 'facts' that changed (apart from the results of any cognitive dissonance) were those generated by the survey. Once one regarded deference as a relationship rather than a set of attitudes, then survey-generated data on the subject became largely worthless unless one assumed the respondent to be deferential in all his relationships with those above him in the social structure. Much of this data I therefore discarded. There seemed little point in constructing elaborate attitude scales of deference, when I had ceased to regard deference as a fixed and immutable attitudinal attribute of the respondents. The data which I presented were therefore selected accordingly.

However, when it came to writing up the research, the survey data in general dominated the monograph and the style of authorship. Since all this information was there – a vast amount, of which I used about 10 per cent – and since much of it was both useful and valid, it seemed imperative to use it. Then, once the writing was under way, the survey data seemed to carry it along of its own volition. Apart from anything else, survey and participant observation require two very different styles of authorship: the former is impersonal, formal and hence usually written in the third person; the latter is more informal and impressionistic and thus written in the first person. Academic convention frowns upon a mixing of the two styles, and even literary consistency makes it difficult to switch suddenly into a first-person anecdotal style in the middle of the measured presentation of hard data. Thus, much to my surprise, the final monograph (Newby 1977) contains little of the material gathered through participant observation, despite my voluminous fieldwork notes which I faithfully wrote up every evening. The participant observation was not, of course, lost altogether. It remains between the lines in my interpretations of the survey data, but I suspect that most readers will not recognise this. This seems unfortunate, for not only did the participant observation crucially affect my theoretical understanding of deference, but also, given my reformulation of the concept, it was this method which was providing me with valid data, and where survey and participant observation data conflicted I instinctively trusted the latter.

CONCLUSION

Doing sociological research on farm workers therefore had a natural history which profoundly affected the outcome of the research itself. In some respects this was inevitable given the length of time which the completion of the study consumed. It was five years to the very day after I had begun as a graduate student that I submitted the manuscript of the monograph for publication. For two years researching into the social situation of agricultural workers had been my sole occupation, but for the remaining three the research had to be fitted in between teaching duties, and the writing of the monograph also coincided with co-directing a further research project on East Anglian farmers. Not surprisingly, over this period many of my own ideas had changed; I had come to know not only a great deal more about agricultural workers, but also more about sociology. Consequently, by the end I was regarding my early written work with a feeling of embarrassment. However, the natural history was also dictated by the reflexivity which is involved in any piece of empirical research. This is why I suspect that much more 'double-fitting' occurs in empirical sociology than is generally acknowledged.

Looking back, the natural history of the research, and with it (which seems to me to be significant) this reflexivity, were as much a product of accident as design. Had I been living with less sympathetic informants than the Hectors I would probably have limited myself almost entirely to the survey and happily set about constructing my attitude scales of deference. Had I actually *played* in the cricket match – as had originally been intended – my doubts about my whole approach to the problem of deference may have remained uncrystallised. Had we sat elsewhere on the boundary I would also have failed to observe what was one of the most crucial of my fieldwork experiences. I could continue in this manner over several pages, for it would be quite easy to construct an account of the fieldwork consisting almost entirely of a series of lurches from one serendipitous event to another. Was I simply lucky, or was it in the nature of the structure of the farm workers' situation that I was in any case bound to bump into a series of analagous occurrences? Obviously I cannot provide a conclusive answer, since it is up to someone else to try and see – yet the answer is in many ways crucial to the validity of my own findings.

In a related form this question has haunted my mind over the entire five years. It has done so in a peculiarly piquant form, since I have often reflected on the precise difference between what I was doing in Suffolk and what Ronald Blythe was doing when he wrote his best-selling book, *Akenfield* (1969). 'Akenfield' – insofar as it consists of any one place – was in my fieldwork area, and I interviewed many of those who appear in the book (and in the subsequent film). Blythe's version of the reality of Akenfield and my own were not entirely similar or even compatible – a problem familiar to those who have previously undertaken restudies of communities (see Bell 1974). I was aware of how Blythe had employed a certain amount of artistic licence, and at first this annoyed me intensely. Later I was not so willing to condemn. I had, after all, utilised a certain sociological licence in both my theoretical development and my selection of the data. But at least I was explicit about my theory, whereas Blythe was not – and obviously had less of an obligation to be so. Was *this* the only difference between doing sociology and writing a semi-fictionalised account? On reflection, however, this difference is not so trivial as it may seem. The theory not only disciplines the data, in the sense of allowing it to 'fit' in Baldamus's (1972) terms; it also disciplines the sociologist by rendering contradictions and incompatibilities more explicit and hence more amenable to investigation. Indeed, if my own experiences are anything to go by, it is these contradictions and incompatibilities which in many respects represent the motor of sociological advance, retrieving it from a sterile flaccidity and allowing it to develop and grow. It also retrieves sociology from, if not a substantial degree of pluralism, then at least a wholesale relativism in which 'anything goes'.

It was in this manner that the theory of deference which I developed from my study of farm workers spawned a whole new series of questions which I was interested in pursuing. There was no lack of theoretical problems now. Much that was crucial to deference I now regarded as being due to the success with which the relationship was handled by those in positions of traditional authority – and for farm workers this principally involved farmers. If I were to really understand the deference of agricultural workers I would have to investigate those, like their employers, to whom they deferred. With this in mind, early in 1973 Colin Bell and I applied to the SSRC for funds to undertake a study of East Anglian farmers. A fortuitous residence in Trunch in 1970 was therefore to determine my future research activities for the following eight years. We received the money, and so, early in 1974, I was back in the forty-four parishes. But that is another story.

6

Playing the Rationality Game: The Sociologist as a Hired Expert

R. E. PAHL

R. E. PAHL

INTRODUCTION [1]

For five years, from 1968 to 1972, I was employed in various capacities for the Department of the Environment. At the beginning of the period I had published an article which argued that real resources were redistributed in cities as a result of managerial decisions in the public and private sector (Pahl 1969). I believed that planners in particular, implicitly or explicitly, redistributed resources, and that if one was personally concerned to shift resources in one way or another, working with such planners would be a way to do it. If one is interested in policy questions it is hard to maintain credibility if one is always in the position of criticising the incompetence, ineptitude, middle-class values or lack of sociological understanding of others. At worst this simply gives rise to resentment on the part of those criticised; at best it encourages them to ask sociologists what they would do to produce 'better' outcomes. If sociologists continually decline such invitations, promising instead to write incisive critiques of how other people make a mess of things, it is understandable when sociologists are less than enthusiastically received by senior decision makers in our society. Many may not mind this; they may feel that their place is with the poor and oppressed (who, as I empirically observe in the world of 1976, are always with us whether or not the state calls itself 'capitalist') and that they should adopt a critical and detached stance in relation to 'those with power in society'. Leaving aside the self-righteous, holier-than-thou aspect of this and noting that sociologists do not refuse to accept the salaries which a bemused society offers them, I believe that such a stance weakens sociology.

If the everyday worlds with which we are most familiar are mainly those of the underdogs or, at best, the middle dogs, we are forced to fall back on accounts of non-sociologists for an understanding of the top dogs. Yet I believe that precise sociological reporting and analysis are extremely necessary if we are to move from fallacy to reality. If one argues that our understanding of the powerless has been greatly improved through sociological analysis, surely our understanding of the powerful could also be improved. In recent years more of such studies have been done. However, the powerful, by definition, need to be convinced that spending their money on someone working with or looking at themselves, as opposed to those well beneath them, is going to be worthwhile.

Looking back on my five years' experience, I realise that I am my own data bank, and that working through my own accounts may be as tortuous and misleading as working through any other respondent's account. Inevitably I became emotionally involved with various aspects of the work, I made some bad judgements, and I have to distance myself from these feelings and mistakes in making my present sociological judgements. Also, what I now consider to be significant in my experience is different from what I thought was significant two years ago, or what I shall doubtless consider to be significant some years hence. Clearly, I am not the first to grapple with these sort of problems, and indeed that, after all, is what this book is about.

In order for my work to be plausible and sociologically interesting, some description of its context is necessary. To describe this briefly within the confines of this chapter inevitably distorts. This is unfortunate, as the different contexts were crucial in determining the limitations and scope of my activities.

THE SOUTH EAST JOINT PLANNING TEAM

From autumn 1968 to spring 1970 I was the sociologist adviser to the South East Joint Planning Team (SEJPT). This was a governmental inter-departmental team set up in collaboration with the local authorities in the South East of England. At the time it was claimed to be the largest exercise in physical planning which had ever been attempted outside the socialist bloc. The original idea of those who established the team was to have a sociologist as a consultant, in the same way that other consultants were being approached to deal with industrial location and transport. The general feeling at that time was that sociology was a 'coming subject' and that it was rather smart to be so forward-looking as to include one in the team. Before we began negotiating, the Director of the study had the idea that the consultant should provide a technical report from which the real planners could create conditions for a maximum variety in lifestyles and for the exercise of personal choice. The consultant was expected to review existing data on housing, personal mobility, service needs, the effects of growth and sizes of communities and to assess the social implications of the employment structure. Later, the consultant was to assess trends in aspirations and patterns of expenditure and to predict the locational effects for 1981 and 1991. Finally, the sociologist was to assess the social constraints of alternative employment and population distributions determined by others.

All this I felt unable to do. In my letter of 23 May 1968 to the Principal Planner in the Ministry of Housing and Local Government, I wrote: 'it does seem to me that I can be of more use in trying to detect the unintended consequences of other people's ideas and plans and also to point out potential problems which will need to be investigated over the next few years'. I went on to stress a focus on social mobility as being perhaps the most useful line to adopt. After a series of meetings with the Director and Deputy Director of the Team, I gradually established an agreed position. I was particularly anxious to stress that I should be appointed as an *adviser* and not as a consultant. By sitting in on the process of analysis I proposed that my job would be to spell out the unintended consequences and sociological implications of the other specialists, such as the economists studying industrial location or the transport consultants. I made it quite clear that sociology is not a form of market research, although I recognised that some members of the team hoped I might do such work. I offered to clarify and advise on the scope and range of my own brief in order that my work and the work of other sociologists after me should be more effective. I also offered to summarise the sociological literature in certain areas, such as 'community' and its relations to urban form, the social styles of 'affluent' manual workers, and so forth; as I put it at the time, 'much of what I would do here would be concerned with *communicating* directly and effectively an academic view to those with a specifically practical brief'. I also felt that it would be useful for me to suggest what data, that were not at present available, should ideally be gathered in the future, although fundamental research on social issues could not be started with the time and resources at my disposal.

My negotiations were successful and I was appointed 'to act as leader of a Sociology Group' to do the kind of work I suggested, but with a further brief 'to predict, so far as possible, the social conditions which are likely to obtain at various dates towards the end of the century'. This latter obligation is the price any sociologist must pay who wants to work with planners. A future orientation suffuses all their work. The role of adviser suited me very well. The rest of the Team gradually accepted me to a greater or lesser degree, and I was greatly aided by my Research Officers – first David Plank then Ted Craven and Jean Conway, who later joined me in the Sociology Group. Being full-time researchers and friendly and agreeable people, they helped enormously to allay the suspicion, if not hostility, of some of the more traditional planners who might have felt a little threatened by what appeared to them as our unconventional approaches and novel jargon. It was very important to gain the confidence of the other group leaders, who met regularly in group leaders' meetings. It was far safer to have one of the traditionalists snort openly about our concern for increasing the employment possibilities for suburban women or coloured school leavers, than for him to stay silent but work against us in other ways. By showing that we did not mind the teasing and joking and by lunching in the pub with our critics, we managed to give them the confidence to condemn themselves out of their own mouths, whereas the moderate majority gradually became more and more willing to listen to the points we were making. If I or my colleagues had been defined as prickly, arrogant or stand-offish we might as well have not been there. We would not have been treated seriously.

My days in my office overlooking St James's Park were spent attending meetings, writing minutes and memoranda and discussing the work of the Sociology Group. I commented on other people's work and visited other government departments, making contacts and gathering information. It was my responsibility to draft the general outlines of a Group report, and then my Research Officers worked up aspects in greater detail. Drafts of the aspect papers, as they were called, were considered by all the group leaders, but after the first round ours got a relatively easy ride because other groups were busy revising their badly mutilated drafts and were too preoccupied with their own problems to raise troubles for others. My position with regard to two conflicting situations was also fortuitously advantageous. Firstly, there was an underlying tension between those seconded from central government departments and those seconded from local authorities through the Standing Conference on London and South East Regional Planning (SCOLSERP). This was partly due to the Team's apparent disregard for the SCOLSERP report, *The South East: A Framework for Regional Planning* (1968). Whatever happened, it was before my appointment, so luckily I was not particularly associated with or seen as a threat to either side. The second tension was between the Team and the transport consultants who sometimes seemed to want to be the tail that wagged the dog. The Team's resistance to the transport consultants' demands for 'inputs' to its model, and its reluctance to have the regional plan dominated by transport considerations, led them to fall back on arguments I was actively canvassing: namely, that people not computer models make plans and that we should acknowledge openly the value judgements we were making.[2]

The Team was also very jealous of its own autonomy and resented it if outside bodies – even its own steering group – made decisions or judgements about what the Team considered to be technical questions. This collective loyalty to the Team when faced with external constraints extended to the Sociology Group. The three of us got on with the others reasonably well, and sociology became a sort of secret weapon which the Team had but the planning authorities and the central government did not have. Hence, when criticism came from outside that there was too much jargon (like 'social mobility') or too much concern with special interests (like 'the poor'), the Team was more prepared to defend its own. This loyalty did not extend to the transport consultants nor to the industrial location consultants. If I had agreed to write some kind of consultant's report my impact would have been much less. As an adviser I interacted with the rest of the Team in a game of intellectual bargaining. I was seen to be listening to them, so they would listen to me. I showed I was committed to the Team as a whole; for example, I took the initiative in arguing for a separate aspect group on housing. This was initially rebuffed on the grounds that housing was a local and not a regional issue. However, I responded with strongly worded minutes, lobbied for support among the group leaders and eventually persuaded the directorate to agree that another member of the Team should produce an aspect paper on housing. Once established, it became evident that the decision was a good one, and this helped to create new allies for the work the Sociology Group was doing. Few group leaders felt qualified to question my judgement about what was 'known' about the social conditions in the South East in 1968. Similarly, when the sociology aspect paper went to other government departments and other external assessors, few felt able or qualified to offer criticism beyond the inevitable concern to avoid 'embarrassing' or potentially contentious phrases or assessments. In the cases of one or two who were able to raise detailed methodological and empirical questions, I could counter that I was engaged in a pragmatic planning exercise, that I had to use my judgement and that were they in my position they would have to do the same.

Using the ambiguity surrounding the role of sociology in this way I was able to guide my 'interest' group more nimbly than might otherwise have been the case. I found it to be an interesting job which did not seem to do much harm, and it perhaps raised some useful ideas which might have led to a wider awareness of the problems of inner London throughout the South East region as a whole. These ideas included the notion of Sector City: a city within a city, stretching along the north bank of the Thames or up the Lea Valley, combining rehabilitation, industrial relocation and limited urban renewal, with new development phased in at both the narrow and broad ends of a wedge-shaped slice into London. This idea had strong organisational and political implications. It was a way to get inner and outer boroughs to work together, and I considered that some body, like a New Town Development Corporation, might be neccessary to get enough energy for something so imaginative to take shape. I also had some knowledge of the problems of inner London housing: the concentration there of low wage earners, and the possibility of imbalances in both labour and housing markets as categories of skilled workers were creamed off to new and expanding towns elsewhere in the region (see Pahl 1976, chs 8 and 11).

It is impossible to assess how useful my work has been; I do not know what might have happened had I not done the job, nor what changes would have taken place anyway whether or not the job was done at all.

THE GREATER LONDON DEVELOPMENT PLAN INQUIRY

Hiring the 'Expert'

Early in April 1970 I received the traditional civil service telephone call asking whether I would meet the Housing Minister to discuss the possibility of being an Assessor to the Panel for the Greater London Development Plan (GLDP) Inquiry. I went along with a vague idea that learning a lot about

London would be useful to me as an urban sociologist and that taking part in such an exercise would give me privileged access to a great deal of information which would otherwise be difficult to get. Mr Crosland, when announcing the setting up of the Inquiry in the House on 10 December 1969, said that 'the panel ... should be assisted by a number of outside assessors to help them to probe and evaluate, fully and searchingly, the policies embodied in the Plan, the objections made to them and possible alternative strategies'. Mr Crosland went on to say in response to a question: 'I should like to emphasise that we do not wish this Inquiry to become a great battle between heavily gunned legal protagonists. I hope that its character will be more informal than that.'

The actual Inquiry was thought likely to last from October 1970 to the following March or April. Time was then needed for writing the report. I agreed to serve as an Assessor on a half-time basis. I was then given a statement about the duties of Assessors at Inquiries. The Assessor's task is to evaluate specialist evidence and to indicate the amount of weight to be put on it. It is for the Assessor to ensure that all the relevant facts in his field are obtained, and the Inspector conducting the Inquiry has a duty to see that the Assessor is afforded every opportunity to obtain these facts. If these facts are particularly complicated it is the Assessor's task to help the Inspector to incorporate them into his final report by providing him with written drafts.

With hindsight, I realise that I was mistaken not to consider my situation more carefully. The rules for Assessors were drawn up for ordinary Inquiries, and this was to be no ordinary Inquiry, as Mr Crosland's announcement clearly indicated. The relationship between the Assessors and the Panel was unclear to everyone, and I should have asked for special conditions. There is always a time during preliminary negotiations when well-thought-out requests are more likely to be accepted lest the negotiations break down, with consequent delay and embarrassment in finding an alternative. I was misled by my earlier experience which had enabled me to use an ambiguous situation to my advantage. It was certainly foolish of me not to consider what my special expertise as a sociologist would be in this context. I soon discovered that, unlike my work with the SEJPT, where *I* decided what was relevant material, here the Plan and the objectors set the agenda. A flood of documents swept upon me from early May, and soon after the end of term I was asked to prepare a paper 'setting out what you see as the major problems you would wish to see explored in any of those strategies which interest you'. Clearly at that time there was no obvious sociological niche for me.

I suspect that I may have been seen by some as an expert concerned with the soft end of the business. Such an impression was fostered in the procedural sessions which preceded the Inquiry, when I was referred to in an embarrassingly adulatory way by one objector.[3] Later, I was told the following story: A leading member of a women's organisation enquired of the Chairman why he didn't have a woman on the Panel. He is said to have replied, 'We haven't got a woman but we've got a sociologist.' It would have been easy to slip into the role of 'token woman' and feel that I ought to be the friend of the underdogs, the poor, the female, the incoherent and the deviant. Clearly, some objectors expected me to be sympathetic to Tower Hamlets but less so to Bromley, to housing charities but not to financial entrepreneurs. I was in danger of becoming the Panel's token soul. However, I do not believe that a sociologist should necessarily be the friend of all populist causes; some of these may be very silly.

The Rationality Game

The day-to-day work involved an enormous amount of reading. Quite apart from the hundreds of technical documents related to the Plan issued by the Greater London Council (GLC), there were also hundreds of proofs of evidence and support documents from the objectors, and these had to be read carefully. Inevitably the GLC had to define its proposals as sensible, based on the best technical judgement. Previous disagreements were covered up, and compromises were patched over to look more rational than they were. Inadequate data were presented in their most favourable light, and the officers defending the Plan rarely acknowledged the political battles on the GLC behind them. A brief reading of GLC minutes soon revealed where the conflicts were between the Conservative majority and the Labour minority.

I was not simply concerned with the apparent logic and technical competence of the various documents; I also became increasingly aware of the ideological assumptions underlying them. Yet, curiously, the Panel did not behave as if it was involved in a political battle at all. Political debate was suspended as we sat through the hearings day after day and week after week. The assumption throughout was that by the rigorous sifting of the evidence and by balancing the logic and quality of one case against another, errors of fact, judgement and supposition would be exposed. Once members of the Panel had decided to take the Plan as a document which could be improved, rather than rejecting it outright, they had to try and discover first what the GLC *really* meant in its Plan and then whether the various objectors could make the odd dents here and there. The aim had to be to produce a workable Plan free from errors and wishful thinking which the Minister, or Secretary of State as he became, could approve. The Plan should be pragmatic, practical and plausible. Rationality would prevail over politics, people would see sense, and Londoners everywhere would understand that fairness and justice had triumphed. Consistently, the Chairman asked objectors what *specific* improvements and amendments they would like to make to the Plan. For them to demonstrate that political considerations had led to the position to which they objected moved him little: what in *practice* would they suggest instead?

Frank Layfield, QC, was a formidable Chairman. He had a seemingly infinite capacity for hard and concentrated work, an incredible memory and a remarkable facility for thinking up new points on any issue. He controlled

Panel meetings very carefully, with a passion for orderliness, punctuality and precision. He could bring together the main points of a discussion in a masterly summary and gave a sense of purpose and achievement to his team. This persistent attention to detail in our work and day-to-day activities did, I think, create some unintended consequences. It helped to underline the Chairman's dominance, and it served to draw him apart from those members of the Panel who did not share his particular social style. He saw things in a particular – lawyer's – way, and for those who shared this approach he was a captivating and charismatic leader. However, those on the Panel who saw things in a different way were not always treated so sympathetically by him, and as a result he might not have got the best out of them. While his concentration and grasp of the issues was truly impressive, perhaps it took him longer to grasp the implications of others' weaknesses.

Turning now to the basic rules and procedures of the public hearings, it is clear that as a *statutory* Inquiry, it had to follow a certain common format. As an Inquiry set up in accordance with the provisions of the Town and Country Planning Acts, there was no question but that those responsible for its organisation had to be meticulous in following legally appropriate procedures. Failure to do so could lead to an appeal by an objector that the lack of proper procedures had prevented his objection from being fairly considered. If such a view were upheld in the courts it could ultimately have the effect of nullifying the Inquiry, and the whole exercise would have to start again. Quite apart from such obligations there are advantages of convenience and logic in following set and established patterns. However, it does not follow that these patterns are without their dangers and difficulties.

The procedures may be described by analogy as a form of game. The main pitch for the game was the Council Chamber of the GLC, a lofty, draughty, domed hall with a raised platform at one end on which sat the members of the Panel and the Assessors. The Panel sat between 10 a.m. and 4.30 p.m. for 237 days over nearly two years. A formal written proof of evidence had to be submitted by objectors well in advance of the appearance, to enable all those concerned to read and discuss it. Those who submitted their proofs late were reprimanded by the Chairman and sometimes were punished by losing their turn to play. Learned Counsel who had tight fixture lists and who did not want to interrupt games elsewhere did not like this. In all, 28,207 objections were considered, and there were 326 appearances before the Panel. These could be heard fully and fairly only if everyone kept to the rules. In truth, the Panel could only hear those who had the time and money to appear before it – but this fact was commented on less often. The range of possible moves in the game were set out in the rules sent to all contestants:

'An objector should first of all outline his objection. If he calls a witness to give supporting evidence, then that witness might be subject to cross examination by the opposing side, and further examination by his own side. If the objector does not call a witness he himself may be subject to cross examination. On the other side, however, GLC witnesses will, at the request of the objector, be recalled, subject to cross examination by him and can thereafter be re-examined in answer to the objection as they require'.

The Panel could ask questions at the end of any round or could recall witnesses at any point. The Panel Counsel also had an opportunity to put a more structured series of questions.

This stylised ritual certainly helped to keep the Inquiry orderly, and it helped evenly matched teams to be unemotional and systematic in presenting their cases and to make their points concisely and clearly. The game was played in the ponderously flowery language beloved of lawyers, with all the traditional mock astonishment, studied politeness and affected wit that that implies. Fulsome speeches of mock modesty in the face of these so-difficult technical questions enabled some barristers to blunder on in considerable style and no doubt at considerable expense. There was plenty of legal toadying to 'M' learned and distinguished Chairman'. And when an elderly worthy of the legal profession went maundering on in an inconsequential way for one objector, he did not receive the expected schoolmasterly reproof of the Chairman or the barbed wit of the GLC Counsel; he was treated deferentially by each, and the rest of us had to put up with the constraints of the status hierarchy of the legal profession with as much patience as we could manage. During the early weeks one or two members of the Panel lingered too long on their trips to the loo, to get a smoke or to avoid cramp. The Chairman sent a note round urging us to be good. He also did his best to discourage long-windedness and flannel, but more by his own example than by reproving some of the worst offenders among his senior colleagues.

After a time we all found ourselves colluding in the desire to get a good game. While the game was on, it did not seem to matter after a time who was winning or losing. The important thing was to get a high standard of play. We could have been corrupted by our natural struggles to avoid boredom, but as we all reread the transcripts of the day's play and picked out further points to follow up or points which had made a substantial impact, the style of play had a less lasting effect than the specific points which were made. Also, we had regular Panel meetings to discuss the evidence as it was presented in order to formulate questions for our Counsel.

The initiative was with the Plan and the objectors. If the objectors missed good arguments we were not expected to give them leading questions. Obviously I was unable to give evidence myself; the best I could do was to prepare a line of questioning which our Counsel could put to a witness whose proof of evidence was not too far from the problems I was concerned with. Many objectors were badly informed; the GLC data were dubious in places; the interest groups were inevitably partial; experts of equal status and authority were locked in fundamental disagreement; professional witnesses were paid by objectors to stick to their lines; the officials from the GLC and from government departments loyally supported as best they could the lines of their political masters. A whole troup of naked emperors appeared before us. To be fair to the GLC professionals, they did admit in a piecemeal fashion that they could not control population, housing and employment. In their evidence they told us, for example, that their population policy stemmed from its housing policy and not the other way round. However, the GLC was not prepared to *force* the outer London boroughs to release the necessary land for those in inner London boroughs who were squeezed out by the reduction in multi-occupation or by the formation of new households. Nor, of course, could the GLC control headship rates, occupancy rates, the condition and allocation of dwellings in the private sector, and much else besides. The GLC witnesses admitted all this, as indeed they admitted that industrial location could not be controlled through the negative powers of floorspace allocation and that the GLC had no means of determining what were the most essential or productive industries which, of necessity, must have a London location. During the period of the Inquiry the population of London continued to decline, adding point to the clear fact that the GLC could do very little, if anything, to prevent it.

As an Assessor, I was supposed to be concerned with 'the facts'. Certainly I did acquire new information in the early days between October and December 1970. The combination of new data supplied by the GLC, the outstanding presentation of an objection by C. J. Holmes, a community worker from North Islington, and the occasional surprise produced by a particularly conscientious barrister who, generally to his own amazement, stumbled on some new area of ambiguity and fudging, all seemed to make the Plan, as it stood, more and more irrelevant. The GLC professionals were not of course generally any less competent than the best planners anywhere; they were simply obliged by the conventions of their trade to wrap up their judgements with a kind of technical certainty which has a superficial capacity to convince. Furthermore, it was not always easy to detect where the political judgements were made. For example, it took me some time to work out the political implications of desirable residential densities.[4] Some of the best matches were between the London boroughs and the GLC. Forced to abandon their own structure plans in 1970, and in general resentful of any interference and any assumptions of superior technical competence on the part of the GLC, the boroughs used the Inquiry to show off their own skills. No doubt many players from the boroughs are now captains or vice-captains as a result of their part in scoring points against the GLC Counsel and witnesses. It was a good proving ground for aspiring talent, and the Inquiry provided an excellent pitch for testing players in down-league boroughs as well as for giving the stars from boroughs like Camden a chance to weigh in against their rivals in the GLC. While I have no evidence to support it, I would guess that some witnesses quite enjoyed playing the game, patiently explaining part of the technical issue but leaving just enough unexplained to stall the non-expert Counsel who painstakingly had to get the point clear before he could logically proceed. Very often a borough would know that the overall political situation was against it, but it did not want to lose without a fight. Expensive Counsel was engaged, the brighter planners prepared their case, and it was off to County Hall for ten days for a good intellectual tussle and a bit of limelight. The Chairman and Panel were attentive, points were scored, and it all made the profession seem important and technical.

The 'rationality game' took longer than anyone expected. The GLC made much of the concept of 'balance', which was their euphemism for 'solution'. Thus, in response to Conservative pressure, a main aim was to provide 'more opportunity for private enterprise' in housing *and* – no doubt in response to pressure from the inner boroughs – 'to direct housing effort towards the area of greatest need'. There was never any resolution of such political incompatibles. Rather, each was used when appropriate to silence an objector who picked up one and neglected the other. After a time, it was easy to see in advance how objectors would be handled, and there would be an exchange of knowing glances as one of the standard tricks of intellectual karate floored an unsuspecting objector. C. J. Holmes's case was effective partly because he managed to talk out the time allotted to him on his first appearance and was able to come back better prepared on a later occasion. Quickly learning the tricks, he started to ask for new information, and by other such ploys he had time to go back over the daily transcript, picking up points and developing counterarguments. He played the game so well that he was congratulated by the GLC Counsel at the end of his case. After all, it's not the winning that counts in sport but a good hard game. Gentlemen can shake hands and have a drink together afterwards. I felt that when the GLC Counsel was struck with one of his own rather soggier witnesses he probably wished he could get a few stronger players such as Holmes in his team.

To be fair, I would not have known what was beneath some of the material in the GLDP's *Report of Studies of the Panel of Inquiry* (1973) unless I had had this ringside seat at the Inquiry. I certainly *was* surprised on occasions since the wrapping round some issues was very cleverly tied up. For a series of pragmatic and prudential reasons I limited myself to acquiring a thorough knowledge of the housing problems, which did not necessarily take very long to do. Such problems, however, are not solved when the 'facts' are free from dispute. They are basically problems of policy and politics. Thus was laid the foundation for a period of acute boredom and frustration, since the Inquiry procedures forced attention on to the statistics. The Plan made statements about how many conversions a year would be possible or desirable or whatever, and such figures could be questioned, probed and argued about. However, the critical *political* issue of the relations between the inner and outer boroughs was always at a delicate stage of negotiation, and all parties were discouraged by the Chairman from pursuing the matter, since it was said that little useful purpose could be achieved at this point in time.

The work of the Panel was suffused by implicit ideologies and political undercurrents. I affirm this intuitively without substantive empirical backing. The very protestations of political neutrality were made rather too strongly. I know the Chairman met with people informally in the evenings and when he was on holiday. The Secretary continued his friendships with colleagues in the department from which he had been seconded. Clearly, I know only some of the people they talked with on these occasions, and I know nothing of what was discussed. However, I am certain that these external and informal meetings did much to colour the Chairman's views about what issues were likely to be acceptable, 'embarrassing' (i.e. not acceptable) or still 'open and undecided'. How far any quasi-judicial inquiry or Royal Commission is ever entirely free from such informal pressures, I do not know. The very fact that an Inquiry or Commission has been established generally implies a delicate political situation. Perhaps some Chairmen are less amenable or sensitive to political pressure than others. I suspect that many would not recognise the informal chats as being the political training sessions that they are. One can be swayed willingly, seeing the sense of the views being implied, or one can be manipulated to believe that one is making up one's own mind, and he who is doing the political sensitising may not be aware he is doing it. This is all very obvious; I believe it to be of crucial importance in creating the 'of course world' of taken-for-granted and unquestioned assumptions into which the Panel was wittingly or unwittingly socialised. I would find the precise documentation of all this extremely difficult to achieve, but this should not minimise its importance. I had no means of knowing what informal contact the Chairman had with the appropriate junior minister responsible for London housing. I suspected that current political discussions were known to the Chairman and to the Secretary of the Panel. The situation was generally mentioned in the form: '*If* the Minister is considering such and such then it would be very embarrassing if ... etc.'.

The most powerful person, in this case the Chairman, can always control the release of ideas and information by claiming superior political judgement. Others can never know whether he really does have special privileges in access to the politically powerful, and they are thus inevitably obliged to accept his judgement. They are further caught in a familiar dilemma: either it is a *technical* issue, in which case the truth will out in time, or it is a *political* issue, and now is a bad time to raise it. The GLDP Inquiry was itself a mammoth stalling device. There were too many reasons for doing nothing, and by law all the objectors had to be heard.

Engineering the Consensus

I felt that my main role as a sociologist was to expose the political or ideological assumptions underlying the policies in the Plan. Once I had grasped these I saw no point in waiting for more numbers, which tended to fog the underlying issues. Yet the Panel could not use the expertise that I could most readily provide. The Chairman assumed, quite probably correctly, that it was for him to make political judgements, not one of his Assessors. He felt that every possible technical argument must be worked through first before coming back to the political issues. I admit that I was bored and wearied by such an exercise which I doubted would serve much useful purpose. There was no reward for me in hearing weak arguments being destroyed, nor did I want to play endless rounds of the numbers game showing that these or those statistics were fudged, incompatible with others or whatever.

With very little enthusiasm I accepted another year out of my university life as the Inquiry rolled into the autumn of 1971. I had written to the Chairman in July urging that the Panel should present an interim report on housing to show the gravity and urgency of the problem and the obvious political constraints. This was stalled in various ways and finally rejected by the Panel in November, which was almost certainly the correct political judgement under the circumstances. I then seriously considered resigning, feeling that there was little more I could usefully add to the deliberations of the Panel and that I would achieve more 'good' if freed from the constraints of my position. I was persuaded that this was a false view, and I stayed on.[5]

The Chairman wanted to do everything possible to avoid the Panel's making up its mind prematurely and to avoid disagreements between the Panel and the Assessors or between members of the Panel itself. Only a unanimous report would have the impact for which he hoped. Hence the orchestration of the final stage of our work was crucial. The preliminary meetings for the final stage began with two residential weekends early in 1972. These were intended to consolidate our knowledge at the time and to point up the unresolved questions still to be tackled. The Chairman's strategy at that time was seemingly to emphasise how little we had in common. He continually opened up topics with a whole string of virtually unanswerable questions. Thus he asked what the Plan should seem to do with regard to certain topics. What importance should we attach to the figures? Should the content of the Plan be determined in terms of existing policies, or should it go beyond them? How would the Secretary of State cope with suggestions not in line with government policy? And so forth. This was a fundamental shift in emphasis from what had been the pattern of the previous eighteen months. Having been trained to narrow down and follow through to the bitter end every technical (and to my mind frequently irrelevant) question, this new wide-ranging approach unsettled some members of the Panel. They were moved away from a position where they would have accepted what I took to be the logic of the situation to one where anything was possible.

In some ways this new freshness was an advantage at the final stage of the Inquiry when questions of general strategy and implementation were to be discussed. However, it certainly prevented the Panel from coming to firm conclusions which might conflict. The fact that Stage III of the Inquiry, on general strategy and implementation, was so different from the previous section, on local effects, and was so close to the drafting of the final *Report* meant that some Panel members had difficulty in keeping their heads clear for this distinctive task.

The next stage began in March 1972, when we were asked to prepare papers to clarify where the Panel needed to make decisions. The logic of such papers was intended to conform to a common pattern. Firstly, would be an account of the logical basis for a given policy: the problem as defined by given facts. Secondly, there would be an assessment of the powers of the GLC and of how far these could handle the problems as outlined. Thirdly, there would be a clear statement of what the GLC said they intended to do. Fourthly there would be an account of some logically possible policies, not in the GLDP but which might more effectively solve the problem. Finally, we were asked to list the constraints on the GLC which inhibited the implementation of existing or putative policies; economic constraints we had previously considered, but now political and administrative constraints were also considered.

The Panel found difficulty in following through this logic, and days and weeks went by in arguing over the 'facts'. At this stage we were divided into subgroups dealing with different topics, and some found it hard to keep in focus what the whole enterprise was about. Detailed discussions about plausible headship rates in 1981 as an ingredient in a housing balance sheet took us a long way from the obduracy of the outer London boroughs in providing homes for inner London people, or from the consideration of the political possibilities for and consequences of widespread municipalisation of housing. Assessors sometimes disagreed with each other on technical points, but there was very little opportunity for trading or bargaining. We found that while we had been treated in most ways like other members of the Panel throughout the Inquiry (apart from not participating in jaunts to other countries, which only the Panel got), at the end we were firmly put back as technical experts. As Panel meetings became more concerned with final drafts of the *Report*, so only certain Assessors were invited for certain topics. Only the Chairman and one or two members of the Panel seemed to have an overall grasp of all sections of the *Report*. The other members had been forced to dig so deeply into the data that all they seemed to want was for their draft to be accepted without the imposition of more work on themselves. The large ideas, the alternatives, the constraints, all these grand logical possibilities were forgotten by them in an attempt to survive. This certainly helped to reduce overt conflict. Much of the very final drafting was done by the Secretary to the Panel, an extremely able assistant secretary seconded from the Department of the Environment. Not being a planner, he maintained the traditional sceptical stance of the senior administrator, which by then most of us were happy to adopt.

Concluding Discussion

I have described something of what I did in two different contexts as a hired expert. In helping to prepare the Strategic Plan for the South East I was able to choose the work I did to a much greater extent than in my GLDP experience. However, I learned much more from the latter than I realised at the time.

Anyone who becomes involved with policy making must be prepared to be a social engineer to some extent. My friends and colleagues assumed that I would use my position to argue for some radical or progressive policy which those without the benefit of sociological understanding could not otherwise see. I have often heard it argued that if more sociologists were involved in the process of government 'better' decisions would be made. My experience is that arguing intervention with interventionists is not easy. The GLDP brought home to me very forcefully how limited are the powers of intervention by a local authority in a market economy. Those objectors who criticised the GLDP for being unrealistic were correct – as the Panel's *Report* concluded: 'the GLDP *Written Statement* [1969] is full of statements of aims which do not mean anything because they can mean anything to anyone . . . Our basic criticism of the Plan is that there are, too often, either no links between its aims and policies, or no policy at all to support a wholly desirable aim'.

In different degrees and in different ways this weakness was grasped by many objectors, from the City of London on the right to the Communist Party on the left. Most of the important questions which we had to resolve were matters of politics and judgement. Now this, of course, is what I and others have often argued in our academic writings. Some may think that, by getting on the inside of a major enterprise like the GLDP Inquiry and pointing out the various value positions that are being held, some benefit will be achieved. First, this assumes that those concerned cannot analyse value positions for themselves; and secondly, by making so much explicit, one's own values become equally well exposed. Putting forward liberal reformist arguments to highly intelligent people who may be market realists or administrative pessimists is a very foolhardy enterprise. Without answers to the questions, 'Do the powers exist to do that?',[6] 'Could you do it if you had the powers?', 'How would it work in practice?' and so on, one quickly loses one's credibility. I suppose one could resign and say 'capitalism does not work'. In another context I suppose equally my counterpart might like to be able to resign and say 'state socialism does not work'. It made better sense to me to be pragmatic and to make judgements about what was feasible within all the constraints I could assess. In a phrase, I started to think like a senior civil servant. I lost my faith in professional expertise, populist enthusiasm and idealist political programmes. 'Will it work and can it be implement?' became the key questions.

Unless one does adopt a 'realistic' attitude one soon loses one's credibility, being seen as a waffler with no practical *alternatives*. Criticising greedy developers, incompetent professionals, self-interested politicians and muddled thinkers everywhere is not really so helpful. 'After the Revolution' I fear there will still be muddled thinkers (some might argue that there will be more). The time must come when one is asked: 'Well, what would *you* do?' Given my values I try to make judgements which are progressive and not reactionary and which I can defend from attacks from very clear minds. The published literature on the sociologist's role in policy making and analysis is slender, but I know of no work which makes clear distinctions between the *levels* at which the sociologist is drawn in. It may be that at lower levels sociological understanding can help to manipulate the situation in a way not possible or desirable at higher levels. It may be helpful to set out some of the putative roles that a sociologist might find him or herself in when working for a government department or local authority.

(1) *The gatekeeper to 'the literature'.* Here the hirer assumes that there is a solid and relatively non-contentious body of knowledge or science which needs to be sifted and summarised. The sociologist, as an omnicompetent abstractor, presents other peoples' ideas clearly and cogently.

(2) *The filterer of the literature.* Here the sociologist is expected to use his/her judgement to select the 'most important' or 'most relevant' material for the non-expert.

(3) *An advocate for a focus of interest.* Here the sociologist takes up poverty, housing, public transport, social mobility, work satisfaction or whatever and points out the implications to the non-expert at all stages of the operation.

(4) *The advocate for a political element.* The sociologist may be concerned with all the implications of a particular political programme, such as increasing participation, devolution of control, development of tenants' or workers' co-operatives or the strengthening of law and order. This is generally quite manifest when a sociologist is hired as a specifically political appointment in order to help implement a given policy. However, it is possible for a sociologist to abuse his/her position and to work covertly for a political end.

(5) *The watchdog or demystifier.* Here the sociologist is solely concerned with unmasking the hidden ideologies and political strategies of all other parties to the enterprise. He/she helps to uncover the self-delusions and mystifications of all, including him/herself and his/her employer.

(6) *The managerialist/technocrat.* This implies that rationality is the true basis of political action and that technocratic tools such as operational research, systems theory, PPBS or some other theory will provide the 'best' policy outcome. This is, in my view, a more unsociological position than some of the others, but nevertheless many who call themselves sociologists do hire themselves out, particularly in industry, to do this sort of thing.

(7) *The fall guy.* Experts are often hired as someone for politicians to

blame for advocating an electorally unpopular policy. This is more likely in other fields, such as government legislation about health or the use of motor cars, where distinguished scientific advisers are quite happy to take responsibility for the implications of their advice.

(8) *The legitimator*. Here the expert is hired to legitimate an expedient policy with the authority of his/her trade. This may not be what the hirer genuinely thinks is happening, but in practice that is the result.

(9) *The social statistician*. The hirer assumes that facts must be measurable and that the more exact the measurement can be the more developed the science must be. The sociologist measures social facts or discovers new facts with surveys. Research means gathering new or better facts.

(10) *The woman*. The sociologist as woman, wild man, people's pal or what have you is a common role on public inquiries. Basically committed to the soft end of an issue, he/she is hired to forestall certain specific criticisms. Again the hirer is not conscious of manipulation but assumes that another interest is being served.

No doubt there are many other roles. It would seem to me to be useful for a sociologist to clarify which particular cluster of roles is expected of him/her before becoming hired. It is also important to know as much as possible about the organisational context of the work. As I have shown, the period of precontract bargaining is absolutely vital to the later effectiveness of the expert's contribution. I believe that sociologists should be prepared to work for official bodies of one sort or another so long as each party knows what to expect from the other. Much of the difficulty lies in the fact that the hirer is often genuinely unsure about what a sociologist can contribute, and so there is frequently more mutual learning of expectations than would be the case with longer established experts such as civil engineers or economists.

These roles I have outlined are not of course mutually exclusive, and many sociologists find that they have to handle a cluster of roles or are lured to fill one but end up playing another. In some cases the role is what the hirer intended; in other cases it is what happens in practice when the hirer expected something else. The list is not by any means exhaustive and is given more to open up a line of analysis than to provide neat bundles of reality.

During the GLDP Inquiry I worked mostly as a reasonably clear-headed interpreter of statistics, much like any other. senior administrator. Sometimes I wrote a paper drawing on 'sociology', but really I did not have much to offer by way of sociological certainties for creating the good life. By and large I believe that poor people want more money and that people with power like to keep and use their power. These great thoughts were well understood by my colleagues. With ability and political will progressive policies can be implemented, but without the ability and the will nothing much happens.

I could have used my experience more calculatingly for my own purposes. With my current interest in political economy I could have focused
on the relationship between the state bureaucracy, the legal system and the
technical experts. The lawyers refused ever to allude to political issues underlying the so-called technical issues they probed, and tended to buttress
the rationality game even though they were so skilled at showing what a
game it was. The lawyers appeared to be obliged to believe in a false order.
They seemed to have to behave as if the continual exposing of errors in the
technical evidence would eventually get us closer to technically determined
truth. The rationality game serves the interests of lawyers very well; experts
fight experts with the aid of their learned Counsel, and everybody gets well
paid for doing so. Even though individually their cases all show the
irrelevance of the game and the fragility of the 'facts', they all support it. The
hidden agenda of the game is to provide a fixture for lawyers and experts to
collude in oppressing those without knowledge. The GLDP Inquiry was a
positive festival in praise of technical rationality, which cost £2–3 million
from the public purse. Individually, all the players knew that political values
and personal judgements determined outcomes; collectively, they all earned
more playing and supporting the rationality game.

At another level I could have done more work on the sociodynamics of
the various teams and off-pitch situations I was in. The use of power in
small-group situations seems to be very similar no matter what the context.
There are always those who count and those who don't. There is always an
informal meeting structure behind a formal one. The most powerful person
(the Chairman in the GLDP Inquiry) has a common cluster of strategems
and ploys to make sure that his team does what he wants them to do. The
same techniques are used everywhere to avoid overt conflicts, to manipulate
and to control. I was doing research of Boards of Directors in British industry during the same period, so inevitably my thoughts went easily along
these lines (Pahl and Winkler 1974).

Clearly, no one would hire me as an expert to do macro- or
microsociology of that order. If I were advising the Secretary of State on
whether he should appoint this or that expert to an official post, I would find
the role of the sociologist hard to specify precisely. However, I would be
confident that in an area where politics or matters of judgement were central, no other professional expertise would be likely to be any more useful.
Given the sociologist's basic scepticism, I would expect that, other things
being equal, it would be more difficult to manipulate, mystify or deceive a
sociologist than any other sort of professional expert. This indeed is the
sociologist's greatest strength. The senior administrator and the sociologist,
sharing a basic scepticism, should be able to work well together. It is most
misleading to judge the usefulness of hired experts by their effectiveness at
lower levels, where the skills of an economist or other expert may be more
appropriate. One way of 'doing sociology' is to maintain one's scepticism in
a variety of different contexts.

NOTES

1 I have greatly benefited from comments on an earlier, longer draft of this chapter. I would like to name those from whom I received much, but to do so might embarrass them.

2 Some time that autumn, discussion with the transport consultant began to be conducted in verse. My reply to their initiative included the following piece of doggerel:

> A question I would like to ask
> Concerns the purpose of our task!
> May not obsession with precision
> O'er cloud a noble vision?
>
> To help the lot of the common man
> Must be the aim of any plan,
> Yet the market sees (tho' some may scoff it)
> That from the poor there's little profit.
>
> One thing's sure I can predict.
> The views of planners will conflict,
> For truly 'twould be an amazing feat
> If one man's poison were another's meat.
>
> But facts ('tis said) speak for themselves
> (And some people believe in fairies and elves)
> But facts — let's face it — we *select*
> And values guide what we detect.

3 *Mr Goodman*: 'I believe that sociology is a subject of the most fundamental importance. I have read and have here Dr Pahl's book . . . and it is one of the most profoundly moving and able documents that I have ever seen in my life . . . I am convinced that this man who by pure chance happens to be on your Panel . . . will not only be a distinguished addition to your Panel but he and he alone — because he is a trained sociologist — will understand and evaluate the points which I and other sociologists will raise . . .'
   The Chairman: 'I would not like you to treasure the mistaken impression that Mr Pahl is one of our associates by accident' (taken from the daily transcript, day 3, p. 8).

4 In the *Draft Studies* (GLDP 1967) it was firmly stated that 200 habitable rooms per acre should be regarded as a maximum density, with 140 hrpa for family accommodation. Yet the *Written Statement* (GLDP 1969) simply states: 'the total residential capacity planned within each London Borough should be at least within the population range (for 1981) shown in Table 1 (para 13.3)'. This clearly is a circular argument since the GLC admitted that the population policy derives from the housing policy. The boroughs simply refused to have density levels imposed upon them.

5 The warm and sympathetic help and encouragement which I received from the friends to whom I turned for advice greatly encouraged me. Without having such friends to turn to in difficult times I would find it impossible to do such jobs. I am deeply grateful to them. I suppose that the Final Report's chapter on housing would have been different had I not been there, but what effect it has had or will have I cannot now judge.

7

The Moral Career of a Research Project

ROY WALLIS

INTRODUCTION [1]

Research on human subjects perennially poses moral and political dilemmas, the diversity and acuteness of which are only rarely matched in the natural sciences. In sociology, a growing awareness of these dilemmas has developed in recent decades. The work of A. Vidich and J. Bensman (1958) on the Springdale community, and more recently that of Laud Humphreys (1970) on homosexual contacts in public facilities, posed in different ways the issue of responsibility to one's subjects. The ill-fated project Camelot raised widespread concern over the dangers of research sponsorship (Horowitz 1967). Studies by L. Festinger et al., (1956), the Humphreys (1970) study and S. Milgram's (1974) study of obedience, all provoked controversy concerning the allowable limits of deception in social research.

Such problems are, indeed, endemic within sociology. The activity itself almost always involves incursion into areas of life which some of those involved are likely to construe as belonging to a private domain. The publication of the results of research almost always contains a potential threat to the public rhetoric or the private self-image of those who have been studied. If components of that rhetoric or self-image are matters of public dispute or debate, the work of the sociologist will inevitably be mobilised or criticised in justification or support of one or another contending party. A great deal of sociology is therefore, in a sense, *subversive*. It inevitably provides an account of features of the social world which will conflict with the beliefs, interests or public assertions of some individuals or groups in a pluralistic society.

The more strongly committed the actors are to the norms, values or beliefs at issue, the more threatening the attentions of social researchers are likely to prove. Those who believe they possess the truth, complete and undefiled, do not need a sociologist to tell them what is going on. Indeed his very pursuit of further or different knowledge, after he has already been informed of the 'truth' of the matter by the individuals or groups concerned, displays the fact that he does not accept the 'self-evident', and perhaps even that motivated by malice he is determined to tell some entirely different story. Few groups are committed to an authoritative conception of reality covering all aspects of their lives. Such totalistic self-conceptions are an extreme case. However, some groups approach very closely this claim to possess complete knowledge. Sectarian collectivities are particularly likely to believe that they possess all-embracing knowledge. Hence, an account of my research into one sectarian collectivity, Scientology, may illustrate the practical and moral (or, broadly, political) problems which some kinds of sociological enterprise can generate. I shall outline the history of my research relationship with Scientology and then make a few general observations deriving from this interaction.

WHY SCIENTOLOGY?

Early in 1971, having exhausted a long list of possible thesis topics, I began work on a range of new religious movements in advanced industrial societies. It seemed to me that while traditional sectarianism had received considerable scholarly attention as a result of Bryan Wilson's research and his stimulation of an active group of graduate students, the new religious movements, many of which were only marginally Christian or altogether non-Christian, had been neglected. I proposed to begin remedying this situation by analysing a number of such movements on a comparative basis. I began to collect literature issued by and concerning such movements and to attend public meetings held by these groups, in order to formulate more precisely the way in which my research should proceed. One of the movements which I included was Scientology.

Scientology is a movement based upon a religious philosophy which now claims a substantial following in all the English-speaking countries and, to a lesser degree, elsewhere. It originated as a lay psychotherapeutic movement, Dianetics, which made its first public appearance in 1950. Dianetics claimed that psychosomatic illness and psychological and social disability were the result of traumatic experiences in early, even intra-uterine, life. By 1952 the movement, which had achieved craze proportions in the USA, had foundered, and L. Ron Hubbard, its inventor, had developed a more inclusive metaphysical system which he later incorporated as a church. Scientology holds that we are all spiritual beings, Thetans, but have lost touch with our spiritual nature and capacities. Through training, and a practice known as 'auditing', we can regain awareness of our true spiritual nature and recover the competence to employ our forgotten supernatural powers. (On the origins, development, membership, ideology, and practices of Scientology, see Wallis 1973a, 1974, 1975a, 1975b, 1976).

Scientology seemed particularly interesting for a number of reasons. To begin with, I must admit to having been attracted by its very 'exoticness'. As I looked over the scant material then available, I found that Scientology proposed a system of beliefs and practices which at that time seemed altogether bizarre to me. How *could* people come to believe such things and undertake the practices they entailed? The common reaction to this puzzle, which I was later to pose to many people in the course of describing my work, was that Scientology's followers must be 'cranks', 'inadequates' or simply 'deluded'. I found these hypotheses sociologically uncompelling. The accounts which I read gave me little reason to believe that, apart from holding some unusual views on the nature of man and how to cope with his problems, the bulk of the following was anything but 'normal'. I wanted, therefore, to find out more about how they came into this movement and came to hold the beliefs to which they displayed such apparently sincere commitment in its publications.

Scientology was especially interesting for another reason. Throughout the English-speaking world it had been a matter of controversy. Why *had* this one movement, out of the luxuriant crop of new religions, become the centre of so much debate and even open conflict with state and private agencies, hostile individuals and the mass media? (It was, of course, followed in this respect within a few years by other new religious movements, most notably by the Children of God.)

There was a further reason for my interest in Scientology. Reflecting upon my motivations, and aware that sociologists rarely interest themselves deeply in phenomena to which they are personally or politically indifferent, I conclude that Scientology partly interested me because as a species of social democrat I was fascinated and repelled by the apparent authoritarianism and even occasional totalitarianism of this movement. I wanted to understand how it came to exercise such extensive control over, and to mobilise such enduring commitment from, so many of its followers.

The Scientologists often accuse me of having had a preconceived idea of Scientology from the outset, which blinded me to those aspects of the movement which I saw as of minimal importance but which they took great pains to convince me were central to their endeavours. This may, of course, be true. No-one can guarantee his objectivity; every researcher is susceptible to bias. There is perhaps even a *necessary* element of truth in their criticism. I did, indeed, formulate quite early a view about Scientology. The material which I read led me to believe that this was a dogmatic movement, intolerant of alternative conceptions of the world and particularly intolerant of interpretations of the nature and meaning of Scientology alternative to that which it provided for general consumption through its own public relations machinery. Whether this theoretical preconception coloured my understanding of the data which I later examined, or was corroborated by it, is always open to debate. That, it seems to me, is as it should be. However, this early working hypothesis was instrumental in moulding my methodological strategy.

CONDUCTING THE RESEARCH

It seemed clear to me that approaching the leaders and officials of such a public-relations-conscious social movement directly, for assistance with my research, was simply to invite public relations. Moreover, should they not approve of the undertaking, there was the possibility that I would even invite overt hostility. The Scientologists had been 'investigated' before. The Federal Food and Drug Administration in America, government inquiries in Australia and New Zealand that I knew of at that time, another inquiry whose report was expected imminently in Britain, and newspapers and magazines throughout the world had all investigated this movement. After reading some of this material later I came to understand better why the Scientologists reacted to public commentary and criticism and to 'investigation' with such aggression, and I even came to sympathise with them to some extent. At that time, however, I merely knew that they *did* react with virulence, and I wished to avoid it in my own case.

Hence, my research initially went little beyond reading the available material and visiting a London Scientology centre for the 'personality test' which the movement provided as a 'loss-leader', to draw further interest. At this stage I still proposed to incorporate Scientology into a broad survey of new religious movements and their social dynamics. At an opportune moment, however, I came across a recently published book by a former member of the movement (Vosper 1971). Having read it, I wrote to him and later met him to discuss the work on which I was engaged. The ex-Scientologist put me into contact with a number of acquaintances, most of whom, initially, had (either permanently or temporarily) ended their connection with Scientology. Many of them agreed to be interviewed by me and even to put me in contact with others who had knowledge of Scientology. A chain sample was developing, and I was beginning to feel that Scientology was both interesting enough, and the source of sufficient information, to make it the sole object of my doctoral research.

Those I interviewed also sometimes made available to me dusty collections of papers and literature. Occasionally in this material were further names and addresses to which I wrote inquiring whether the individual concerned would be willing to see me. Or a name would reappear through many old documents, and I would badger my informants for information about how I might contact the people in question. One informant made available a mailing list of a Scientology organisation, some years out of date, on which she had indicated those whom she believed no longer to be active Scientologists and who might therefore be willing to discuss their experiences with me. I prepared and despatched a questionnaire to a sample of the names, although not restricting myself to those indicated by my informant.

I did not ask myself until some time later whether I had any right to employ this list. The donor was aware of my intentions, and I fully intended to maintain the confidentiality of the respondents, yet it might be said that this list was an internal document of the movement and should not have been employed for this purpose without the permission of its officials. During the course of my research, I was to read many documents not meant for public consumption, and I believe the status of this mailing list differed little from other such material. I did not come by any of it dishonestly; hence I felt entitled to use it.

The questionnaire was not successful as a means of generating a random or even a representative sample of Scientologists. It was so far out of date that many of those sampled were no longer at the same address. A number of those to whom questionnaires were sent had only got on to the list as a result of buying a single book on Scientology and had had no further contact. Nevertheless, some completed questionnaires were returned, and some of my respondents subsequently indicated that they were willing to be interviewed. A grant was made available by the Social Science Research Council, which enabled me to travel around Britain conducting interviews, and later to visit the United States to conduct more and to examine documentary sources. The interviews took various forms. Whenever possible I tape-recorded my conversation with respondents. I began with a fairly well-formalised list of questions but gradually developed a looser, more flexible and open-ended style, talking round various themes of interest to me and allowing the respondent to converse at length on matters which he regarded as important. These interviews were conducted in locations as diverse as a London taxi-cab and a Japanese restaurant in Oakland, California. Some respondents were unwilling to be tape-recorded, and in these cases I sought to recall the content of the conversation as soon afterwards as I conveniently could.

Scientology provides a wide range of courses on its theories and methods, some acquaintance with which would, I believed, prove indispensable to my research. I proposed to secure some insight into this aspect of the movement by engaging in participant observation. Because I had left my name and address when taking the 'personality test' and had purchased books by mail from the organisation, my name had appeared on their current mailing list. In consequence I received several dozen circulars and letters, many of which encouraged me to visit the headquarters at Saint Hill Manor, East Grinstead, in order to take the introductory Communications Course.

One letter, dated 1 July 1971, for example, ended: 'Should you ever be near East Grinstead, come up and see us and have a look round. You will be welcome.' A further letter in July 1971 concluded: 'I hope you will take the first basic course in Scientology as soon as you can. This is the Communications Course which costs only £5 and the results are invaluable. It takes only three weeks to do.' The literature which accompanied such letters indicated no constraints upon who would be acceptable to take the course. I therefore concluded that it was open to the public at large and that I could in good conscience participate in it without revealing any more than that I was an interested outsider.

Early in 1972 I visited East Grinstead, registered for the Communications Course and arranged lodgings at a Scientology boarding house. This seemed an ideal opportunity to engage in participant observation on the movement. When I registered for the course and paid my fee I was shown a list of conditions to which I was asked to agree. Due to the character of my role and the circumstances in which this took place, I was unable to make any note of the nature of these conditions. I recall, however, that I had early decided that, while I did not feel covert participant observation to be unethical in this context, I was, nevertheless, not prepared to lie about my interest in Scientology. I was only prepared to represent it less than fully. Hence, I believe that the conditions were not such that my assent to them would have been a lie. Much later in the history of my relationship with this movement its officials claimed that, among other things, I had agreed to 'use knowledge gained from the course for Scientology purposes only'. A copy of a list containing conditions for course entry was sent to me. I now have no way of telling whether or not this was a duplicate of the list to which my assent was requested. My feeling is that this list and the one to which I gave my assent were *not* the same, but clearly this *could* be rationalisation.

Would it have been unethical behaviour to agree to such a list of conditions and then to break them? I do not believe there is a general answer to the question of whether or not certain kinds of behaviour are ethically impermissible in all situations. The ethics of social research involve a complex weighing of values in relation to particular situations. In *this* particular situation I feel that agreeing to constraints one did not intend to keep would have been morally reprehensible and that if such were the case the information required should have been secured some other way. It is important to note, however, that the facts of the case are not altogether clear on this occasion. My own view is that I did not agree to my conditions which I could not keep.

Having registered for the course I spent two days at Saint Hill Manor working on the materials, stapled in folders, which I would have to assimilate in order to complete it. I early felt uncomfortable in my role. Prior to this piece of fieldwork I had engaged in participant observation at services and meetings of various groups, but there I had been one of a (usually small) crowd. My presence signified nothing beyond an interest in what was taking place. On those occasions too I had felt uncomfortable when I was approached on a personal basis, when a group leader or speaker would stop for a few words of welcome to a new face among the regulars. Disguised or convert participant observation is easy when no participation beyond mere presence is required. When the interaction moves to a more personal basis and participation of a more active kind is necessitated, role-playing dilemmas present themselves.

How should one exhibit oneself? As an interested newcomer, seeking some transcendental commodity which this group or individual may be able to provide? Or as a disinterested observer, viewing this group or individual as one case of a general class and personally indifferent to, perhaps even sceptical of, the transcendental knowledge which is being offered? Good participant observation required a particular personality or discipline which I did not possess. Outside a 'mass' context I felt uncomfortable in my role. It felt like spying and a little dishonest. In general, I tried to shift the situation to an 'open' interaction context as quickly as possible. As early as was conveniently possible I generally conveyed that I was a sociologist, that I worked in a university and that, while I was interested in what my informant had to say, my *personal* interest was tempered and directed by wider *sociological* concerns.

To take that step in this situation would, however, have been self-defeating. I had come to Saint Hill Manor to learn how 'anyman' coming in off the street would be received, not how a visiting sociologist doing a thesis on Scientology would be treated. In some research situations such a distinction would have been of little importance. Everything I knew about Scientology suggested that in *this* instance it would make a good deal of difference.

At the Scientology lodging house the problem was equally difficult. The other residents with whom I dined and breakfasted were committed Scientologists and in a friendly way sought to draw me into their conversations. I found it difficult to participate without suggesting a commitment similar to their own, which I did not feel. Returning to the course material, I found as I progressed that I would shortly have to convey — either aloud or by my continued presence — assent to claims made by Ron Hubbard, the movement's founder, with which I could not agree and of which I could sometimes make little sense. I indicated my disagreement with some point in the course material to the instructor and thereby mobilised a series of remedies which Scientology has available to manage disagreement with the 'data'. I was asked to look up all the words in the contentious phrase in a dictionary to ensure that I understood them. When this did not help I was asked to make some visual configuration out of available bric-à-brac of my disagreement with the phrase. There is not space here to detail all the remedies that were applied. It became clear, however, that were I to proceed with the course I should finally have to convey some agreement with the statement in question. I felt this would have been dishonest and, more pragmatically, my discomfort in doing so would have been too great. I therefore quietly slipped away from Saint Hill Manor at a dinner break, rueing perhaps that I was not made of sterner stuff.

Later in 1972, I wrote for the first time to the movement's leaders, indicating that I was a sociologist engaged upon research into Scientology for a thesis. I acknowledged that previous studies of the movement had rarely been models of academic objectivity and that they had often resulted in bad publicity and occasionally in intolerant political action against the movement. I therefore suggested, with all the pretentiousness of a novice graduate student, that they consider the possibility that my own research might be

more advantageous than some of the earlier studies. I suggested three
reasons why this might be so:

(1) I pointed out that I was 'independent'. By this I meant that I had not
been commissioned by the state or by any interest group opposed to
Scientology. (I was at that time a student at Nuffield College, Oxford.)
Nor could I, I felt, be subjected to pressure by such groups.

(2) I pointed out that I was 'an academic' and did not therefore have to
produce a popular work. I did not have to aim to sensationalise in order
to achieve sales.

(3) I pointed out that, while I was independent, I was also a 'professional
sociologist' and had therefore to maintain standards of objectivity,
neutrality and ethics to which some other authors do not owe responsibility. I also believed that by providing an objective account of the
movement and its history I might be able to refute some of the more extreme claims directed at the movement by interests hostile to it. I stressed, however, that my work would not only involve rebuttals of critical
claims. I wrote: 'It would be wrong to suggest that my intention is simply to produce an eulogy of Scientology. Rather my aim is to produce a
balanced and reasoned appraisal and since I have no axe to grind I . . .
think that with your assistance this might be entirely possible.'

I offered to visit East Grinstead to discuss my research with officials of the
movement.

In mid 1972 I paid this visit to the headquarters and there discussed my
research with a member of its Guardian's Office. (This office is concerned
with the movement's external relations.) The official, an Assistant Guardian,
was clearly puzzled and concerned about my having spent two days on the
Communications Course and having then left in the middle of it. I attempted
to explain the reasons for my departure. He had also received various of the
questionnaires which I had sent to names on the list of Scientologists of
earlier years, and it was evident that he was suspicious of the fact that the
questionnaires seemed to be directed particularly towards apostates and
former members rather than towards current members. In subsequent
mailings of this questionnaire I modified some of the questions so that they
read less as if directed solely at apostates. The Assistant Guardian agreed to
provide me with materials of various kinds on the movement, although he
declined to give me any direct access to its archives. He also agreed to allow
me to interview some staff members and students at the headquarters and to
provide me with the names and addresses of people I might visit on a then
forthcoming research trip to the United States.

I entered into no obligations with this official about the nature of my
research. He insisted on laying certain 'ground rules', which were that he
would not give me blanket access to materials on Scientology and that he
would pursue legally any publication of 'advanced course' materials. Apart

from these stipulations he requested no undertakings from me as to the nature of my research, and none were offered. No promises of any kind were made.

EARLY PUBLICATIONS AND REACTIONS TO THEM

I had been formulating some of my early conclusions regarding Scientology in a paper in which I discussed this movement in the context of models of sectarianism that were currently available in the extant literature. The main drift of my discussion was to point to the inadequacy of the prevailing formulations of the concept of sect and to attempt to produce an argument for those dimensions which seemed to me still to be of utility, employing Scientology in illustration. After my discussions with the Assistant Guardian I sent to him a draft copy of this paper entitled 'The sectarianism of Scientology' (Wallis 1973a). He was altogether unenthusiastic about the paper, objecting to my use of the terms 'sectarianism' and 'totalitarianism' in the Scientology context, to aspects of my characterisation of the movement's founder, and to my account of the movement's development.

In retrospect, given the degree to which Scientology had in the past suffered from investigation by journalists and agencies of the state, it is not difficult to see why my own behaviour and writings should have led to considerable suspicion and some hostility on the part of the movement. I appeared to be behaving in ways reminiscent of earlier investigations of Scientology which had led to persecution of the movement. I had approached apostates and those who were hostile towards Scientology before I had approached the movement's leaders or those who were currently taught by the movement, without declaring my ulterior motive; and then, apparently, I had written a paper which its leaders viewed as hostile and which departed to a considerable extent from their own interpretations of the movement's reality.

It was shortly after the Scientology officials had commented unfavourably on my paper that a series of events occurred which led me to believe that I was the object of a campaign of harassment designed both to cause me inconvenience and to discredit me in the eyes of fellow sociologists. The events which transpired are recorded in detail elsewhere (Wallis 1973b). In brief, they involved the activities of a staff member of the Scientology organisation who visited my university (I had by then become a lecturer at the University of Stirling), presenting himself as a student wishing to undertake some study or research into Scottish religion. He asked to attend my classes and lectures and inquired whether I could put him up at my home for a few days! This naturally aroused my suspicion, and I shortly recalled having seen him in a staff member's uniform when I had taken the Communications Course at the Scientology headquarters. However, I took no action at this stage, not knowing precisely how to react. During his short stay in Stirling he made visits to my home in my absence and, unknown to me at that time, presented himself to students and others as a friend of mine in order to make inquiries concerning whether or not I was involved in the 'drug scene'. After a couple of days I confronted him with my knowledge of his background.

At this point he changed his story, claiming now to be a defector from Scientology, come to sell me information. I informed him that I was not buying information and gave him to understand that I believed his present story as little as his earlier one. While I checked up on his credentials he disappeared. I was subsequently able to discover the man's real name and observed that he was later listed in a Scientology publication as a graduate of one of the movement's many courses.

In the weeks following his visit a number of forged letters came to light, some of which were supposedly written by me. These letters, sent to my university employers, colleagues and others, implicated me in a variety of acts, from a homosexual love affair to spying for the drug squad. Because I had few enemies and because this attention followed so closely upon the receipt of my paper by the Scientology organisation, it did not seem too difficult to infer the source of these attempts to inconvenience me.

In fact some of the forged letters *were* a source of considerable inconvenience. One set of letters, containing homosexual declarations of love supposedly written by me, were sent to my university employers. They were received during a period in which disciplinary proceedings were being pursued against a number of students for allegedly disruptive activities during the visit by the Queen to the University. My own part in the ensuing debate had not endeared me to the University authorities, whose first action was to show the letters to the University's lawyer, present for the disciplinary hearings, to determine whether or not I had committed any offence against the University's regulations by writing such letters on official notepaper. I should add, however, that they readily accepted that the letters were forgeries and offered the services of the University solicitor to enable me to decide what was to be done about them. Since the police were not able to take any worthwhile steps in locating the culprit, I determined to publicise what had transpired.

Consequently I drafted another article in which I discussed my own experience and the experiences of several other writers on Scientology, who had suffered either from 'mysterious and unpleasant' happenings or from extensive litigation. Before publishing, I visited the movement's East Grinstead headquarters again in April 1973, where I had arranged through the official of the Guardian's Office to interview staff members and students. These interviews I tape-recorded, while a member of the Guardian's staff tape-recorded me conducting them. I was not surprised that a number of my interviewees were engaged upon courses concerned with public relations; meeting me was doubtless a useful practical exercise for them. I also had a lengthy conversation with the Assistant Guardian concerning the research. Towards the end of this conversation I broached the matter of the spy and the forged letters. The Assistant Guardian did not take this matter up, except to say that he knew nothing about it and would look into it.

I reminded him of this in a subsequent letter, but no admission of any knowledge of, or responsibility for, the events was ever made, and indeed such knowledge and responsibility were subsequently denied. I therefore went ahead with the publication of my article, bravely undertaken by Paul Barker, editor of *New Society* (Wallis 1973b). The Scientologists' response was to write to my funding body, the SSRC, complaining of my 'unethical' behaviour in writing this article and in the conduct of my research and threatening legal action. The SSRC acknowledged the Scientologists' letter but took no further steps, accepting my account of the preceding events. *New Society* also published a letter from a Scientology official disputing my account.

In September 1973 the Scientologists themselves published an article concerning my research in a widely distributed news-sheet which they produced (Spittell 1973). They quoted the Panel on Privacy and Behavioural Research (1967), established by the US President's Office of Science and Technology, whose preliminary report had stressed the doctrine of 'informed consent' as an ethical principle which should be adopted by researchers on human subjects. The Scientologists argued that I had not obtained *their* informed consent at the beginning of my study. They also argued that 'an allegedly authoritative paper on the nature of Scientology' (alleged only by the Scientologists, I might add) had been based 'on information gained solely from a few people openly hostile to the Church of Scientology'. They also claimed that my completed questionnaires were to go into a data bank and implied some sinister collection of information on my respondents' political leanings. Further allegations were: that I planned to write a popular book on Scientology; that I was conducting a 'campaign' against it; that I aspired 'to make a name and to make money out of sensationalising a non-selling subject'; that I had 'extracted information' under a 'pretence of guaranteed privacy'; that I had distorted the truth; and that I was conducting a 'trial by innuendo'.

Some of these allegations were not totally without foundation. I did hope to 'make a name' out of my study of Scientology, although with a professional rather than a lay audience, and I even hoped I might make the nominal, but nonetheless useful, royalties that academics usually make from their books. I had never intended to write a popular book, but I can now see the Scientologists' grounds for this claim. I had originally told them I was writing a *doctoral thesis* on Scientology, and I think they had perhaps not realised that doctoral theses are sometimes published, and indeed I had not thought seriously of this myself until my work was some way advanced.

On the issues of 'informed consent' and 'pretended privacy', it is true that I had not informed the *organisation* from the beginning that I was conducting the research, nor do I see why I should have done so, but I did always fully inform interview and questionnaire respondents of the character of my research. I also gave respondents a guarantee of confidentiality, i.e. an undertaking not to publish their names without their permission. This guarantee has been completely fulfilled. Contrary to the Scientologists' claim, many of my interviews were with individuals openly *favourable* to Scientology. None of my material was appropriate for data bank purposes. The only 'campaigning' or 'trial by innuendo' that I could be accused of conducting was my *New Society* article (Wallis 1973b), the cautious conclusions of which were, I believe, only what any man on the top of the Clapham omnibus would also have drawn. Finally there is the assertion that I 'distorted the truth'. I claim no privileged access to the truth; I believe all knowledge to be conjectural, and it is not impossible that some of my conjectures may prove to be false. 'Distortion' rather implies something stronger, however; it suggests that I recognise as true something other than what I wrote, or that my perceptions were in some way biased by an animus against the Scientologists. Of course, I dispute this. I have at times been irritated, even angered, by the Scientologists' behaviour, but I detect in myself no permanent hostility towards them. I would, indeed, feel impelled to defend them against legislative intolerance such as they had experienced in Australia, where in some states they were briefly banned.

I replied to the article which criticised my research, in a letter which reminded the Scientologists that they had often in the past complained of being allowed no right of reply to hostile articles. They kindly published my letter in their paper.

EMENDATIONS IN THE FINAL REPORT

The year following these events was spent in analysing and writing up my data. This work was completed in the summer of 1974, and my thesis was presented at the end of August. A publisher had exhibited some interest in the manuscript, and a contract for *The Road to Total Freedom: A Sociological Analysis of Scientology* (Wallis 1976) was signed a month or so before presentation of the thesis.

I had for some months thought that Scientology's treatment of its critics and commentators was largely directed at the suppression and censorship of works they construed as hostile to their interests. At first, therefore, I planned not to send them my manuscript, but the completion of my work led me to reflect on this matter. Suppose some of my 'facts' and interpretations were untrue and were a source of harm to the Scientologists. They surely had a right not to be publicised in a false light. It seemed to me that a sociologist owed his subjects an obligation not to cause them *undeserved* harm. There was, therefore, a major ethical dilemma here, a tension between the obligation to one's subjects and the possibility of censorship. I reasoned that, although Scientologists might sometimes act against commentators in ways that seemed malevolent, perhaps this was because they had been given no prior opportunity to comment. Were they not, after all, reasonable men?

Would they not recognise and respect my aspiration to objectivity, and therefore approach my work with an open-mindedness which they were unwilling to exhibit towards more sensationalising, journalistic or openly hostile works? I decided to send them my manuscript. I should add, however, that this action was not motivated solely by altruism. I thought the manuscript quite a good one and wanted to see it published. I also wanted to avoid lengthy and astronomically expensive litigation, which I could ill afford. My contract with the publisher stipulated that, in the event of a libel action which we lost, I would be responsible for any costs and damages. Perhaps such an action could be avoided by letting the movement's leaders see my manuscript, comment upon it, and provide any further evidence which would support their interpretation. For both ethical and pragmatic reasons it seemed sensible to allow them an opportunity to comment on the work before it appeared in print.

Early in September 1974 I sent them the manuscript. Later that month I met with an official of the Scientology organisation in London, and we discussed in an amicable way the contentious issues which it posed. He provided me with a preliminary list of points which had emerged from his reading of the thesis. These six pages I found heartening. My judgement was vindicated. We could begin to discuss the contentious points and consider the evidence. Where my view was changed, I would modify the manuscript. Where it remained unchanged, we could perhaps agree to differ.

I examined the manuscript in the light of these comments, and some of them seemed to me to contain reasonable foundations. For example, I strengthened in various places the sense that some things which had originally read as facts were only various people's *interpretations* of the facts. At one point I changed a statement that people had done something because of Hubbard's authoritarianism to read that they had done it because of 'what some of them viewed as his . . . authoritarianism'. I modified some descriptions which seemed to read more evaluatively than I could justify; at one point, for example, I had claimed that Hubbard was 'obsessed' by the threat of communism, and I now changed this to read that he was 'exercised' by communism. I added further commentary on Scientology's religious practices and contemporary social-reform activities, which I had possibly underemphasised in my original version. I also deleted a section in which I had drawn parallels between Scientology and the Nazi party; while I continued to believe that these parallels were sociologically viable, they were not crucial to my discussion, and I felt that they both lent themselves to sensationalistic interpretation and were *unnecessarily* offensive to ordinary Scientologists. In all I made some twenty-seven changes (the exact number depending on how one defines a change).

Early in November the Scientology organisation sent me a more detailed commentary which comprised some 12,000 words. I again turned to the manuscript. This time I found little in my text which I thought I had reason to change. However, I felt the Scientologists' disagreements with my interpretations should be known. I therefore incorporated a number of foot-notes setting out their arguments, later transposed into the text, to enable the reader to compare them with my own. My emendations to the manuscript now numbered around forty-six.

I also had what seemed to me to be a bright idea. What the Scientologists wanted, I reasoned, was for their version of events to be known. Therefore why should we not let them have some right of reply. Having discussed the idea with my publishers I wrote to the Scientologists early in November 1974, sending my latest revisions and offering to include in the book a 5,000-word commentary or reply to the book by them, in return for an undertaking to refrain from litigation in connection with its publication. They replied that they noted my proposal and, 'provided there is no legal barrier and subject to the determination of certain fundamental issues which will result in a partial rewrite', they were prepared to give it favourable consideration. They also sent a further thirty-eight pages of comments and 148 items of supporting documentation. I found the talk of a 'partial rewrite' slightly ominous but again turned to the manuscript. I found only a few minor points which I could, in good conscience, amend. Once again, however, I inserted a number of additional sentences stating the Scientologists' arguments. I had now made eighty modifications.

I sent these to the organisation and pointed out that 'If you have further specific commentary and corrections I will be glad to look at these, but there has to be some limit to the length of time this can drag on.' The Scientologists' reply contained the following specification of what they had in mind: 'Before we can agree to your proposals all libelous [sic] statements will be corrected, not by footnotes.'

I now suspected that the organisation was in fact determined to see only one interpretation of the matters discussed in my book prevail. A right of reply was not sufficient. The law of libel was to be invoked as a weapon in an attempt to censor my book into a form which rendered it compatible with the Scientologists' views. I naturally protested, to the effect that their allegation that certain passages were libellous did not make them so. At this point the Scientologists took the step of submitting the manuscript, with the emendations already agreed upon, to an eminent Queen's Counsel who had considerable experience in libel cases and was of known liberal sympathies. This move was a singularly astute one. Should the lawyer construe the items which they pointed out to him, and complained of, as libellous, my publisher and I would not have been able to claim that this was an attempt to suppress freedom of speech, when so notable a civil rights campaigner had found the passages of which they complained to be defamatory.

In the event, however, only one substantial section was held to be defamatory in the Opinion rendered by the barrister, of which the Scientologists sent me a copy. This section comprised some eight pages in which instances of the mysterious and unpleasant things which had not infrequently occurred to commentators on Scientology were discussed. In providing an account of these phenomena I offered an interpretation which, while certainly a plausible, and conceivably a true, explanation for what had transpired, was not in the nature of the case provable. The passages involved were therefore *prima facie* libellous in content. The circumstances involved in the events in question were often obscure in some respects. The responsibility for their occurrence was always a matter of controversy. Hence, while I could satisfy myself that the bulk of the cases cited indicated a particular explanation, it appeared to be a distinct possibility that I would not convince a libel jury that all of the cases could thus be accounted for. Moreover, it seemed to me that my responsibilities were more extensive than merely remaining within the bounds of the law. Whatever my personal feelings about Scientology and its organisations, I owed a responsibility as a sociologist towards the subjects of my research. Scientology is viewed with hostility in some quarters, and my responsibility extended to ensuring that I did not impute to the movement and its following behaviour for which adequate evidence was unavailable and which might rouse further hostility towards the movement. At the same time, however, I owed a responsibility to the SSRC as grantors of my research funds, my colleagues and my readers, not to submit to censorship in the sense of suppressing adequately supported evidence concerning the subjects of my research.

The matter was ultimately resolved in the following manner. Two cases which I felt lacked sufficient substantiation were deleted. In two other instances sentences were included which incorporated statements by the organisation's representatives bearing on the events or persons involved. Throughout the section, any statements attributing responsibility for the events, which I had made in explanation, were removed. Otherwise the pages remained unchanged. The changes which I made, and which after further discussion were agreed by the Scientology organisation, seemed a reasonable and honourable compromise to both parties.

With these changes, negotiations between myself and the Scientologists were all but concluded. A comment on my book was commissioned by them from a sociologist who was also a practising Scientologist. This comment the publishers and I happily incorporated into the book as an appendix. An agreement was drawn up between the Church of Scientology, the publishers and myself specifying that the Church of Scientology, its officials and its members would refrain from litigation connected with the publication of the book, in consideration of the modifications I had made – ultimately totalling well over 100 – and further specifying the inclusion of the commissioned Scientology comment as an appendix.

Honour had been preserved on all sides, and a legal action – which none of the parties concerned seemed eager should take place – had been averted. My book would appear without mutilation or fear of legal consequences (Wallis 1976), and the Scientologists could confound their enemies by exhibiting our final amicable resolution of the controversy as evidence of their reasonableness and good faith.

CONCLUSIONS

The course of this research project appeared to undergo a particular moral career (Goffman 1968, p. 24). In this, both researcher and researched sought not only to define the behaviour of the other, but also to locate the other within a conceptual framework and theoretical schema, thereby rendering the other party's behaviour understandable and predictable and providing guidelines for reacting to it.

Both parties began with a certain suspicion of the other, based on stereotypes which were culturally available. This researcher had much in common with other 'researchers' who turned out to be agents of hostile groups (e.g. psychiatrists, the state, the mass media). The researched had features in common with totalitarian groups which do not concede the possibility of a non-member's having any valid view on their structure or behaviour. The researcher's behaviour, motivated by what he saw as sensible caution, was interpreted by the researched as underhandedness, prevarication or spying. Their reaction, whatever its motivation, was construed by the researcher as harassment and an attempt to limit investigation or public discussion of their affairs. Hence, relations between researcher and researched escalated to a point of open hostility.

Actions taken to correct the stereotype by one side were viewed as public relations exercises by the other. However, if that is as true for me as it is for them, what validity can the final work claim to have? My answer to this, I think, has to be that the question cannot be settled in the abstract. It is always possible for someone else to conduct research on Scientology and to come to different conclusions. At such a time, of course, evidence can be compared and weighed again where necessary. I do not claim absolute objectivity because to me this seems an ideal to which we can only try to approximate; I rather claim to have attempted to be objective. I am sure that there are occasions upon which objectivity has eluded me. I note, for example, a recent paper in which I did not, until it was too late to amend it before publication, find it amiss or even odd to refer to Scientology ministers as wearing 'dog-collars' (Wallis 1975a). Why did I use that term? Of course, I meant 'clerical collars', but I must have read and reread the paper a dozen times over the course of more than a year before this struck me as a curious vulgarity. Did this 'amnesia' display a disrespect for ministers of religion in general or Scientology ministers in particular? Without a depth analysis of the researcher I will probably never know.

The central conclusion to be drawn from this account is that the sociologist's interaction with his subjects forms a part of, and takes place in the context of, the overall interaction between those subjects and the wider society. He may be seen as a potential legitimator and defender of their public image, or as a threat to it. Those groups which are, or have been, in conflict with agencies of the wider society are likely to view a potential threat to their public image with hostility. If they are wealthy and well organised, they have available a powerful weapon with which to defend themselves against the publication of commentary of which they disapprove. The law of libel provides an important protection of individual and corporate character. Its remedies are, however, particularly costly for both plaintiff and defendant. Hence the threat of invoking such remedies is a weighty sanction mobilisable by the wealthy to censor or suppress accounts of themselves which they view as unflattering. As a spokesman for the Scientologists once said: 'Whatever else we may have been called, no-one has ever accused us of being poor.'

The law of libel is an arcane mystery to the layman and a severe constraint – although not perhaps for that reason an unwarranted constraint – on the author of accounts of contemporary individuals and groups. It poses the problem of the relationship between sociological evidence and legal proof. As far as I understand it, the English law of libel requires 'that he who asserts must prove, and the proof required is proof up to the hilt, and the author will fail if he can show only that the defamatory statement was true on the balance of probability based on the evidence before him' (Kimber 1972, p. 74). Yet, of course, this is precisely the kind of evidential circumstance with which the sociologist is typically faced. In my analysis of the Scientology material I took every precaution that I thought possible. Interview statements were weighed for the possible bias of the informant, and the more extreme and unlikely statements were rejected. Information from one interview was checked against information from other interviews and against documentary sources. Documents for external publication were weighed against documents for purely internal circulation and where possible against documents from independent sources (e.g. court records). All of this clearly involved selection on two bases: a theory or model of the nature of the information source, and the purpose for which the material was produced. This kind of theoretically based weighing and sifting of evidence is precisely the kind of intuitive skill that professional training in research is designed to inculcate. It is unlikely in most research situations, even under the most auspicious circumstances, to provide 'proof up to the hilt'.

There were two other problems in relation to the law of libel. First, some features of the background of Scientology have been obscured by its officials whose wish it is that only their own version of certain affairs will become public knowledge. Information on such matters was hard to come by, and my account necessarily relied on a degree of more or less indirect inference. Secondly, the presentation of evidence in court in defending a libel action might require infringing upon the anonymity of respondents. Information was provided by many respondents on the understanding that their names would not be revealed. Probably most of these would have been loath to risk any repercussions by testifying in court to what they told me in private. Sometimes they still had friends or relatives in Scientology. Sometimes they were themselves members and wished to remain so, while nonetheless having reservations about some of its practices. Sometimes the

individuals concerned had found their break with Scientology traumatic or
had begun entirely new lives, and in either case would not have wished to
draw attention to themselves in connection with this movement. Hence while
my material might be more or less adequate sociologically, there was reason
to suspect that it might not be adequate to proving my comments on the
movement 'up to the hilt' in every instance.

The problems of a potential libel action do not lie simply in the possibility
of losing such an action. My publishers were insured against libel. A require-
ment of such an insurance policy is that the author undertakes to indemnify
the publisher in the event of losses' being sustained from a libel claim. The
author typically has no resources adequate to defending, or indemnifying
the publisher against, a libel action. Hence if the publishers do not wish to
renounce the benefits of their insurance policy, they must be responsive to
the wishes of the insurers. A major interest of the insurer must inevitably be
that of minimising costs to his company. This interest may often best be
secured by achieving an early apology and settlement in favour of the alleged libel victim and, if necessary, the withdrawal of the offending book,
rather than undertaking to support the cost of defending the action, *even*
when there is a good chance of winning (Kimber 1972). For even when an
award of costs is made, the successful defendant rarely recovers all his expenses. Libel cases are notoriously expensive. Juries are liable to be swayed
by a variety of unpredictable circumstances, and the award of damages is
subject to so many imponderables as often to defeat prediction.

Hence the weight of pressure in the case of a study such as my own is
towards modifying and emasculating the final work, i.e. towards censorship.
Publishers and insurers have a common interest in minimising legal conflict
and therefore in eliminating controversial material; the Scientologists
similarly have an interest in eliminating controversial material. Hence at this
point they share an interest with the publishers and insurers which may conflict with the interest of the author. Fortunately, as a result of extensive
negotiation and some compromise by the parties concerned, in the present
case the matter was finally resolved without either litigation or censorship.[2]

Howard Becker (1964) pointed out some years ago, that 'A study that
purports to deal with social structure ... inevitably will reveal that the
organisation or community is not all it claims to be, not all it would like to
be able to feel itself to be. A good study, therefore will make somebody
angry.' The sociologist who undertakes to study the social structure and
dynamics of powerful groups firmly committed to some particular view of
themselves must expect his revelations to result in hostility and the mobilisation of strategies to censor or even prohibit the publication of his work. He
is likely to be drawn into a power struggle over which versions of the
movement's history, morphology and behaviour are to become publicly
available, and he may indeed be drawn into open conflict with his research
subjects. While in the past sociologists have, rightly in my view, displayed
concern over the dangers of harming the interests of powerless groups which

they have chosen to study, they should not altogether forget the problems of the relatively powerless sociologist faced with the threat of censorship.[3]

NOTES

1 I am grateful to the SSRC for a grant in support of the research discussed in this chapter.
2 The notion of 'censorship' is not an easy one to explicate, and I have no space here to explore its manifold possibilities. I have used the term in what seems to me a fairly 'commonsense' manner, to indicate some form of constraint upon what an author may say which *runs contrary to his wishes and/or his conscience*. My satisfaction with the outcome in this case arises from the fact that none of the changes made to my book violated either my methodological criteria or my conscience. It may always be said, of course, and indeed almost certainly *will* be said by those who would have wished me to take a more hostile stance *vis-à-vis* Scientology, that this is because my conscience was more malleable than their own would have been under similar circumstances. My own feeling is that my modifications were made precisely in virtue of the fact that in the light of subsequent discussions I could not in good conscience publish material or interpretations of a controversial and potentially damaging character for which I lacked sufficient evidence. Pre-'censorship', or self-'censorship', in the sense of allowing oneself to be persuaded that certain things should not be said, was of course extensive. But this seems to me a matter for neither apology nor self-recrimination. The exercise of selection is a fundamental component of any scientific or scholarly enterprise. The pursuit of objectivity does not entail that moral criteria should not guide and inform the selection that takes place. They clearly do influence the topics which sociologists study and the aspects of those topics which they choose to discuss, and hence they are inherently involved in both what the sociologist says and what he leaves unsaid. There is no necessary conflict between objectivity and responsibility. An aspiration to objectivity does not require one to say *everything*; rather it requires that as far as possible everything one *does* say should be available to criticism and refutation. Objectivity requires that acceptance of an account does not *depend* upon prior acceptance of a particular set of moral assumptions. There are, however, no simple means of deciding how well an author approximates the ideal of objectivity. The matter is always open to dispute, and this – if I may now venture an explicit value-judgement – appears to me both rational and healthy.
3 It should be mentioned that this chapter was a source of considerable anxiety to the publishers of this volume. They believed that it too contained potentially libellous matter and sought to secure radical changes in content, failing which they subtly suggested that this chapter should not be allowed to endanger the whole volume and could perhaps be omitted entirely. The editors resisted these blandishments, and the publishers were finally convinced, after several months' delay, that the Scientologists had no intention of suing a piece in which my research was exhibited as more art than science. Indeed, a Scientology spokesman admitted that in his view this was the best piece I had written about Scientology – and it is not hard to see why.

Appendix: A Scientologist's Comment

DAVID GAIMAN, *Church of Scientology*

I believe that *The Moral Career of a Research Project* is a fairly factual account of Roy Wallis's experiences as a sociological researcher into Scientology and a statement of his ethical position from his viewpoint. I have been invited to comment on this chapter and do so as a layman and a member of the Church of Scientology. There was a temptation to pass the task to a better qualified member of the Church of Scientology – a sociologist or noted academic. I did not do so for two reasons: I had been in contact with Wallis from the receipt of his first letter, and I wanted to make some observations on the sociologist from the position of the 'victim'.

The sociologist plays a role in which he sees himself as the social scientist inquiring into various social phenomena occurring within the society; this is, in my submission, not the case. Further, I submit that the value of this social science in terms of exchange with society is limited or perhaps non-existent, for too often the conclusions are anything but scientific, being opinions presented as scientific findings. An analogy is the difference between a medical diagnosis, based on symptoms, and a psychiatric diagnosis by an institutional psychiatrist, based on opinion. For the institutional psychiatrist to make his diagnosis stick it is necessary that he assume or be granted authority, that there be a passive audience who will concur with his diagnosis, and that there be a minority (in this case the patient) whose disagreement or protest or acceptance of his classification is used to confirm that diagnosis. There is no argument with a diagnosis of pneumonia or a fractured bone; the condition exists. But there are apparently as many definitions of schizophrenia or manic depression as there are psychiatrists. In the present case, Wallis, the sociologist, came with formulated opinions which coloured his approach and what he looked into and what he disgarded. I suggest that the reader would be misled to treat his work as anything other than Scientology as viewed by Wallis.

Wallis's initial approach to a Scientology organisation as a sociologist investigating the movement followed very extensive conversations with apostates and enrolment on a Scientology course. I could not understand at that time, and still do not understand, the ethics of his failing to declare this to me in his initial approach. One does not have to lie to mislead; a half-truth will do. Indeed, it was not admitted until put directly to him during his first visit to my office.

Wallis deals with events which he has alleged occurred to him prior to April 73. An account of these was published in *New Society* (Wallis 1973b), where the allegations were couched in legally careful terms. It is my view that for Scientology to have taken any other action than making it clear that we had no knowledge nor evidence of the allegations Wallis made, would have put us in the position of issuing a denial to the question: 'Have you ceased beating your wife?'

Wallis states that he detects in himself no permanent hostility to Scientologists; the veracity of this statement is best determined by the reader. I detect in myself no permanent hostility towards sociologists or institutional psychiatrists but I find both subjects authoritarian, unscientific and pretentious. This view colours anything I write on either subject.

In the matter of the complaint to the SSRC, I would make two points. Firstly, I asked for satisfaction and stated that if it was not available then the matter would be taken to a more public place. This was done by a publication in our journal, Freedom (Spittell 1973); there was no threat of legal action. Secondly, I studied the terms of the funding grants by the SSRC, and from my reading it became quite clear that data gathered under grant from the SSRC are subject to the condition that they may be used for programing into the SSRC's computerised data bank (I have in mind the completed questionnaires). This raised a privacy issue to which neither Wallis nor the SSRC has yet replied. If there is a possibility of a question-naire's being programed into a computer, the respondent surely has the right to know before determining whether he wishes to answer the questionnaire. It also tends to torpedo the undertaking of confidentiality given by the originator of the questionnaire. It is my opinion that sometime prior to September 1974, perhaps as a result of self-inspection or perhaps because we allowed Wallis a right of reply to our criticisms of him in our journal, Wallis became more aware of his ethical position and his responsibilities to his subject.

Much has been made of the laws of libel and the problems facing the researcher. I would mention the laws of libel in this country and the problem facing the defamed. One goes into a libel court knowing that as plaintiff one is to be 'put on trial' by the defendant's counsel. It is also to be expected that the emotional climate of any case will be determined to some degree by yesterday's headlines. Moreover, a publisher sometimes may feel that the publicity resulting from a legal action justifies the finan-cial risks involved. I am not suggesting that this is the case in regard to Wallis's publishers. It is perhaps a subject for some new sociological work, that in this case all parties emerged relatively unscathed and unbowed.

For my part, the entire exercise is of very little consequence, for the researcher was presented with a social movement of phenomenal growth and increasing im-pingement upon society in areas of social reform, yet he chose to paint, in dark tones, a small square in the lower left-hand corner of the canvas.

Epilogue

COLIN BELL and HOWARD NEWBY

When we began the task of compiling this book, although we were convinced of the necessity and validity of such an exercise we were also aware of two principal dangers to our original conception. One was the basis of selection of our contributors; we had originally envisaged a selection as wide as P. Hammond's in *Sociologists at Work* (1964), but the economic realities of the publishing industry during a period of hyperinflation so restricted the size of the book that our selection was forced to become more arbitrary than we wished. Our second concern was to prevent the accounts presented by our contributors (including ourselves) from sliding into self-indulgence and self-justification. In the event, neither of these problems has caused us anything like as much trouble as the British libel laws (although it must be left to the reader to judge how successfully we have overcome the problems).

In what seems in retrospect to be an incredibly naive and other-worldly manner, we hardly considered, let alone discussed, the threat which the British libel laws presented to a book of this kind. While we agonised over whether, for example, these accounts would merely replace one set of methodological formulae with another set, more disingenuous but equally selective, we remained blissfully oblivious of the real nature of the problems which lay ahead. Academics – particularly in a subject like sociology, which lacks any widespread paradigmatic consensus – come to accept or indeed welcome debate, even though it may often be tinged with acrimony; and they are rightly suspicious of the suppression of any evidence which would be relevant to such arguments. Such considerations, however, count for little in the labrynthine complexities of the current libel laws. 'Truth', for example, is not a concept which carries any weight in the current libel lexicon; if published truth is littered with an intent to defame it becomes libellous. The law of libel is now so restrictive that we were advised by one leading academic authority on the subject that any litigant who cares to pursue a case into the courts is almost guaranteed success; the only doubtful issue relates to the size of damages. As David Caute has remarked: 'Our own wretched condition is both to know less and to be able to report less than we know; to be forced, whenever the participants are alive and liable to litigate, to resort to pallid circumlocutions and stock formulas, erasing the real figures from print' (1976, p. 683).

In the Introduction we deliberately refused to make prescriptive statements about how sociologists should go about their work – yet we now discover that the law will do this for us. We do not, of course, want to make the case that sociologists or anybody else should be above the law; nor do we wish to deny that the freedom to publish must, like all freedoms, be subject to certain limitations. Equally, however, a vital component of freedom in a democratic society is, to use I. L. Horowitz's (1970) phrase, 'the right to know', and it is quite apparent that the libel laws currently curtail this right to an extent which to us seems quite unjustified. This, of course, is hardly news to investigative journalists (with whom, since at least the days of Robert Park, some sociologists have retained an affinity); to them it is a commonplace that Woodward and Bernstein could not have revealed as much as they did if they had been forced to operate within the constraints set by the British libel laws. Because, however, the focus of sociological research in Britain has hitherto been directed away from the centres of power in British society, the problems of libel have only rarely been encountered. Instead a good deal of effort has been expended on drafting a code of conduct which regulates the relationship between sociologists and their generally powerless 'objects of study'. Both the British and American Sociological Associations have done just that, and we do not dispute for a moment that it is necessary. However, if British sociologists are to direct more research effort towards the powerful, they should be more aware of what they are letting themselves in for; we have seen in recent years that the writ is now a standard weapon used to suppress knowledge. The implications of this for sociologists require far wider discussion, if only because to be forewarned is to be forearmed.

Producing this book has at least made us a little wiser. What these essays have forcibly brought home to us is that the shape of the sociological product is not just an issue of epistemology, nor even, in H. S. Becker's sense (1964), the product of collective action; it is also moulded by the risk of a writ. As a consequence, our objectives as stated in the Introduction – of providing the materials on which could be based a descriptive methodology – have suffered considerable setbacks and distortion. Moreover, these distortions are fairly difficult for the outsider to detect – so much so that we rather whimsically considered going to press with blank spaces, like some sociological *Rhodesian Herald*, in order to indicate how much had been removed. Sadly, it has proved impossible to publish accounts that are completely forthcoming about how the research was carried out. We now realise that it is not only the objects of study who need protecting from 'sociological snoopers'; there are occasions when sociologists also require protection from harassment by powerful sponsors and gatekeepers who may conspire to frustrate legitimate academic objectives. The current laws are so restrictive, and thus lawyers are so cautious, that publishers – for what we recognise are good commercial reasons – are likely to kill a book stone dead at the slightest whiff of libel. This particularly applies to books for the academic market. A book like this one does not sell many copies, and nobody, not even the publishers (and certainly not the editors and contributors), is going to make much money out of it. In fact, as we have discovered, legal opinion costs more than a single contributor will make for writing the piece in the first place. So unless authors are rich or stupid or stubborn they do not take the risk – and unless they *are* Woodward and Bernstein, with the prospect of huge sales, neither does a publisher.

So one or two accounts are rather anodyne. We apologise to our readers; there were and are even better stories to tell than some of these found in this book. In one case we have lost a complete chapter, and it is not even clear to us that we can safely discuss it or the reasons for its removal. However, we would like it to be known that it proved to be impossible to describe the behaviour of some of the institutionally powerful within British sociology – even though the behaviour was so adequately documented that even we would, under other circumstances, have risked going to court – because the accusation that the piece was malicious in intent would have been enormously difficult to refute. As it is, a piece of research, published by a very responsible university press, is not reported here. So yet another empirical monograph has appeared whose readers can frankly have no real perception of why the research is presented in the way in which it is. Furthermore, the actions of those involved are very good data about the institution which was studied and therefore add to the empirical findings – yet we cannot tell you about these findings, the parties involved or what the issues are. We do not wish to maintain that there can ever be only one true account of what occurs; but where certain events do not figure in these accounts, yet all involved agree that they occurred, then there is cause for concern.

Where this agreement is absent the preferred alternative is to resort to publishing alternative accounts, e.g. the Comment by David Gaiman, from the Church of Scientology, on Roy Wallis's chapter. The publication of Colin Bell's chapter on the Banbury restudy, however, presented more of a problem, for, as the Editorial Note which follows that chapter makes clear, we were faced with demands for up to three alternative accounts. There is no intrinsic objection to this whatsoever, but the current situation in academic publishing is such that it does not seem possible to publish such a series of accounts which would simultaneously allow the book to be a viable commercial proposition. This implies that, if the suggestion which we made in the Introduction is taken up and more accounts of sociological research such as the ones in this book are made available, then a less formal means of dissemination may be more appropriate than a commercially published book. In any case, perhaps this Epilogue will alert any prospective editors to the problems which they are likely to face.

Perhaps, on the other hand, libel may be the least of their worries. The chapter in this book by Stan Cohen and Laurie Taylor has had a number of sentences deleted at the publisher's request. The proper epilogue to their chapter, however, is a report in the *Guardian* of 8 October 1976. This refers to a Home Office ban on Professor Taylor, preventing him from entering borstals or remand centres in order to conduct interviews for a BBC documentary on delinquency: 'The reason for the ban', the report continues, 'was a book he wrote several years ago about how long-term prisoners coped psychologically with their years inside. "I thought it was a mild psychological work", he said, "but I was told I had contravened the Official Secrets Act Section II...".'

At times like this it seems tempting to carry on publishing the sanitised appendices that we are so accustomed to finding at the end of empirical monographs, and so to perpetuate the myths about doing sociological research which threaten to distort its teaching and development. This situation is obviously far from satisfactory. However, the reasons for this Epilogue are clear. You have in this volume all the news that fits the British libel laws and the Official Secrets Act – and no more. But more did go on and does go on – only we are not allowed to tell you about it. Why don't you protest too?

Notes on Contributors

MAXWELL ATKINSON graduated with a BA in Social Theory and Institutions from the University of Reading in 1965 and a PhD in Sociology from the University of Essex in 1974. He has held research positions at the Home Office Research Unit and the University of Essex and has taught sociology at the Universities of Lancaster and of Manchester. He is author of a number of articles on suicide, social isolation, deviance and the elderly, and of *Suicide and the Social Organization of Sudden Death* (1977). Currently he is Senior Research Fellow at the Centre for Socio-legal Studies, Oxford, and a Research Fellow of Wolfson College.

COLIN BELL, born in 1942 in London, attended a local grammar school and is a graduate of the Universities of Keele and of Wales. Currently Professor of Sociology at the University of New South Wales, he was previously Reader and Chairman of the Department of Sociology at the University of Essex. He is author of *Middle Class Families* (1968); co-author of *The Disruption of Community Life* (1969), with Peter Abell and Patrick Doreian, of *Community Studies* (1972), with Howard Newby, and of *Power, Persistence and Change: A Second Study of Banbury* (1975), with Margaret Stacey, Eric Batstone and Anne Murcott; and co-editor of *The Sociology of Community* (1974), with Howard Newby. He has published papers on the family, kinship, methodology and social stratification. For the past few years he has been engaged in research into the sociology of British agriculture.

STANLEY COHEN is Professor of Sociology at the University of Essex. He has carried out research and written on the sociology of deviance, youth culture, prisons, mass media and social work. His main publications include: *Images of Deviance* (1971); *Folk Devils and Moral Panics* (1972); with Laurie Taylor, *Psychological Survival: The Experience of Long-Term Imprisonment* (1973) and *Escape Attempts: The Sociology of Resistance to Everyday Life* (1976); and with Jock Young, *The Manufacture of News: Deviance, Social Problems and the Mass Media* (1973).

ROBERT MOORE is Reader in Sociology at the University of Aberdeen, and was previously Lecturer at the University of Durham and Research Associate at the University of Birmingham. His publications include: *Race, Community and Conflict* (1967), with John Rex; *Pitmen, Preachers and Politics* (1974); *Racism and Black Resistance in Britain* (1975a); and *Slamming the Door: The Administration of Immigration Control* (1975b), with Tina Wallace. He is currently working on the social impact of migrant workers in the oil industry in the north-east of Scotland.

HOWARD NEWBY is Senior Lecturer in Sociology at the University of Essex. He is author of a number of articles on various aspects of farmers, farm workers and rural communities. In addition to his book on farm workers, *The Deferential Worker* (1977), he is co-author, with Colin Bell, of *Community Studies* (1972) and co-editor, with Colin Bell, of *The Sociology of Community* (1974), he is currently carrying out research on large-scale farmers in East Anglia.

R. E. PAHL is Professor of Sociology at the University of Kent at Canterbury, where he is also Director of the Centre for Research in the Social Sciences. His empirical research in urban sociology has been published in *Urbs in Rure* (1965) and *Whose City?* (1976). Other research on managers in industry has been published jointly with J. M. Pahl in *Managers and Their Wives* (1971); and work on directors in industry has been published jointly with J. T. Winkler (1974) in *Elites and Power in British Society*, edited by P. Stanworth and A. Giddens. Professor Pahl is a member of the Sociology Committee of the Social Science Research Council, and is President of the Research Committee on the Sociology of Urban and Regional Development of the International Sociological Association.

LAURIE TAYLOR graduated in Psychology from the University of London and completed postgraduate studies in Sociology at the University of Leicester. His principal publications include: *Deviance and Society* (1971); *Psychological Survival: The Experience of Long-Term Imprisonment* (1972) and *Escape Attempts: The Theory and Practice of Resistance to Everyday Life* (1976), both with Stanley Cohen; and *Crime, Deviance and Socio-Legal Control* (1973), with Roland Robertson. At present he is Professor and Head of the Department of Sociology at the University of York.

ROY WALLIS was born in 1945 in London, where he subsequently lived and received his education. After an inauspicious grammar school career he left school at seventeen to become an office boy, then pump attendant, barman, factory hand, etc. Tiring of honest toil he became a student at the University of Essex, where he graduated in 1970 with a First Class Honours Degree in Sociology. After a period of post-graduate research at Nuffield College, Oxford, he was awarded his PhD in 1974. He has been Lecturer in Sociology at Stirling University since 1972, and in 1976 was Morris Ginsberg Fellow at the London School of Economics. He is author of *The Road to Total Freedom: A Sociological Analysis of Scientology* (1976) and editor of *Sectarianism: Analyses of Religious and Non-religious Sects* (1975b).

References

Abell, P., Bell, C. R. and Doreian, P. (1969), *The Disruption of Community Life* (London: HMSO).

Atkinson, J. M. (1968), 'On the sociology of suicide', *Sociological Review*, vol. 16, pp. 83–92.

Atkinson, J. M. (1969), 'Suicide and the student', *Universities Quarterly*, vol. 23, pp. 213–24.

Atkinson, J. M. (1970), 'Social isolation and communication in old age' (The Post Office, mimeo).

Atkinson, J. M. (1971a), 'Social isolation, class and social mobility in old age', *Population et Famille*, vol. 23–4 pp. 183–200.

Atkinson, J. M. (1971b), 'The Samaritans and the elderly: some problems in communication between a suicide prevention scheme and a group with a high suicide rate', *Social Science and Medicine*, vol. 5, pp. 483–90.

Atkinson, J. M. (1971c), 'Societal reactions to deviance: the role of coroners' definitions', in Cohen (1971), pp. 165–91.

Atkinson, J. M. (1973a), 'Patterns of face to face communication of the elderly', *Zeitschrift fur Gerontologie*, vol. 6, pp. 251–64.

Atkinson, J. M. (1973b and 1977), 'Suicide and the social organization of sudden death', unpublished PhD thesis (University of Essex); to be published under the same title (London: Collier Macmillan).

Atkinson, J. M. (1974a), 'Versions of deviance', *Sociological Review*, vol. 22, pp. 616–25.

Atkinson, J. M. (1974b), 'Community reactions to deviance', unpublished report on Social Science Research Council Grant HR 149/1 (London: SSRC, mimeo).

Baldamus, W. (1972), 'The role of discoveries in social science', in T. Shanin (ed.), *The Rules of the Game* (London: Tavistock), pp. 276–302.

Barry, B. (1966), 'The roots of social injustice', *Oxford Review* (Michaelmas), pp. 33–46.

Batstone, E. V. (1975), 'Deference and the ethos of small town capitalism', in M. Bulmer (ed.) (1975), *Working Class Images of Society* (London: Routledge and Kegan Paul), pp. 116–30.

Becker, H. S. (1964), 'Problems in the publication of field studies', in Vidich, Bensman and Stein (1964).

Becker, H. S. (1967), 'Whose side are we on?', *Social Problems*, vol. 14 (Winter), pp. 239–47.

Becker, H. S. (1974), 'Art as collective action', *American Sociological Review*, vol. 39, pp. 767–76.

Bell, C. R. (1968), *Middle Class Families* (London: Routledge & Kegan Paul).

Bell, C. R. (1969a), 'The middle class tribe', *New Society*, no. 333, pp. 238–9.

Bell, C. R. (1969b), 'A note on participant observation', *Sociology*, vol. 3, pp. 417–18.

Bell, C. R. (1971), 'Occupational career, family cycle and extended family relations', *Human Relations*, vol. 24, pp. 463–75.

Bell, C. R. (1974), 'Replication and reality', *Futures*, vol. 6, pp. 253–60.

Bell, C. R. and Newby, H. (1972), *Community Studies* (London: George Allen & Unwin).

Bell, C. R. and Newby, H. (1973), 'The sources of variation in agricultural workers' images of society', *Sociological Review*, vol. 21, no. 2, pp. 229–53.

Bell, C. R. and Newby, H. (1974) (eds), *The Sociology of Community* (London: Frank Cass).

Benson, D. (1974), 'A revolution in sociology', *Sociology*, vol. 8, pp. 125–9.

Berger, J. and Mohr, J. (1975), *A Seventh Man* (Harmondsworth: Pelican Books).

Bernstein, B. (1974), 'Sociology and the sociology of education', in J. Rex (ed.), *Approaches to Sociology* (London: Routledge & Kegan Paul), pp. 153–70.

Bittner, E. (1967a), 'Police discretion in emergency apprehension of mentally ill persons', *Social Problems*, vol. 14, pp. 278–92.

Bittner, E. (1967b), 'The police on skid-row: a study of peace keeping', *American Sociological Review*, vol. 32, pp. 699–715.

Blauner, R. (1964), *Alienation and Freedom* (Chicago: Chicago University Press).

Blythe, R. (1969), *Akenfield* (London: Allen Lane).

Bohannan, L. (1964), *Return to Laughter* (New York: Random House); first published 1954 under the pseudonym E. S. Bowen.

Bottomore, T. B. and Rubel, M. (1956), *Karl Marx: Selected Writings in Sociology and Social Philosophy* (London: C. A. Watts).

Brockway, F. and Hobhouse, S. (1922), *English Prison Today* (London: HMSO).

Bulmer, M. I. A. (1973) (ed), Proceedings of the SSRC conference on 'The Occupational Community of the Traditional Worker' (London: SSRC).

Burns, T. (1967), Review of Runciman (1966), *British Journal of Sociology*, vol. 18, pp. 430–4.

Caute, D. (1976), 'Eye-witness in hell', *New Statesman* (21 May), pp. 682–3.

Cicourel, A. V. (1964), *Method and Measurement in Sociology* (New York: Free Press).

Cicourel, A. V. (1968), *The Social Organization of Juvenile Justice* (New York: Wiley).

Cicourel, A. V. (1973), *Argentine Fertility* (New York: Wiley).

Clarke, M. (1975), 'Survival in the field: implications of personal experience in field work', *Theory and society*, vol. 2, no. 1, pp. 95–123.

Cohen, S. (1971) (ed.), *Images of Deviance* (Harmondsworth: Penguin).

Cohen, S. (1972), *Folk Devils and Moral Panics* (London: Paladin).

Cohen, S. (1974a), 'Criminology and the sociology of deviance in Britain: a recent history and current report', in P. Rock and M. McIntosh (eds), *Deviance and Social Control* (London: Tavistock), pp. 1–40.

Cohen, S. (1974b), 'Human warehouses: the future of prisons', *New Society*, vol. 30, no. 14, pp. 407–11.

Cohen, S. and Taylor, L. (1970), 'The experience of time in long-term imprisonment', *New Society* (31 December).

Cohen, S. and Taylor, L. (1972), *Psychological Survival: The Experience of Long-Term Imprisonment* (Harmondsworth: Penguin).

Cohen, S. and Taylor, L. (1975), 'Prison research: a cautionary tale', *New Society*, vol. 31, no. 643, pp. 253–5.

Cohen, S. and Taylor, L. (1976), *Escape Attempts: The Theory and Practice of Resistance to Everyday Life* (London: Allen Lane).

Cohen, S. and Young, J. (1973), *The Manufacture of News: Deviance, Social Problems and the Mass Media* (London: Constable).

Collingwood, R. G. (1943), *The Idea of History* (Oxford: OUP).

Coulter, J. (1973), *Approaches to Insanity* (London: Martin Robertson).

Coulter, J. (1974), 'What's wrong with the new criminology', *Sociological Review*, vol. 22, pp. 119–35.

Davis, M. S. (1971), 'That's interesting: towards a phenomenology of sociology and a sociology of phenomenology', *Philosophy of the Social Sciences*, vol. 1, pp. 309–46.

Douglas, J. D. (1965), 'The sociological study of suicide: suicidal actions as socially meaningful actions', unpublished PhD dissertation (Princeton, NJ: Princeton University).

Douglas, J. D. (1966), 'The sociological analysis of the social meanings of suicide', *European Journal of Sociology*, vol. 7, pp. 249–98.

Douglas, J. D. (1967), *The Social Meanings of Suicide* (Princeton, NJ: Princeton University Press).

Dumont, L. (1972), *Homo Hierarchicus* (London: Paladin).

Durkheim, E. (1952), trans. by J. A. Spaulding and G. Simpson, *Suicide: A Study in Sociology*, (London: Routledge & Kegan Paul).

Evans-Pritchard, E. E. (1973), *Journal of the Anthropological Society of Oxford*.

Eysenck, H. (1970), *Crime and Personality* (London: Paladin).

Farberow, N. L. and Shneidman, E. S. (1961) (eds), *The Cry for Help* (New York: McGraw-Hill).

Faris, R. (1967), *Chicago Sociology* (Chicago: Chicago University Press).

Festinger, L., Riecken, H. W. and Schachter, S. (1956), *When Prophecy Fails* (New York: Harper & Row).

Feyerabend, P. (1975), *Against Method* (London: New Left Editions).

Filmer, P., Phillipson, M., Silverman, D. and Walsh, D. (1972), *New Directions in Sociological Theory* (London: Collier–Macmillan).

Fletcher, C. (1974), *Beneath the Surface* (London: Routledge & Kegan Paul).

Ford, J. (1975), *Paradigms and Fairytales* (London: Routledge & Kegan Paul).

Fortes, M. (1940) (ed.), *African Political Systems* (Oxford: OUP).

Frankenberg, R. (1966), *Communities in Britain* (Harmondsworth: Penguin).

Friedrichs, R. K. (1970), *A Sociology of Sociology* (New York: Free Press).

Fryer, R. and Martin, R. (1973), 'The deferential worker: persistence and disintegration in paternalist capitalism', Bulmer (ed.) (1973), pp. 326–64.

Gallaher, A. (1961), *Plainville: Fifteen Years Later* (New York: Columbia University Press).

Gallaher, A. (1964), essay in Vidich, Bensman and Stein (1964).

Garfinkel, H. (1967), *Studies in Ethnomethodology* (Englewood Cliffs, NJ: Prentice Hall).

Genovese, E. (1971), *In Red and Black* (London: Allen Lane).

Giddens, A. (1971) (ed.), *The Sociology of Suicide* (London: Frank Cass).

Goffman, E. (1968), *Asylums* (Harmondsworth: Penguin).

Goffman, E. (1973), 'The nature of deference and demeanor', in E. Goffman, *Interaction Ritual* (Harmondsworth: Penguin).

Goldthorpe, J. H. (1973), 'A revolution in sociology?', *Sociology*, vol. 7, pp. 449–62.

Gouldner, A. (1967), *Enter Plato* (London: Routledge & Kegan Paul).

Gouldner, A. (1975), 'The sociologist as partisan: sociology and the welfare state' in his *For Sociology* (Harmondsworth, Pelican Books).

Greater London Development Plan (GLDP) (1967), *Draft Studies* (London: Department of the Environment, HMSO).

Greater London Development Plan (GLDP) (1969), *Written Statement* (London: Department of the Environment: HMSO).

Greater London Development Plan (GLDP) (1973), *Report of Studies of the Panel of Inquiry: vol. 1 Report, vol. 2 Appendices* (London: Department of the Environment, HMSO).

Hagman, D. G. (1971), 'The Greater London Development Plan Inquiry', *Journal of the American Institute of Planners* (September), pp. 290–6.

Hammond, P. (1964), *Sociologists at Work* (New York: Basic Books).

Hindess, B. (1973), *The Use of Official Statistics* (London: Macmillan).

Horowitz, I. L. (1967) (ed.), *The Rise and Fall of Project Camelot* (Cambridge, Mass.: MIT Press).

Horowitz, I. L. (1970), 'Sociological snoopers and journalistic moralizers', *Transaction*, vol. 7 (May), pp. 4–8.

Humphreys, L. (1970), *Tearoom Trade* (London: Duckworth).

Johnson, V. (1975), 'Violence in marriage', MA qualifying thesis (Sydney, NSW: University of New South Wales, School of Sociology).

Kimber, W. (1972), 'Libel: a book publisher's view', in M. Rubinstein (ed.), *Wicked, Wicked Libels* (London: Routledge & Kegan Paul).

Kitsuse, J. I. and Cicourel, A. V. (1963), 'A note on the uses of official statistics', *Social Problems*, vol. 12, pp. 131–9.

Kuhn, T. S. (1962), *The Structure of Scientific Revolutions* (Chicago: Chicago University Press).

Lakatos, I. and Musgrave, A. (1970), *Criticism and the Growth of Knowledge* (Cambridge: CUP).

Lewis, O. (1951), *Life in a Mexican Village* (Urbana, Ill.: Illinois University Press).

Lukes, S. (1975), Review in *New Statesman* (15 September).

Lynd, R. S. and Lynd, H. M. (1937), *Middletown in Transition* (New York: Harcourt Brace).

Marshall, T. H. (1965), *Class Citizenship and Social Development* (New York: Anchor Books).

Martins, H. (1971), 'The Kuhnian revolution and its implications for sociology', in A. H. Hanson, T. Nossiter and S. Rokkan (eds), *Imagination and Precision in Political Analysis* (London: Faber).

Merton, R. K. (1967), *On Theoretical Sociology* (New York: Free Press).

Merton, R. K., Broom, L. and Cottrell, L. S. (1959) (eds), *Sociology Today* (New York: Basic Books).

Milgram, S. (1974), *Obedience and Authority* (London: Tavistock).

Miliband, R. (1969), *The State in Capitalist Society* (London: Weidenfeld & Nicolson).

Mills, C. W. (1959), *The Sociological Imagination* (New York: OUP).

Mitchell, A. (1973), *The Import of Labour* (Rotterdam: Rotterdam University Press).

Mitchell, J. (1971), *Woman's Estate* (London: Allen Lane).

Moore, R. (1974), *Pitmen, Preachers and Politics* (Cambridge: CUP).

Moore, R. (1975a), *Racism and Black Resistance in Britain* (London: Pluto Press).

Moore, R. (1975b) with T. Wallace, *Slamming the Door: The Administration of Immigration Control* (London: Martin Robertson).

Moore, R. (1977), 'Migrants and the class structure of Western Europe', in R. Scase (ed.), *Industrial Society: Class, Cleavage and Control* (London: George Allen & Unwin).

Morris, T. (1975), 'Some thoughts on the politics of criminology', *Times Literary Supplement*, no. 3837 (26 September), pp. 1103–4.

Morris, T. and Morris, P. (1962), *Pentonville: A Sociological Study of an English Prison* (London: Routledge & Kegan Paul).

Moser, C. and Kalton, G. (1958), *Survey Methods of Social Investigation* London: Heinemann Educational).

Newby, H. (1972a), 'The low earnings of agricultural workers: a sociological approach', *Journal of Agricultural Economics*, vol. 23, no. 1, pp. 15–24.

Newby, H. (1972b), 'Agricultural workers in the class structure', *Sociological Review*, vol. 20, no. 3, pp. 413–39.

Newby, H. (1975), 'The deferential dialectic', *Comparative Studies in Society and History*, vol. 17, no. 2, pp. 139–64.

Newby, H. (1977), *The Deferential Worker* (London: Allen Lane).

Pahl, R. E. (1965), *Urbs in Rure* (London: Weidenfeld & Nicolson).

Pahl, R. E. (1969), 'Urban social theory and research', *Environment and Planning* (November).

Pahl, R. E. (1976), *Whose City?* (Harmondsworth: Penguin).

Pahl, R. E. and Pahl, J. M. (1971), *Managers and Their Wives* (London: Allen Lane).

Pahl, R. E. and Winkler, J. T. (1974), 'The economic elite: theory and practice', in P. Stanworth and A. Giddens (eds), *Elites and Power in British Society* (Cambridge: CUP).

Paine, S. (1974), *Exporting Labour: The Turkish Case* (Cambridge: CUP).

Panel on Privacy and Behavioural Research (1967), 'Privacy and behavioural research: preliminary summary of the report of the Panel on Privacy and Behavioural Research', *Science*, vol. 155, pp. 535–8.

Phillips, D. (1971), *Knowledge from What?* (San Francisco: Jossey Bass).

Phillips, D. (1973), *Abandoning Method: Sociological Studies in Methodology* (San Francisco: Jossey Bass).

Platt, J. (1976), *The Realities of Research* (London: University of Sussex Press).

Popper, Karl (1963), *Conjectures and Refutations* (London: Routledge & Kegan Paul).

Poulantzas, N. (1973), *Political Power and Social Classes* (London: New Left Editors).

Reisman, D. (1964), Introduction to Bohannan.

Rex, J. (1961), *Key Problems of Sociological Theory* (London: Routledge & Kegan Paul).

Rex, J. and Moore, R. (1967), *Race, Community and Conflict* (Oxford OUP).

Robertson, R. and Taylor, L. (1973), *Crime, Deviance and Socio-Legal Control* (Oxford: Blackwell).

Rosenthal, R. and Rosnow, R. (1970) (eds), *Sources of Artefact in Social Research* (New York: Academic Press).

Rost, H. (1927), *Bibliographie des Selbstmords* (Augsburg: Haas und Grabherr).

Runciman, W. G. (1966), *Relative Deprivation and Social Justice* (London: Routledge & Kegan Paul).

Sacks, H. (1963), 'Sociological description', *Berkeley Journal of Sociology*, vol. 8, pp. 1–16.

Sacks, H. (1966), 'The search for help: no-one to turn to', unpublished PhD dissertation (Berkeley, Calif.: University of California at Berkeley, Department of Sociology).

Sacks, H. (1972a), 'On the analyzability of stories by children', in J. J. Gumpertz and D. Hymes (eds), *Directions in Sociolinguistics: The Ethnography of Communication* (New York: Holt, Rinehart & Winston), pp. 329–45.

Sacks, H. (1972b), 'An initial investigation of the usability of conversational data for doing sociology', in D. Sudnow (ed.), *Studies in Social Interaction* (New York: Free Press), pp. 31–74.

Sacks, H., Schegloff, E. and Jefferson, G. (1974), 'A simplistic systematics for the organization of turn-taking in conversation', *Language*, vol. 50, pp. 696–735.

Sayre, A. (1975), *Rosalind Franklin and D. N. A.* (New York: Norton).

Schegloff, E. (1972), 'Notes on a conversational practice: formulating place', in Sudnow (1972), pp. 75–119.

Self, P. and Storing, H. (1962), *The State and the Farmer* (London: George Allen & Unwin).

Spittell, F. (1973), 'Sociological research: production or destruction', *Freedom*, p. 4.

Stacey, M. (1960), *Tradition and Change: A Study of Banbury* (London: OUP).

Stacey, M., Batstone, E., Bell, C. and Murcott, A. (1975), *Power, Persistance and Change: A Second Study of Banbury* (London: Routledge & Kegan Paul).

Standing Conference on London and South East Regional Planning (SCOLSERP) (1968), *The South East: A Framework for Regional Planning* (London: HMSO, 17 July).

Strategic Plan for the South East (1970), *Report and Studies* Volumes (London: HMSO).

Sudnow, D. (1965), 'Normal crimes: sociological features of the penal code in a public defender's office', *Social Problems*, vol. 12, pp. 255–72.

Sudnow, D. (1967), *Passing On: The Social Organization of Dying* (Englewood Cliffs, NJ: Prentice Hall).

Taylor, I, Walton, P. and Young, J. (1973), *The New Criminology: For a Social Theory of Deviance* (London: Routledge & Kegan Paul).

Taylor, L. (1971), *Deviance and Society* (London: Michael Joseph).

Trasler, G. (1962), *The Explanation of Criminality* (London: Routledge & Kegan Paul).

Turner, V. W. (1957), *Schism and Continuity in an African Society* (Manchester: Manchester University Press).

Urry, J. (1971), 'Role performance and social comparison processes', in J. A. Jackson (ed.), *Role* (Cambridge: CUP).

Urry, J. (1973), 'Thomas S. Kuhn as sociologist of knowledge', *British Journal of Sociology*, vol. 24, no. 4, pp. 462–73.

Vidich, A. and Bensman, J. (1958), *Small Town in Mass Society* (Princeton, NJ: Princeton University Press).

Vidich, A. Bensman, J. and Stein, M. R. (1964) (eds), *Reflections on Community Studies* (New York: Wiley).

Vilar, P. (1973), 'Writing Marxist history', *New Left Review*, no. 80, pp. 65–106.

Vosper, C. (1971), *The Mind Benders* (London: Neville Spearman).

Wallis, R. (1973a), 'The sectarianism of scientology', in M. Hill (ed.), *A Sociological Yearbook of Religion in Britain*, no. 6 (London: SCM Press).

Wallis, R. (1973b), 'Religious sects and the fear of publicity', *New Society*, vol. 24, pp. 545–7.

Wallis, R. (1974), 'Ideology, authority and the development of cultic movements', *Social Research*, vol. 41, pp. 299–327.

Wallis, R. (1975a), 'Scientology: therapeutic cult to religious sect', *Sociology*, vol. 9, pp. 89–100.

Wallis, R. (1975b), 'Societal reactions to scientology: a study in the sociology of deviant religion', in R. Wallis (ed.), *Sectarianism: Analyses of Religious and Non-religious Sects* (London: Peter Owen; New York: Halsted Press).

Wallis, R. (1976), *The Road to Total Freedom: A Sociological Analysis of Scientology* (London: Heinemann Educational).

Watkins, J. W. N. (1963), 'Confession is good for ideas', *Listener*, 69, 18 April, pp. 667–8.

Watson, D. R. (1975), 'Calls for help: a sociological analysis of telephone communications to a crisis intervention centre', unpublished PhD thesis (Warwick: University of Warwick).

Webb, E. J., Campbell, D. T., Schevartz, R. D. and Sechrest, L. (1966), *Unobtrusive Measures* (Chicago: Rand McNally).

Weber, M. (1949), trans. by E. Shils, *The Methodology of the Social Sciences* (New York: Free Press).

Whyte, W. F. (1955), *Street Corner Society* (Chicago: Chicago University Press).

Wilkins, J. (1967), 'Suicidal behaviour', *American Sociological Review*, vol. 32, pp. 286–98.

Wilkinson, P. and Grace, C. (1975), 'Reforms as revolutions', *Sociology*, vol. 9, pp. 397–418.

Willer, J. (1971), *The Social Determination of Knowledge* (New York: Prentice Hall).

Willer, D. and Willer, J. (1973), *Systematic Empiricism* (New York: Prentice Hall).

Williams, W. M. (1963), *A West Country Village* (London: Routledge & Kegan Paul).

Wolff, K. H. (ed.) (1950), *The Sociology of Georg Simmel* (Glencoe, Ill.: Free Press).

Worsley, P. M. (1974), 'The state of theory and the status of theory', *Sociology*, vol. 8, pp. 1–17.

Zubaida, S. (1974), 'What's scientific sociology?', *Economy and Society*, vol. 3, no. 1, 71–83.

Index